Josephine

From Washington Working Girl To Fisherman's Wife

A MEMOIR: 1917 TO 1959

MARGARET
THOMAS
BUCHHOLZ

DOWN THE SHORE
PUBLISHING
WEST CREEK, NJ

The words "Down The Shore" and the Down The Shore Publishing logo are registered U.S. Trademarks.

For information, address:
Down The Shore Publishing Corp., Box 100, West Creek, NJ 08092
www.down-the-shore.com

Printed in the United States of America on recycled paper, 30% PCW.
10 9 8 7 6 5 4 3 2 1

Book design by Leslee Ganss.

Library of Congress Cataloging-in-Publication Data

Buchholz, Margaret Thomas, 1933-
Josephine : from Washington working girl to fisherman's wife / by Margaret Thomas Buchholz.
    p. cm.
ISBN 978-1-59322-062-4
1. Thomas, Josephine Lehman, d. 1959. 2. Thomas, Josephine Lehman, d. 1959--Diaries.
3. Thomas, Josephine Lehman, d. 1959--Travel--Europe. 4. Women ghostwriters--United States--Biography. 5. Women in the civil service--Washington (D.C.)--Biography. 6. World War, 1914-1918--Washington (D.C.) 7. Fishers' spouses--New Jersey--Barnegat Bay Region--Biography. 8. Ionia (Mich.)--Biography. 9. Washington (D.C.)--Biography. 10. Barnegat Bay Region (N.J.)--Biography. I. Thomas, Josephine Lehman, d. 1959. II. Title.
CT275.T55395B82 2012
973.91092--dc23
[B]
                              2012022665

CONTENTS

FOREWORD

Who hasn't fantasized going back in time to see our parents, young and uncertain, choosing the paths that led to the Mother and Father who shaped our own lives. Margaret Buchholz has done exactly that with this book. It is a vivid and fascinating journey through her mother's life, lived in a series of worlds that couldn't be more different than each other, or the life that she finally embraced.

Beginning with a trip to the attic, Margaret not only travels these worlds through the writings and diaries her mother left behind, but later retraces her steps through research and her own travel.

Josephine Lehman, later Thomas, was born in 1898 in Ionia, Michigan. Her first job after high school was at the *Ionia Sentinel* where she ascended to a reporter's post. Intuitively, she had found the profession that embodied the goals she had set herself at thirteen, to serve her country, to write and travel.

Swept up in the eruption of national patriotism after President Wilson's call to enter World War I, Josephine was eager to take part, as her two enlisted brothers did. The opportunity came swiftly. Spotting a government advertisement for "Stenographers and Typewriters" needed in Washington D.C., she took the civil service test and was soon embedded in the frenzy of our nation's capital. Her remarkable eye for detail and her curiosity about every person and challenge she encounters is so engaging that we see her world as if we were colleagues at her side, enjoying her humor and insights. She's "Jo" to us by now, we know her too well to call her "Josephine." She gives us her own unique perspective on Washington in wartime. We're there as she plays hooky from work to watch the Liberty Loan Parade from the Capitol to the White House. We stand on the packed sidewalk, wave and cheer on the fundraising efforts of Mary Pickford, Douglas Fairbanks and Charlie Chaplin and hear the complaints of a man shoulder to shoulder with us, "Aw, 'dat ain't Charlie Chaplin! Where's his mustache?"

Jo takes us to dances at the Neighborhood House where she bonds with returning soldiers who tell her their painful stories of being gassed and under constant fire. We meet Jo's suitors; just as empathetically observed and unforgettable as our own best and most miserable dates.

When the war ends, Jo's skill as a writer leads her to a job with adventurer and journalist Lowell Thomas, a perfect match. She travels the globe interviewing fascinating military leaders such as Captain Georg von Trapp, best known later through Rodgers and Hammerstein's musical "The Sound of Music." Her travels expose her to yet another world just as alien: the world of silk hats and monocles and Caribbean cruises, a "whirling maze of wild improbabilities — of cliques, scandals, gossip, too much drinking — as well as of tropic nights so lovely that one hurts, and falls in love with whomever has the nearest deck chair."

Love leads Jo into another world she would build herself, that of a wife and mother. This chapter explores Jo's family so vividly that its domestic triumphs and challenges are as compelling as any that came before it, maybe more so. Jo marries Reynold Thomas, who had served in the war, ran a dairy in Chincoteague, Virginia, and worked at his uncle's eelgrass business in Harvey Cedars. This was a true honeymoon period, with touching love letters, work for both, and a prosperity that ended as unexpectedly as the coming of the Great Depression.

There couldn't be a greater contrast between Jo's earlier, elegant life than this life she now lived as frugally as possible: The move from Manhattan to Harvey Cedars, where Reynold made a meager living as a deep-sea fisherman in the boat he once started building as a pleasure craft; Jo, watching the clock, waiting and hoping for him to come home safely. She captured the essence of her daily life in a beautifully written article she sold to *Scribner's* magazine for $500 in July 1933. She didn't use her real name, she didn't want her New York friends to identify her and learn how her life, often desperate, was so different than theirs. Clear eyed, she chronicled the experience.

"It was a satisfaction to Tom to know he was providing a living for us, even by manual labor, and some answering primitive instinct made me content to cook and tend the hearth and breed … something much finer was welded between us than we found in the first prosperous days of our
marriage, when our lives followed two distinct paths and we couldn't afford a baby."

Jo's situation was not to continue in this contented state. First came the deprivations of World War II, and we experience it first hand as vividly on their small island as we did World War I in Washington. German ships sank tankers near Long Beach Island's Barnegat Inlet. Bodies were pulled from the ocean. Jo assumed the role of tax collector and Reynold was called away to work in the defense industry. Jo worked hard to keep an atmosphere of normalcy for Margaret and her younger brother Michael. Her equanimity was tested daily. Jo's acceptance of the fact the Island had no coal and that her children were freezing as she thoughtfully sifted through which of her favorite books she needed to burn to keep her family warm is an example of her spirit.

Life after the war had bitter surprises of its own. A hurricane destroyed twenty percent of Harvey Cedars. Margaret's fight with polio, and then the return of Jo's breast cancer. This, too, she confronted with her usual mixture of humor and astute observation, "Even when I'm dying no one will believe me, saying I look so damn healthy."

Jo's life as a writer came full circle, linking with her daughter's, when both worked at the *Beachcomber,* a seasonal, weekly newspaper that started in 1950. Jo wrote essays, garden and cooking columns, "little bits of this and that." Margaret sold advertising and wrote copy when needed.

In 1955 Margaret met and married Bill Douglas, editor of the *Beach Haven Times,* and they bought the *Beachcomber.* Jo and Margaret continued to work together. Again, we hope for the happy ending.

Margaret's marriage ended with Bill's devastating and unexpected suicide two years later. Jo came to the rescue, helping her daughter raise her two children and keeping the newspaper afloat.

"Josephine" is as much a biography as it is an exploration of the bond between mother and daughter. Jo is fascinating and a terrific writer. It is riveting reading, one of the rare and wonderful times when journalism and memoir merge and become compelling literature. In these too brief pages we are given the gift of feeling that we know an extraordinary human being.

Two, actually. I had the privilege to work with Margaret on the *Beachcomber* as my first writing job, so I know her firsthand. What I didn't know is how she became the inspiring editor, writer and traveler she is. Now I know. Her mother, Jo. And now you have the opportunity to meet them both.

Mark St. Germain
Playwright, author, film and television writer.

PROLOGUE

In 1988, after my parents had both died, I moved back into my childhood home in Harvey Cedars, on Long Beach, a barrier island six miles off the New Jersey coast. It is a joy to live in a house that has the comfort of a childhood home. Something about this spit of sand on Barnegat Bay, where the sound of the Atlantic Ocean had been the lullaby of my youth, drew me here. My parents felt the pull, too, when they moved here as a refuge from New York City's joblessness, choosing Long Beach Island as "a serene place" to wait out the Depression. "Just for a few years," my mother said. They never left.

But their stories remained. Some tucked away in the window seat overlooking the bay; others in the attic. There was a quilt of fog that afternoon, when at last I went to the window seat and lifted the lid. For the past few years it had beckoned to me, but I'd procrastinated, as if I sensed the contents would reawaken suppressed emotions. I did not want to postpone this any longer. I pulled the cushion off the weathered cedar top and raised the cover. The seat yawned open on its old hinge. I saw layers of cardboard accordion files, yellowed manila folders, and large envelopes that bulged with unknown documents and creased letters — my mother's archive.

Where to start? Probing the layers in the window seat, my hand touched a journal with a smooth-grained, leather cover about the size of my hand. I pulled it into the light. It was my mother's 1917 diary, about a hundred pages filled with her writing. Then I spotted a bulky packet of typewritten pages, almost four inches thick. I flipped for a peek at the final date, June 1920. In my mother's clear script on the cover I read, "Josephine Lehman, Washington DC." This find exceeded my expectations. What would I discover? For good or ill, my view of my mother, who died in 1959 when I was 26, would be forever revised.

In a few days I had read enough to make me think that there was more of my mother's writing in the attic. Once started, it was impossible to stop. Now that I was on the trail I wanted to explore all that I could find. I remembered that whenever my mother didn't know what to do with something, she stashed it in the attic. I climbed up on the iron ladder that my father had found on the beach after a schooner wrecked. I must have been four years old when I first scampered up this ladder. "Like a little monkey," my mother said.

I pushed aside an old record player, discarded toys, a box of 1950s bark-cloth curtains, a mahogany card table, dozens of paintings and boxes of Limoges china. I opened carton after carton, many filled with my teenage scrapbooks and high school yearbooks, until I found a softened cardboard box, sides weakened by damp and age. It was filled with photographs from my mother's childhood in Michigan, scrapbooks and photo albums from her Washington years, and folders containing typewritten manuscript fragments from the 1930s and 1940s. Carbon copies of long narrative letters she wrote to her family and friends between 1920 and 1938 were clipped together. In another large packet, labeled in my father's handwriting "Letters to Marian," were about sixty letters my mother wrote between 1928 and 1957 to her sister. Marian sent them to my father after my mother died. I was startled and thrilled.

Reading late into the night, I fell into a trance of the past; the familiar living room seemed to expand with my mother's presence — not the mother I had known, but a tall, lithe young woman I wished I'd known, who loved to dance as much as I did, who fussed with her clothes — who flirted and chatted — a woman as ripe for adventure as I was. The Josephine on these pages did not at all resemble the mother I remembered — a serious, introverted, middle-aged woman, content in her marriage, but worn down by the Depression, war and deteriorating health. I had never seen my mother dance, but during her Washington years she went to dances three times a week, and rated the men she met on their dancing ability. The mother I remember read for pleasure the 1890 edition of the *Encyclopedia Britannica*. I did not know the young woman who had a professional career as researcher and ghostwriter, who in the 1920s crisscrossed the Atlantic Ocean in luxurious ocean liners, who in 1927 had a harrowing first airplane flight across the English Channel, and who, just before the stock market crashed in 1929, cruised the Caribbean on an outrageously extravagant trip aboard Count Felix Von Luckner's four-masted windjammer. Nor did I appreciate the mother who juggled the demands of motherhood with work.

As I read the words on the brittle onionskin paper I felt a vague flicker of familiarity, remembering what little she had told me about the years she worked before she met my father in 1931, and wondered why she hadn't told me more. How I would have loved to know this when I, too, was young and dancing. Or had she told me, and had I not paid attention, wrapped up as I was in my teenage world?

On Decoration Day in 1917, six weeks after the United States entered World War I, my mother began her diary; the tightly woven pages are yellowed, but her penciled script is graceful and clear, the perfect penmanship taught a century ago. In 1917, when war news dominated the newspaper for which she worked, and her brothers and friends enlisted, she must have realized that her life would change, and that it would be enhanced as she participated in history in the making. She entered wartime Washington with high spirits—a young woman seeking and exploring life.

The handwritten entries end on June 20, 1918; from then on she typed her journal. Until June 1920, my mother wrote almost daily and interspersed copies of her long, typewritten letters to friends and family in chronological order. The early diary entries are brief but they lengthened during the first five months in Washington when she was in the thick of the excitement of the nation's capital at war — with all its soldiers. It culminated in the voluminous typewritten sheets she produced in the postwar period, when any one event could take on the narrative form of a short story.

Reading and rereading my mother's letters and diaries, I became intimately involved with the vibrant, independent young woman who started to make her own way even before women had the vote — who in the 1920s had a career unique not only for her generation, but for the next to follow. I can share her life before I was born with an intimacy impossible when she was alive. Through these letters and diaries I met someone other than the mother I thought I knew — happy with her husband and children — but a writer with her hands tied to domestic chores, an exile from the glamorous life she had once led. She recorded her experiences, both the work itself and her life surrounding it, with wit and acuity that startled me — she would make me see the world through her eyes. I would re-encounter my mother as if her spirit had been imprisoned in that window seat, in those boxes.

By lifting the lid I let loose not a Pandora's Box of wicked mischief, but something far more profound and pleasurable. I freed my mother's spirit through her words. And while I could not realize this when I began to read her private papers, she, and this place, so long her home, would renew the love between us. I no longer have to imagine my mother before I knew her; she comes to life through her writing.

1898 TO 1918

Growing Up in Ionia, Michigan

Josephine Lehman when she attended Ionia High School.

"Miss Lehman was notified that she was to report to the War Department in Washington at her earliest convenience and that the salary would be $1,100 per annum to start. She is the first girl from Ionia to enlist for this work at the front."

My mother was born in 1898, and the *Ionia Sentinel*, the Michigan town's daily newspaper where she would get her first job, announced her birth: "Dr. Joslin reports a 12-pound girl at the home of Michael Lehman, whose future birthday surprise parties will be on March 16." Josephine was the first daughter; she followed seven boys who had appeared regularly since 1887, four years after their parents emigrated from Germany as teenagers. After my mother, another boy and three more girls, Marian, Lillian and Helen, who died when she was three, filled the family farmhouse near the Nickleplate crossroad, about five miles outside the central Michigan town of Ionia, a substantial county seat populated by about 9,000 citizens.[1]

Under the onslaught of a farmhouse full of boisterous boys, my mother learned to take care of herself, either when she participated in their pranks or, encouraged by her father, retreated into her beloved books. Her mother had learned English employed as a domestic and never understood her husband's desire to read, but Jo absorbed her father's love of reading and history. The fall after her fifth birthday, with three of her brothers still in school, she walked several miles down the unpaved country lane to the one-room stone schoolhouse.

Years later my mother remembered this school: "Its teacher was an eighteen-year-old girl whose pedagogical training had been six weeks at a state normal school. She had twenty-three pupils in eight grades and every one of them learned how to read. If one were backward about it, her smartest eighth grade girl — it was always a girl — kept after him — it was always a him — until he read what his class was reading."

My mother was a perceptive child, diligent and studious, but like so many young girls, she agonized about her looks; by the eighth grade she was already taller than most of the boys, and would grow to five feet ten inches. On one of the scraps of typewritten copy in her files I found: "My best friend in the seventh grade had naturally golden hair curled every morning by loving fingers and tied by those spanking big taffeta bows; a best friend with a peach bloom skin and doll features compared to my own dust brown hair skinned back so tightly into braids it was a wonder I could still shut my eyes. I agonized over my freckles for years, the serviceable dresses my mother made for me, and the way visitors to school looked at the best friend and said 'what a beautiful little girl' but never looked at me and said 'what a beautiful speller, what a beautiful reader, what a beautiful multiplier and subtractor'."

Compulsory education ended with eighth grade, and for many children this was the end of learning and the start of laboring. None of my uncles went to high school; several stayed home to work the farm with their father. Jo saved the large, embossed diploma she received when she graduated eighth grade. It attested that on May 13, 1911, she had completed orthography, reading, writing, arithmetic, English grammar, geography, physiology, United States history, and civics.

In the spring of 1911, Jo's freshman year at Ionia High School, she penned this prescient essay, a progressive vision of her future. The core of my mother's thirteen-year-old vision — the service to her country, writing, traveling, disease, keeping a diary, and even her "fairy prince" — forecast her reality.

My Future: During the long hot summer of 1927 I volunteered as a nurse in a hospital in California. It was when the war between the United States and Japan was raging most fiercely, and I had become a nurse, partly because they were scarce and partly to gather material for a new book, for I had chosen as my vocation that of an authoress.

When I arrived at the hospital the scene of the wounded and the dying inspired in me a resolution to be of use to my country, and to those men who were fighting and dying for that country, and not merely to gather material for a book. At last came the joyful news that Japan had surrendered. This did not surprise me, because I did not think that anybody could beat Uncle Sam. After resting for a time I started my book, which I intended to make a sort of diary containing my experiences, but after I had written only a few chapters my eyes were afflicted with a disease, which the doctors pronounced almost incurable. I had my eyes treated for about six months by one of the most skillful specialists in Europe and they were completely cured.

During my stay near Florence, Italy, I had seen a beautiful little villa that I longed to possess. I found to my great joy that it was for sale, made the necessary transactions for purchasing it, and returned to America. I finished the book I had started, saw it published and made popular, then sailed for Europe to make my home in the villa, devoting my time to writing, and also to wait for my fairy prince to appear.

By her senior year Jo had studied chemistry, English, German, civics, trigonometry and, as she wanted to get a job, typewriting and stenography. Her final marks ranged from a low of 96 percent in English to 100 percent in typewriting. When she graduated in 1915, she and her thirty-two classmates were in a group of fewer than 1.5 million students in the country who completed high school. My mother was eager to have a career, and that summer took a job with the *Ionia Sentinel*, the county's largest daily paper. She rapidly worked her way up from general front-office duties to reporter.

The World She Lived In

In August 1914, the European war started, and in February 1915, Germany announced an aggressive policy of submarine warfare against all ships — which included those of neutral countries such as the United States — in an "area of war" demarcated around Great Britain and Ireland. The United States protested, and said it would take any steps necessary if American lives were lost as a result of this policy. On May 7th the Germans torpedoed the *Lusitania* and 128 Americans were among the 1,198 persons drowned; the nation experienced "mingled horror and rage." The *Sentinel's* headline, **"Sinking of Lusitania is Deliberate Murder,"** echoed that of newspapers across the country.

America's anti-German reaction was so strong that even Count Johann-Heinrich von Bernstorff, the German ambassador in Washington, said the *Lusitania* sinking could have carried the United States into the war; President Wilson needed only "to nod to induce his country to fight." But Wilson believed his higher moral purpose justified continued neutrality. Wary of United States entry into the war, Germany backed down and promised it would not attack American ships.

The first week of February 1917, Ionia prepared to welcome Company E of the National Guard home from Mexico, where American troops under General John J. Pershing were engaged in a "punitive operation" against Pancho Villa. Jo was on the story: "Company E will be met properly and as is very fitting will be escorted to their armory by that gallant remnant of the Boys of '61. The band will be out to greet them, Ionia merchants will join heartily in decorating the street with flags... The citizens en masse will assemble at the depot to cheer the boys and accompany them to the armory, where the company will be dismissed." For several days she followed this story and ended the final one on this ominous note: "So the welcome which Ionia is to extend to its soldiers is not exactly in the nature of a joyous homecoming. It is a homecoming to be sure, but one which is likely at any time to be again turned into a marching forth for further services somewhere else."

A week later, Germany terminated the grace period that allowed safe passage for American shipping: U.S. ships would be torpedoed without warning. Immediately a German U-boat prowling off New Jersey sank five in one day. Almost every day, new sinkings were reported. President Wilson broke diplomatic relations with Germany, and Ambassador von Bernstorff was ordered to leave the country. Wilson signed the War Resolution on April 6th, and the *Sentinel* announced what everyone had expected: "The world is notified that United States is at war with Germany."

On May 26th, 1,500 American combat troops arrived in France. By Decoration Day, Ionia residents followed the war on a daily basis. The *Sentinel* printed upbeat letters from men already at camp and started a column called "Our Boys in the War." A *Sentinel* editorial hinted at the horrors to come and asked Ionians: "What will you say to yourself when the casualty lists come in? Will you be able to stand erect in your own mind and say I did what I could to make their sacrifice worthwhile?"

Company E was mustered into the regular army as a National Guard unit and awaited a remobilization call. Jo was back at her typewriter: "Company E enlisted for service, and service in the world today does not mean just weeks or months spent in training camp. That is but the necessary preliminary to bloodier work that is expected will follow." In an editorial, the paper exhorted its readers: "Wake up to the magnitude of the task before you. Wake up to the power and the far-flung resourcefulness of the enemy. Wake up to the fact that it is a man's fight and it is only just beginning."

It was also a woman's fight. Two weeks after the war declaration, Wilson met with the first National Women's Committee, and women were called to fight on the home front. The federal government distributed registration cards to state women's committees, which in turn fanned them out to local groups. If a woman wished to serve, she stated her age, dependants, education and/or work experience, and whether or not she would relocate. President Wilson said, "We cannot win this war by shutting up women's energies in a garbage can."

The Navy enlisted "Yeomanettes" for duty at wireless stations; factories needed women to sew the cloth wrapping on airplane wings, which, it was felt, required a "delicate touch." The new science of occupational therapy drafted women adept in handicrafts to retrain shell-shocked soldiers in rehabilitation hospitals. New York City hired ten women letter carriers and the District of Columbia one traffic policewoman. Banks put the first women behind the barred teller's windows, and women were trained to replace the men who previously dominated the ranks of typists, and telephone and telegraph operators. The Labor Department enlisted women as "draftsmen, bookkeepers, fingerprint specialists, topographers, shipping clerks, and other new lines."

In a government bulletin on the status of women's war work, popular author Ida Tarbell wrote: "Quietly, almost unconsciously, there is going on in this country, an extraordinary gathering of its woman power ... multitudes of organizations and of individual women are flowing together in a great union. This movement is a natural response to a need which was scarcely recognized until it was suggested."

The same week that my mother reported Company E's remobilization, she started her handwritten diary, where she kept track of her social activities and unusual work assignments. That first wartime summer she covered song recitals, football banquets and Chautauqua entertainments; she organized a newsboys club, read proofs, and wrote the obituary for her classmate Frieda Hausserman, dead from typhoid fever.

My mother was "miserable and glum" as two of her brothers and more and more friends enlisted in the Army. She made candy and knitted scarves and sweaters for her soldier friends, and complained that a spy scare had canceled a dance: "Owing to the suspicion that the Germans were going to blow up the pavilion, there was no dance, so we visited the Kiesters. Sat on piano stools and talked about the Red Cross, German spies and the IWW [Industrial Workers of the World]."

At the end of August, Company E left: "Tuesday morning was a grand rush for the train depot to see Company E off for France. Rather depressing and a number of tears shed. But they finally departed and Helen, Elsie and I went to the Sugar Bowl and got some breakfast then went to work. It is surely lonesome without some of the fellows with whom we had so much fun."

During the fall, my mother tried to decide which kind of war work would suit her best, and whether or not to leave Michigan. On November 17th she told her diary: "Have fifteen inches knitted on my sweater. Lawrence Hale came home from Ft. Sheridan this morning looking splendid in his uniform and title of lieutenant. Have been trying to decide whether to give up my job and take the civil service examination."

Caught up in the fervent patriotism as she proofread war dispatches and reams of nationalistic government propaganda releases, she could not have missed the full-page advertisements in women's magazines circulated from one coast to the other: "Stenographers and Typewriters Wanted. Men and Women. The United States Government is in urgent need of thousands of typewriter operators and stenographers. All who pass examinations for the departments and offices at Washington D.C. are assured of certification for appointment." The annual salary ranged from $1,000 to $1,200. My mother earned $500 at the *Sentinel*.

She took the rigorous seven-hour civil service test on December 20th and recorded: "Am informed I will come through in flying colors. Have started to look up railroad schedules and places of interest in Washington."

Six weeks later a telegram confirmed her appointment. Page one of the February 12th *Sentinel* carried the story under a boldface, three-deck headline: "**Miss Lehman Is Called To Washington, *Sentinel* Loses an Efficient Employee Who is Called to the War Department.**"

Miss Josephine Lehman, for two years and a half in the employ of the *Sentinel*, received telegraph notice Saturday night that she had been called to the service of the government... Several weeks ago she took the civil service examination here and when her papers came back from Washington her credit was high. Miss Lehman was notified that she was to report to the War Department in Washington at her earliest convenience and that the salary would be $1100 per annum to start. She is the first girl from Ionia to enlist for this work at the front. Her good fortune is well deserved by efficiency and a determination to do well whatever she undertakes. It is that kind of an army Uncle Sam is enlisting for the glorious cause of world freedom.

Jo's last diary entry in Ionia was on February 17: "I am nearly ready to leave and my only hope is that I don't cry like a baby at the station. That would be too awful. Have thought of a fine plot for a short story. Perhaps I'll be an author before I know it." Her next entry was written on the train from Ionia to Washington.

February 20: A berth is a lot of fun, just like going to sleep in the bottom cupboard shelf if all fixed up nicely. I was no sooner under the covers than rap-rap-rap came the conductor saying, "Tickets please." I couldn't in the least remember where that ticket was, so lifted down my furs, winter coat, baggage and knitting bag, dug out my purse and extracted my ticket.

All this time the conductor was continuing his infernal rapping, repeating, "Tickets please lower six. Lower six please." After satisfying him that I had a legal right to be on this train, and restoring my ticket to its hiding place and me under the covers, some other guy came along and went through the same program. I dropped off to sleep for a few minutes but wakened again because of the electric light in my eyes, at first not being able to discover how it was turned off. I then found I could see the country we were passing through by the light of the moon, and could not sleep for watching it. I have a blurred recollection of hundreds of towns, several mammoth bridges looming in the darkness, innumerable freight trains thundering by, and clearest, most clearest of all, the snoring of the man in upper six and the squeakiness of his berth.

Finally dropped off to sleep about three o'clock only to have the porter yank at my covering a while later and inform me it was quarter of five, and we would reach Pittsburgh shortly. Oh! How I hated that porter at that moment, but I loved him immediately afterward for he had polished my shoes, stood me in the hall and brushed my suit and coat, helped me off the train and generally looked after me. In spite of the unearthly hour I had to get up, we did not get into Pittsburgh until 8:00 and out again at 9:40, about three hours late. Had breakfast there in the loveliest place ever. Was shown to my table by a magnificent darky who took charge of my wraps and pulled out my chair. I also paid a magnificent price for some grapefruit, rolls and coffee, irreproachably served, and I remembered to dip my fingers into the finger bowl instead of drinking its contents. Tipped the waiter, too. Altogether, I've paid out a sizeable amount in tips so far but have gotten fine results. A nice boy in khaki was opposite me in the Pullman and I talked to a friendly Burroughs adding machine man, in spite of my parents' admonitions not to talk to strangers; both gave me some fatherly advice about Washington.

Pittsburgh is just what it is cracked up to be; only a dozen times worse. Such smoke I never dreamed of. For miles all I could see was smokestacks and blast furnaces glowing red, oil wells, and dirty, drab little houses perched on the hillside. Then more smoke, more blast furnaces, more smoke. Smoke and dirt over everything. Oil wells and brickworks stuck up all over the landscape by the hundreds. Everywhere were bare spots, no grass, just black, dirty earth. There did not seem to be any pretty houses until we reached the outskirts, where I saw beautiful large estates and houses up on the hills, out of the nasty dirtiness of the valley. Until we got into the mountains all the villages we passed were grimy little burgs with plenty of smokestacks and smelting works with coalmines sprinkled throughout.

We traveled through Pennsylvania until late afternoon. At Johnstown, the place of the big flood in 1889, the river was within an inch of being even with the streets. Johnstown seemed even dirtier than Pittsburgh. The whole city was smoky, saffron yellow, and I could see the glowing smelting works, the flames and sparks from the huge furnaces shooting high into the sky. And it seemed like I saw a brick factory every two minutes.

We passed the famous horseshoe curve during the day. It was the most wonderful sight! The country is very mountainous and the train is way high up betwixt Heaven and Earth. The mountainside is a wall of rock and dirt sheer above us in strata of orange and brown and black with the river in the valley seemingly miles below. The track turns sharply around so that in the first car one can look across the valley and see the last car on the other mountain. There is no snow here and it is almost like spring. We followed the river from Harrisburg through much of Maryland and got into Baltimore at 7 o'clock. We were only three hours late into Washington, arriving Wednesday night at 8 o'clock into the Union Station.

NOTE

[1] *In 1994 I went to Ionia, Michigan for the first time and met Marian's son Mickey Hurd and his wife Marie, who showed me the farm where my mother had grown up and the small school she attended, still standing at the Nickleplate intersection. The* Ionia Sentinel *offices were in the same building where my mother worked; Ionia is a beautifully preserved town. I met other cousins, and felt cheated of a whole family that I had never met.*

Josephine's mother takes the reins on a ride from the family farm into town.

1
FEBRUARY TO JUNE 1918
A New Government Girl In Washington

Jo and her friends visit the National Zoo on May 20, 1918.

"There were six military five-ton trucks filled with girls from Washington. The soldiers came down from camp and brought us back. The six trucks went right down Pennsylvania Avenue and past the Capitol. It is a common sight to see truckloads of soldiers, but truckloads of girls are rather unusual."

My mother rushed through the gate and into the ten-year-old Union Station's cavernous, vaulted concourse, and was awe-struck when she entered the waiting room to search for the housing information booth. She clutched her furs and knitting bag and dragged her bags over the marble and granite floor — no redcap was to be found. The buzz of the crowd reverberated around the vast space. She didn't know then that the Washington Monument could lie sideways in this concourse; but she did know that she wasn't in Michigan anymore and recorded that the "station could swallow half of Ionia."

Various agencies set up booths inside the waiting room to help incoming war workers find rooms, and to ease their transition from small towns to swollen city. As the government agencies expanded, the local District Council of Defense launched a campaign in the daily press, which explained the need for housing and asked homeowners, as a patriotic service, to list any rooms in their homes that could be spared to house an expected tens of thousands incoming government employees. An editorial in *The Washington Evening Star* complained that not enough help was coming from Congress and urged it to realize that Washington was "the main war shop." The federal government finally appropriated $50 million to build and acquire adequate housing.

In a 1918 letter, longtime resident Henry Adams, the country's elder statesman of letters, noted Washington's crowds and confusion: "Everything is camp and hospital... This little town has returned to its old habits of the Civil War... The railways are all running wild, every train is six or eight hours late, and every house is crowded beyond all reckoning by people arriving without notice and departing without good-byes. As for the young women, they are too numerous and too charming for cataloguing. I believe that all the prettiest girls in this country are now seeking jobs under government or in the Red Cross."

Before the United States entered the war, about 360,000 people lived in Washington, and the city had the atmosphere of a provincial Southern town. Ten months later, in a burst of explosive growth, another 75,000 persons lived in the financial and diplomatic center of a world allied against Germany. It was impossible to get a hotel room. A single room in a boarding house or private home cost as much as the rental of a whole house before the war; three or four persons occupied a room intended for one, and few young women got a bed to themselves. When the Union Station Plaza women's dormitory opened in December, a double room cost $20 a month per person. Even then, some girls were crowded three to a bed in rooming houses and paid 25 cents to bathe at the Central High School pool at 13th and Clifton Streets N.W. My mother shared a bed with Marie Smith, who would become her best friend, and be recorded as Smittie.

On February 21, 1918, Jo went to work at the War Department's massive three-story temporary building on the Mall. It faced B Street, now Constitution Avenue. Until the end of May, when she was transferred to the shell-loading division as a private stenographer, she maintained a hectic schedule and rarely stayed home more than one evening a week. Jo always found time to write in her diary, however, and often typed both entries and letters at the office. She inserted the long letters into her diary, and sometimes apologized to the recipient for the carbon, explaining that she needed a copy for her diary.

A few days later, my mother transcribed her diary into a long letter to her parents, who, unknown to her, passed it on to her former boss at the *Sentinel*. He wrote a patriotic introduction and gave it page one space: "Thousands of American girls are flocking to Washington to do their part in the winning of the war. To many of them, the experience of the journey to the nation's capital and the sights of the feverish wartime activities, which are the life of Washington today, are new. The experience of one of these girls is the experience of all, and in the following letter Miss Josephine Lehman has voiced the thoughts that must have come to a great army of those who have gone there with the same aim. ... It is not a letter from just one young woman, but a letter from the composite type of true young American womanhood which finds its expression in the massing of thousands of individuals in the great heart of the Union."

February 24: Heah Ah am, and it appeahs that if Ah stay heah ve'y long A'll jes nach'lly talk like this all the time. I just love it here!

At the station I obtained the address of a rooming house only two blocks from the depot but I didn't want to attempt getting lost so let a taxicab driver soak me for forty cents. The house was overflowing, but the lady of the house was kind enough to rout out a lieutenant and he carried down a small bed so she could bunk me in the parlor, which I considered extremely kind of her. Thanked the Lord I am gifted with an iron constitution so managed to get up for a formal breakfast and report to work by nine o'clock.

I was sworn into the Civil Service and sent over to the ordnance war building for work. A thin, middle-aged man and a big, young man argued over which should get me, both wanting a stenographer with business experience. I watched the fray in silence, mentally rooting for the young man. He won. My job is in the supply division of the ordnance department. The building is a mammoth new one and I have to have a pass to get in and out. This is the hardest department to work in, as they are so busy. The girls don't get many holidays but pay and promotions are good.

The government room registration office sent me to 1415 Massachusetts Avenue and I can't tell you how much I like it. The people who run it are real southerners, something like the old aristocracy one reads about. They have a daughter, Margaret Dudley, as pretty as her name and one of the sweetest girls I ever met. She has a southern accent, in fact, almost everybody does.

We have twenty-three girls living here, two, three, or four to a room, so don't worry about my being lonely. The rooms are large, so we don't mind it. I have two others in my room, Miss Dell Brokaw from Illinois, a tall, stunning blond and awfully dear, and Miss Grace Leonard from New York, also a big girl, with the most beautiful gown you ever saw. They call us the "Big Four Minus One," "Amazons" and other endearing names. All the girls are the finest kind, splendid, and very congenial. They are pretty and have stylish clothes. We take our breakfasts and dinners here and lunch downtown. No one eats supper here. Negro servants serve dinner in courses, clear from soup to dessert and finger bowls. We have a piano and Victrola downstairs which we can use any time and the girls in the next room have a ukulele.

And soldiers! There are about fifteen camps within a short radius of Washington. It seems the soldiers I have seen would make an army big enough to demolish the Kaiser in a day — Sailors, Marines, aviators, cavalry, infantry and artillerymen, plain desk-holder-downs and many IWTGBCs. The initials stand for a certain order, which is going to petition to wear buttons that say "I Want To Go But Can't."

Our house is a three-story brick and stone residence fronted with turrets and bay windows, situated high on a tree-lined terrace looking down six streets diverging from Thomas Circle, just a few minutes ride from work by electric car. It has old-fashioned furniture, grandfather clocks, big mirrors, cozy corners and fireplaces galore. It seems just like a college dormitory. On Saturday nights Miss "Mahgahret," as the servants call her, gives dances and invites enough young men to go around. We roll back the living room rugs, or drawing room, as they call it, and have piano and Victrola music and refreshments and the entire wherewithal to make a real party. The German Embassy is next door; the joke is that it's the only empty building in Washington.

My hours are from nine to four-thirty with double pay for overtime. There is a movement to lengthen the federal employees working law to eight or nine hours and all the department clerks went to protest, but even if they do give us longer hours I can realize that we still are not sacrificing much. One morning I went to work without my pass and had a difficult time getting into the war building, but talked my way in. Will have picture taken Tuesday for a permanent pass.

February 25: The weather is beautiful here, almost warm enough to go without a coat, and so sunny. Went to a Billy Sunday meeting the other day.

The evangelist, William "Billy" Sunday was a well-known personality. He had made a name as a baseball player, but gave it up to "work for Jesus Christ." Sunday toured the country with his supercharged revival meetings; they brought a new combination of old doctrine and up-to-date salesmanship. He ignored the higher-toned literary style in vogue, and used common speech: "I loaded my Gospel gun with rough-on-rats, ipecac, dynamite and barbed wire." President Wilson approved of Sunday, and he conducted an eight-week revival in a long, wooden tabernacle set up in front of Union Station, and drew adoring crowds, including society people, diplomats and government officials. He stimulated the prevalent anti-German feeling when he led his flock in such prayers as "God damn the Germans' stinking hide."

February 26: Mrs. Dudley had a dance at the house last night. Seventy-five there and excellent time. Sat out a dance with Sergeant Kenyon of the British Royal Flying Corps, who is in Washington as an instructor. As soon as his machine arrives he is going to do some stunts over the city. Nearly every day I see daring exhibition aeroplane flights over the city and at night the sky is shot through with many searchlights playing on the dome of the Capitol. Some thrilling thing is going on all the time and the city is full of soldiers, sailors, aviators, etc. A dozen or more were at the dance, from privates to lieutenants, and Marines. Also a civil engineer from the Navy Yard. The gowns were of the real evening variety. I have gotten over being shocked by such a display of arms and necks. After I have some new glad rags I am going to have some large pictures taken to astonish the native Ionians by the general absentness of the upper part of my gown.

March 10: Friday night Dell and I talked love affairs until twelve o'clock while I sewed my evening gown. Saturday night we resolved to go to bed early and end the week respectably. We started it, however by going to see "So Long, Letty" where we had seats of honor in that locality known to users of slang as "peanut heaven." We were geographically defined as a small body of girls entirely surrounded by soldiers. The play was very good, or so the morning paper said. Every time the audience laughed I had to peer around a large post directly in front of me; everything that happened seemed to be on the other side of it. To fully enjoy the sight of Letty's lengthy limbs I had to lean over on Dell or the soldier man on the other side. He didn't seem to be adverse to it; on the contrary I had some little trouble keeping away from him. That paved the way for an intermittent conversation that we kept up during the show. At the end of the play however, it was exit one soldier, enter two other soldiers, who sat in front of us. They first offered us some candy, which we accepted with hungry stomachs and thankful hearts. They escorted us home and talked a while on the steps; then we went inside and talked some more. They were nice boys, not objectionable.

March 24: I went to a dance at Camp Laurel last night, a big military camp about twenty-five miles north of Washington, between here and Baltimore. There were six military five-ton trucks filled with girls from Washington, twenty-five going from our house, accompanied by Mrs. Dudley. The soldiers came down from camp and brought us back. The six trucks went right down Pennsylvania Avenue and past the Capitol. It is a common sight to see truckloads of soldiers, but truckloads of girls are rather unusual. Got back at three this morning and didn't have breakfast until eleven. It was a farewell party for the boys who are leaving for France this week. Now I am so sleepy I can't write any more.

The War Department's Committee on Training Camp Activities took enough of an interest in its workers' leisure-time activities to issue a warning in the *Evening Star* against "pick-up soldier acquaintances." The warning was not intended to reflect on the character of the servicemen, who, it stated, as a whole were "clean and upstanding," but the War Department did not want its girls to converse familiarly with men in uniform unless introduced by a mutual friend or vouched for by a community organization. Nor did Uncle Sam want his boys loose to the temptations of the big city. For many of the young recruits who came from all over a very rural United States, it was not only the first time in the nation's capital, but the first time out of their state. Brothels in the vicinity of military bases were closed, and thousands of prostitutes were interred in federal prisons. "Wholesome" activities — Ping-Pong, pool, track, boxing, baseball, swimming, and dances — were offered. Keeping the boys "fit to fight" became a patriotic duty. YWCA lectures warned young women against the hazards of illicit love; the slogan "Do Your Bit to Keep Him Fit" attempted to foster a "higher standard of personal conduct and civil cleanliness." Posters reminded men and women: "Men must live straight if they would shoot straight."

March 31: Clocks turned ahead today so I lost an hour's sleep somewhere.[1]

April 6: One year ago today the United States entered the war and today the third Liberty Loan campaign was launched. Only by being delinquent did I see the great Liberty Loan parade from the Capitol to the White House.[2]

At four o'clock, although we were not supposed to have leave, we took advantage of Mr. Brady's absence and walked out en masse, leaving Mr. Sachs, the mail distributor, alone and helplessly furious, as he dared not leave his post. By dint of much pushing and shoving, and by judicious use of elbows, I jostled my way to Pennsylvania Avenue through the dense crowd. For about sixteen blocks the Avenue was lined on either side with a mass of people. My height was in my favor in looking over the crowds, and I held a place near the edge of the throng. All affairs of war were pushed from my mind because I was soon to see probably the best-known people in the country. My anxiety to have the parade reach our vantage point was almost as great as the urchins in front of us, who jumped up and down at the thought that at last they would see their hero with the cocky mustache and voluminous trousers — Charlie Chaplin. A forward guard was composed of twelve mounted police with immaculate uniforms, brass buttons glittering in the bright sunlight, a cavalry troupe, and then the famous United States Marine Band. The music was the signal for anticipatory little shivers to start dancing the length of my spinal column. This, however, was but the prologue.

Storms of applause arose when Mary Pickford appeared in the first carriage. She is very tiny and I can now see how she can appear as a child of ten. She looked very sweet and charming, wearing a large droopy hat of two shades of blue with long streamers, a heavy motor coat of grayish blue, brown tie oxfords and a corsage of orchids. Her hair is a bright yellow, much lighter than it appears in pictures. But as she rode along, kissing her hands and dimpling at the crowd, she was the same Mary we have known on the screen.

In the next carriage, rotund, robust Marie Dressler was enveloping the crowd with the same wide smile and good-natured appearance that make her comedies so much fun. When the next carriage appeared my sympathies were entirely with the little chap down in front who exclaimed derisively, "Aw, dat guy ain't Charlie Chaplin. Where's his mustache?" The Charlie of the movies, minus diminutive derby, enormous trousers and shoes and the ever-present mustache appeared as an attractive, dark-haired young man with an unusually likeable smile, unhampered by mustache.

Douglas Fairbanks, in the same car, came up to expectations by looking exactly like I always supposed he did. His famous grin was all wool and a yard wide. He was tanned and jocular and slangy and a hit with the crowd. "Please Mr. Fairbanks will you shake hands with me?" piped up a tiny girl in the crowd. "Gosh darn it, I believe I will," he answered with his big smile.

Following the movie stars were company after company and rank upon rank of infantry, engineers, Marines, artillery and the US Cavalry band. Overhead were the best aviators from the aviation field dipping, curving, whirling and showering thousands of Liberty Bells upon the crowd. It was a fitting beginning for the Liberty Loan drive and a celebration that I shall never forget. I had an hour's worth of work to catch up when I returned to the office.

May 7: Thursday night Grace and I went to Poli's to see "Hearts of the World," for which some scenes were taken along the French front; it's on the same scale as "Birth of a Nation."

"Hearts of the World," starring Lillian and Dorothy Gish, was innovative director D.W. Griffith's latest movie. With full orchestra and stage effects, the silent film was presented in the former opera house. Griffith incorporated military footage when he shot this story of a family who lived just behind the lines in France. For the benefit of an audience not used to the language of war, an eight-page program defined words and phrases such as barrage, dugout, hand grenade, shrapnel and heavy artillery. A ticket cost from 25 cents to a dollar fifty.

May 9: Cooler today. A most wonderful brass band leading a Knights of Templar parade went right by our house. We girls in nighties hung out the windows while the wind billowed us out like balloons so that thrills had sufficient room to run up and down our backbones.

May 10: I observe as never before the infallibility of that old chestnut, "Oh what a tangled web we weave, when first we practice to deceive." It started with my seeing Mr. Siegel and a friend in the lower hall and trying to persuade Mrs. Dudley to tell him I was out. Failing that, I went downstairs with a sad tale entitled "A Previous Engagement." I hope he fell for it. While they waited for Miss Waterbury, I did a little dodging act trying to get out of the house and went for a walk up Massachusetts Avenue with Dell and Mabel Simpson. We strolled through Dupont Circle to Twenty-second Street, past the Walsh and McLean homes and others.[3]

Home again and they were still on the porch, cutting off the only entrance. Our facile brains conceived the idea of entering from N Street at the rear, although that vicinity was untrodden territory, as we realized when we found ourselves wandering in a maze of alleys, paths, ash piles, wagons, garages and fences. We realized the futility of finding our own back door and we ran into an exclusively masculine back veranda party, so backed out to the street, and by the time we reached our own front door the men had departed.

May 12: Went with Dell to the Neighborhood House. The evening began with the girls sixteen to one but it ended better and I had a fairly good time, was escorted home by Mr. Radcliffe, a nice boy who was deeply grateful (so he said) for the dancing instruction I gave him.

For the next two years, Neighborhood House at 468-470 N Street, SW, would play a large part in Jo's life, even after the servicemen who made Washington so exciting returned home. Opened in 1901, it was the oldest settlement house in the District. She was sometimes nervous when she came into this slum area, but the Ninth Street trolley rolled to within a few blocks of the door. During the war, Neighborhood House opened its doors to servicemen, and provided a space for dances, reading, writing, crafts, and holiday dinners. Jo became fond of resident directors John and Clara Neligh, and after the war she volunteered at the District's first public library branch, which the city opened in the building.

May 14: Made my first visit to Arlington Cemetery with Dell, David Blanchard and Mr. David Miller, a soldier from Philadelphia. Regaled ourselves with refreshments twice and filled up the spaces with candy. At the urgent request of Blanchard and Dell, Miller and I obligingly went into the house. We looked around and saw nothing, thus giving them time to get comfortably ensconced under a tree down the hill. Being generous souls, we walked around some time before disturbing them. We visited the Confederate Monument, the anchor of battleship Maine, the monument to the Maine Sailors, the grave of the unknown dead, and about a million graves of the Boys of 1865.[4] Strolled past Ft. Myer and through the officers' quarters and had more refreshments. The mosquitoes were out for refreshment too. Mr. Miller insisted on paying me compliments, stock ones, and barely kept his distance; he just escaped being fresh.

May 20: On Sunday Mr. John Henry, a delightful sailor boy, Miss Ada Smith and I and Mabel and Miles Connors visited our kith and kin at the zoo, the monkeys especially. We had ourselves snapshotted eighteen times so I trust at least a few will show what we looked like. Although Henry is Miss Smith's property, I like him very much and it's a relief to have a natural good time with a nice chap, after some of the men I have met.

June 10: Put in a strenuous day doing copy work. Lt. Munro said I might be placed as a private secretary.[5]

June 23: Worked two days last week for Monsieur Capitaine de Roquelaine and love him, really. It was a wonder he let me work, he was so polite, and he brought me a box of candy, too. He has just arrived from France on a confidential mission and asked for a private stenographer "with intelligence" and they sent me to him. I was chosen out of fifty stenographers. He is at the head of all the French military experts in the US and his work is very important. For the past two weeks I have been working in the section dealing with high explosives and I know how to blow up just about anything.

June 28: Another hot day and circumstances are slowly bringing me to the realization that I am in for a stretch of work and not much play. Much of the exuberance I felt upon my arrival has vanished and the novelty of Washington is wearing away. I think I shall go in for some serious reading and some lectures. There is one consolation, or rather more than one — there are always men and dances and places to go. I wonder what has happened to the innocent unsophisticated child I was last winter? However, this is my life, and I am glad I am in Washington.

NOTES

[1] *Daylight Saving Time began on the last day of March as a fuel conservation measure. The government expected to save $40 million in the nation's lighting bills.*

[2] *Five Liberty Loan Drives to sell bonds helped finance the more than $1 billion a month war. The parades that launched each drive were a patriotic and popular form of entertainment. The Secretary of the Treasury received a letter suggesting a solid week of fund raising parades because, according to the writer, "Nearly everyone seems blind to the hell that's facing us... music will make everyone step out, even the slackers' blood will warm up." Tens of thousands of people turned out for the biggest parades.*

[3] *Dupont Circle was larger then, and more like a park, with flower-lined, pebble paths and little traffic noise except for the clang of the streetcars rounding the curve. The bustle of the war-clogged city didn't extend to this residential area.*

[4] *Visitors were free to roam through the ground floor rooms of Arlington House, principal residence of Robert E. Lee until 1861, when he resigned his commission in the U.S. Army to join the southern rebellion. The Grave of the Unknown Dead contained 211 bodies from the Civil War battles of Bull Run and Rappahannock. The Four Unknown Servicemen from WWI would not be interred until 1921.*

[5] *My mother hated filing and making copies on the new mimeograph machine. She requested the less boring job of stenographer. She told me that her assertiveness got her out of the secretarial pool.*

2
JUNE TO SEPTEMBER 1918
Long Hours
At the War Department

Jo's future husband, U.S. Marine Reynold Thomas, with his mother and sister.

*"I have just finished typing a long report. Our office is a continual uproar.
Two dozen typewriters are going at the same time, forty-seven people are
yelling over the different telephones to places from New York to Chicago, men
are shouting at each other across the room, and workers are rushing back and
forth until I can't hear myself think. This is the life."*

At about the time Jo was transferred from Administration to the Shell-Loading section, and wrote that she could blow up just about anything, news reports of American soldiers who had suffered that fate in France were on the front page of Washington newspapers. In March, the Germans launched a major push to Paris, and Big Bertha, their new long-range gun, barraged the French capital from a distance of seventy-four miles; when they advanced to within forty miles of the city, Parisians began to evacuate. The Allies begged General Pershing for more manpower, but he insisted that the morale of his soldiers depended upon their fighting under the American flag. However, on May 30th the Germans crossed the Marne River, and when it seemed they would enter Paris, Pershing reluctantly turned over 170,000 men, who included the recently arrived third Marine replacement battalion. A week later, 10,000 still-green men were sent to Chateau-Thierry, a town near Belleau Wood, and ordered to hold the line against the advancing Hun. Jo's future husband was one of these Marines. He wrote home, "The Boche has been shelling a most ungodly storm... the days are not so bad, but Oh God, the nights are worse than mad hell in darkness." The Americans held that line at a cost of more than half the brigade killed or wounded. Headlines throughout the United States blazed: "Germans Stopped at Chateau-Thierry with Help of God and Few Marines." This battle marked a turning point, and numerous posters all over Washington proclaimed, "The Hun is on the Run." (My father was one of a small percentage of that brigade to survive the attack.)

Washington was now on an all-out military basis. Even though President Wilson still took occasional walks to his bank or a shop, military policemen with rifles bayonet-ready guarded the two White House gates. No longer could casual sightseers walk up to the presidential mansion. Soldiers kept watch over the Potomac rail bridge and bunked in tents along the riverbank. Further down the river the polo field was converted to a landing strip. The section of Potomac Park not covered by temporary government buildings sprouted vegetables; a District resident could lease a garden plot for two dollars and fifty cents a season. Construction of the Lincoln Memorial continued, and plans for "speedily erected, readily taken down" workers' housing between it and the river were on the drawing board.

Emergency war measures staggered Washington and citizens stood in line everywhere. Lines formed in restaurants, cafeterias and street corner food carts, at banks, at theater and movie box offices, at butcher shops and greengrocers, to read war bulletins in front of the Star building, and at the imposing green marble lobby of the new post office next to Union Station. Long lines crisscrossed the station's waiting room as would-be train passengers hoped to book a seat rather than standing room. Lines formed around public telephone exchanges and frustrated residents besieged overworked operators.

Private automobiles brought to the city by the dollar-a-year-men — industrialists who donated their services to the government for the duration of the war — challenged the trolleys and horse-drawn carriages, and congested downtown. The city's traffic police held their stop-and-go signs at major intersections, and could no longer daydream on the job. Speed limits for the high, bulky, black automobiles ranged from six miles an hour in the alleys to a racy twenty-two on the outskirts.

Flags fluttered high against the sky, draped over doors, or fell in folds from a window. And not just the American flag, but service flags, the Red Cross flag, the Liberty Loan flag and flags of the Allies. Patriotic posters authorized by the Committee for Public Information, many of them masterpieces of the illustrators' art, were at eye level on street corners and in the multitude of small, grassy triangle parks at intersections of tree-lined streets and avenues. Beginning in August, a flag-draped siren, "sounding like the wail of lost souls," blew every day at noon, and all Washington stopped work to pray for victory. Department stores and small shops still closed on Saturday, but stayed open later on weekdays to serve government employees who had to work Saturdays.

Civilians heard a new vocabulary. They became accustomed to military talk and used words like liaison, communiqué, propaganda and sector in their conversations; phrases like "over the top" and "carry on" entered common usage. Cigarette smoking gained popularity with soldiers; a pack fit neatly into a uniform pocket, but a pocket watch did not. The new wristwatch, $13.50 with a khaki strap, became the favored gift for a husband, son, or lover off to war. Uniformed men mingled with smartly dressed crowds in restaurants, theaters and dances. War-weary English, French and Italian officers, many lame or battle-scarred, were billeted in private homes. Officers in dress uniforms added panache to the dinner parties of fashionable women. Battalions of soldiers on their way "over there" trained, and more and more Americans in khaki or Navy blue flowed through the camps that surrounded Washington.

To support this manpower, Pershing asked the War Department for twenty-two million rounds of ammunition by December 1st, and the Shell Loading Section was on full alert. Jo, caught up in the excitement, worked at a hectic pace. In early July she wrote: "I have just finished typing a long report. Our office is a continual uproar. Two dozen typewriters are going at the same time, forty-seven people are yelling over the different telephones to places from New York to Chicago, men are shouting at each other across the room, and workers are rushing back and forth until I can't hear myself think. This is the life. Everything short of a riot or the New York Stock Exchange will be too tame for me when I get out of here."

Jo took dictation and typed reams of neat letters. Correspondence concerned everything from how soldiers assigned to the Dupont engineering plant would be paid, to a request for 2,000 more "white" troops, to appeals for "soldier labor" at various shipping plants. Another letter told how it was "impossible to get nurses as the country has been combed for same, and there are none available." There were, but "colored" nurses were refused permission to go to France. She coordinated highly technical reports, and documents about shipping high explosives between Washington, district offices and munitions plants around the country. She sent Safety Operating Rules for manufacturing, loading, handling, and storing explosives to the various munitions plants. She confirmed shipments of grenades, detonators, shells, drop bombs, gas shells, and hand and rifle grenades, and typed endless inventories of explosives.

President Wilson declared that it was time for America "to correct her unpardonable fault of wastefulness and extravagance," and waged a home front war on waste. Herbert Hoover designed propaganda to help women, men, and children feel a glow of pleasure when they participated in the process that Hoover called food conservation, but which came to be known affectionately as Hooverizing. Hoover's appeals were read out from pulpits, schools, and motion picture theaters. Newspapers, posters, placards, and billboards shouted the slogan, "Food Will Win the War." The nation shared wheatless Mondays and Wednesdays, meatless Tuesdays and porkless Thursdays and Saturdays. Fish was marketed as a valuable and inexpensive food (trout was only five cents a pound, compared to thirty-five cents for lamb). Some restaurants added horse, rabbit, and even whale meat to the menu; they served no bread until after the first course and allowed only one-half ounce of butter per person. Hoover urged homemakers not to purchase more food than they were certain to use. *Life* magazine editorialized: "Do not permit your child to take a bite or two from an apple and throw the rest away; nowadays even children must be taught to be patriotic to the core."

From the time she was ten Josephine wrote jingles and verse. She contributed the following to *Intowin*, a magazine published by the Ordnance Civilians' Association. This house organ stressed patriotism and duty, gave housing updates and information on entertainments for the lonely war worker — riding parties, roller-skating, volleyball, rhythmic and social dancing, shooting, and nutting parties. (The nuts would be shipped to the soldiers in France.) Humor was included, too; short takes, essays, and lots of verse.

August 12: Dear Mother: The weather for the past week has been the hottest I ever have gone through. It got as high as 120 in the street, the asphalt pavements were soft as putty and the cement pavements burned my feet through the soles of my shoes.[1] All the girls did wear dresses, but they didn't wear any more under them than the law required, and the sun shone right through. It was a matter of choice between roasting to death and looking indecent. It's a little better now, but just enough so that we manage to sleep at night. I have so many white skirts in the wash, my laundry bill is bankrupting me. I wash all my underclothes myself every night, but even at that I can't wear them more than two or three days without sending them to the washwoman. It is impossible to wear silk waists as the perspiration shrinks them, and if they are colored they get streaked, and a heavy skirt is out of the question entirely. Last night it was so hot that I wrung out a towel in cold water and put it on my head (I suppose you'll tell me that is a good way to catch cold) and when I went to sleep the towel would get out of place and I would wake up again with my face dripping and have to rescue the wet towel in some corner of the bed. It was a good thing that Smittie, my bedmate, was away on her vacation or she would have been drowned.

The suffragettes have been having high old times picketing the White House to ask for the vote and laying for the President whenever he comes out.[2] The police are arresting them by the hundreds and giving them free rides to the lockup, where their husbands and fathers have to bail them out.

Have you anything good to eat at home? You might telegraph me some. Sugar is so scarce in Washington that we can only have it once a day and no one can make ice cream for a week on account of ice scarcity.

Write soon, and put it in German if English is too slow, although I wouldn't dare show the letter in the house. My service pin with four stars is the only thing that redeems the fact that I am German. Auf wiedersehen. With Love, Jo.

A woman whose husband, son or brother was in the service wore a little gold bar pin with a hanging red and white ribbon and one embroidered blue star for each man. Four of Jo's brothers served in Europe. Notwithstanding their German heritage, the family was intensely patriotic. Her parents immigrated when they were teenagers and were naturalized before 1900 and, with the exception of several cousins, had no family in Germany. My mother and her brothers felt no connection to Germany; their roots were irrelevant to their only goal — to defeat the country where their parents were born.

September 17: I didn't work last week, being able to get six days off in one stretch. Nellie and Ferne arrived from Ionia on Thursday and will stay if they can find suitable work, but they didn't take the government examination before they came. All day Friday we spent looking for rooms, and if there is a street in Washington that we didn't visit I wish someone would show me to it. After all our searching we found only two vacant rooms. One of them was beautiful, with furniture of bird's eye maple and mahogany leather rockers and couch with Oriental pillows and draperies, big window seat, bookcase, desk, etc. But we let it slide when the owner informed us that it was $200 a month without board. The other room was in a good-looking house but it was kept by a woman of too dark a complexion to suit us, and was in a neighborhood settled entirely by others whose skin was of the same shade.[3] However, as the girls had to have something they took it, and I am trying to get them a place in our house, which already has a large waiting list.

NOTES

[1]*Even for Washington, August 1918 was a fryer and, except for the unique system devised by Connecticut Avenue homeowner Alexander Graham Bell, air-conditioning was in the future.*

[2] *The suffrage amendment to the Constitution finally passed Congress in the spring of 1919 and the states ratified it in 1920.*

[3] *My mother's casual racism is typical of the attitude of the era, especially in segregated Washington. When I was in high school and said that one of the girls on the basketball team lived in "Niggertown" — the African-American section of Barnegat — I was sharply reprimanded; my mother said, "We do not ever use that word."*

3
SEPTEMBER 1918 TO MARCH 1919
Adventures with Boys

Jo poses on the roof of her boarding house before a Halloween party.

"The two women heard newsboys as they yelled, "Extree — War's over," at the top of their voices, and people hung flags from their windows ... Josephine and her friends flocked out of their offices when the sirens and whistles blew and joined thousands of laughing, crying, dancing revelers who thronged onto Pennsylvania Avenue and surrounded the White House. Wilson emerged briefly, waved his handkerchief, and received a cheering ovation."

The fall of 1918 was a time of hard work and long hours. Overtime pay was eliminated, and government employees worked as many hours as "national necessity" required; those few who protested were quickly labeled slackers. My mother saved a special after-hours pass from the State, War, and Navy Department dated September 11. Her notation with it reads: "In memory of the 'good old days' when I worked day and night AND Sundays." The deadly Spanish influenza epidemic curtailed social activities. The Dudley girls planned an elaborate Halloween party, but, as the *Star* reported, Halloween would be "overshadowed by war and influenza" this year, and Jo and her housemates didn't have their costume ball until after the armistice.

In September the Spanish flu reached eastern seaboard cities, after it ravaged the armies in Europe, and killed half as many soldiers as were killed in the war; those between the ages of 20 and 40 were most vulnerable. The first week of October, the disease entered Washington from surrounding camps with such force that federal office shifts were staggered. More than half the streetcar operators sickened. Stores limited their hours. Saloons, schools, churches, and theaters closed; public gatherings were prohibited. The government set up nursing centers in the vacated schools, and transformed a Western Union office into a Red Cross training center. A requisitioned government building became an emergency hospital, and forty-five society women commandeered a garage and cranked up a volunteer ambulance corps that used donated Model-T trucks and their own chauffeured limousines to transport sick and dying residents to emergency centers. Even though not one nurse was available, patients filled every bed at George Washington University. For lack of gravediggers, bodies in coffins piled up in cemeteries; for lack of coffins, some dead lay where they died.

In his autobiography, District Commissioner Louis Brownlow recalled the epidemic's uncontrollable horror: "A girl had called to say that she and three other girls had a room together, that two of the girls were dead, another was dying and she was the only one not stricken; would I please get some help there. I managed to get the police department, and it found someone to go to that house. When the policeman got there, there were four dead girls in the room."

Jo wrote a letter to the *Sentinel* about the epidemic in which she said, "Out of the twenty-five girls at my boarding house, about twenty were ill, and it was a young hospital all by itself."

About 35,000 Washingtonians caught the flu and it killed 10 percent of them. The epidemic spread quickly throughout the forty-eight states. (In October 1919, it was declared a pandemic.) Journalist Mark Sullivan wrote: "In the age of microbiology, serums, and enlightened medicine, here were death lists three or four times as long as those of the Black Death in London, the terrible plague of 1665."

In August, the Allies started their last big push against the Germans; Americans in the Argonne Forest were in the middle of their largest and most costly battle. Both nations counted more than 100,000 dead in the six-week action, and the Germans retreated to a line that would demarcate boundaries at the time of the armistice. Germany's starving population threatened a socialist revolution, and its desperate Chancellor cabled President Wilson on October 8th to ask for an armistice to negotiate peace, but the President demanded unconditional surrender.

On November 7th, Mrs. Dudley, Jo's landlady, heard a steam whistle above the clatter of her sewing machine, then another, and another. Her maid came in and asked, "Could they be peace whistles?" And they were. The two women heard newsboys as they yelled, "Extree — War's over" at the top of their voices, and people hung flags from their windows. Her husband came home from work and said at the Capitol, congressmen romped like boys, officers and privates embraced, and the streets were so full that the cars couldn't move. People carried flags, shouted and sang, and long lines of dancing young women joined hands and wound in and out of the crowds.

Jo and her friends flocked out of their offices when the sirens and whistles blew and joined thousands of laughing, crying, dancing revelers who thronged onto Pennsylvania Avenue and the Ellipse, and surrounded the White House. Wilson emerged briefly, waved his handkerchief, and received a cheering ovation. Good-natured pandemonium took over as soldiers and sailors joined the young women, and a serpentine dance started on Ninth Street. Battalions of marchers shrieked their joy and shouted patriotic songs. Crowds surged around the newspaper offices to wait for the latest word. People piled into military trucks; bands led long processions; horns, cowbells, pans, drums, anvils and iron pipes scored the revelers' jubilation; airplanes dipped and looped over the crowd. The fury of celebration went on until midnight, and regained momentum after theater crowds let out. Motormen in jammed trolleys clanged their gongs; automobiles overflowed with riders balanced on the running boards.

But the news was premature and not confirmed by the White House. On November 11th at 11 am, the actual armistice was signed, and the second celebration was mild in comparison, although President and Mrs. Wilson rode up and down Pennsylvania Avenue in an open car, surrounded by a densely packed crowd.

December 2: Things are in such a mixed up condition since the armistice. Half of the office workers have already resigned, been discharged or transferred; I was transferred and am now working for a Major. I have worked for the Colonel at times; maybe I'll have a chance to work for the General before long. Almost half the Section personnel have left and someone is going every day. I am starting to wonder what this old town will be like when nearly all the wartime government employees are gone and the soldiers and sailors leave.

December 12: Reached home just in time to snatch some dinner, dress, and off to the Neighborhood House. Mr. Neligh is a fat old gentleman who wears a black frock coat and a black satin flowing bow tie and combs his hair à la the 19th-century mode, and he is equally at home whether capering around in a waltz with one of the girls or sitting in a corner talking anything from political science to the psychology of thought. Mrs. Neligh is a friend of Dell's fiancé, so the girls in our room have a standing invitation to the Saturday night dances. Practically the same bunch of girls is there each time, but the men are always different, as the soldier and sailor and Marine population of Washington is constantly shifting. The dances are very informal. One is usually introduced to all the men present, but if you are not, you are supposed to be nice and cordial to them just the same.

Am back in Major Gardiner's office again. Fussed around all the afternoon with a cablegram from General Pershing, which I got in proper form for the Major.

December 13: Corporal Brenn and Dell's Billy came for a dancing lesson. Dell did her best but Billy refused to take her efforts seriously, so didn't make much headway but Corporal Brenn surprised me by acquitting himself as a decidedly good dancer before the evening was over. Such an apt pupil I never had.

My mother entered her teens at the same time the ragtime dance craze bopped across the country. In 1910, Irving Berlin wrote "Doing the Grizzly Bear," and a series of animal dances had young people hopping, jerking, limping, and flopping; the grizzly bear, bunny hop, turkey trot, lame duck, camel walk and chicken scratch turned dance floors into a menagerie of graceless movements. Then dancers Irene and Vernon Castle glided across the floor in the 1914 Broadway show, "Watch Your Step" and the stage was set for a new style. Awkward gyrations were abandoned, and debutantes and working girls alike learned the graceful Castle walk and fox trot, and the intimate tango. My mother's dance programs list a few obscure dances — "blind feed the blind" and "blind boxing" — but at the more formal dances the Paul Jones, a circle dance with changing partners, waltz, fox trot, and one step were the most popular.

December 18: Major Harkness has been promoted to Chief of the Loading Section so I am now in the private office with him. I can hardly believe I am working in the same place. Everyone has gone out of the three private offices except ours, and the man for whom I work, Major Harkness, is the only one in a private office now.[1] I am some pumpkins — secretary to the chief. The stenographers who were in the other private offices were discharged, transferred or resigned, and nearly all the girls in the outer offices have gone. The work will be steadily cleaned up until about next May when nothing more will be left and the Shell Loading Section will die a natural death. That also means I am out of a job. I was recommended for $1,520 a year, but I am not counting on it until I see that first $63.33 coming in for two weeks' pay.

The Captain told me that if I was ever in need of a job here I was to call up his former roommate who is the Director General of the US Employment Service, to whom he has already recommended me. He also told me that if he got established in his business in Boston and needed a good stenographer and secretary, he would remember me. As he won't be here, he gave me $5 for Christmas. All Uncle Sam gives is a half day before Christmas. I can't believe how money goes in this city. I am hoping that my raise will take effect very soon, as the money surely will be needed.

Jo's money would have gone like this: newspaper two cents, bottle of aspirin 70 cents, hat $5 to $25, petticoat $2 to $5, shoes $8 to $15, suits and dresses $25 to $50, skirts and sweaters $4 to $6. Fabric cost only 19 cents a yard, so she made many of her clothes. A round-trip boat excursion to Marshall Hall cost 50 cents, including war tax; candy was 30 cents a pound and a typewriter $50 to $100.

January 6: Stayed home all day with a cold and as I was dead broke didn't have any money to buy lunch so ate the remainder of my Christmas candy. In the evening, Grace and I declared it too cold to remain in our room, so went to Thomson's to keep warm.[2] We got what we wanted, as the usual hot, packed Thomson crowd was present.

January 11: Spent the morning at the office packing our belongings preparatory to moving to E Building. Came back after lunch and found the furniture still there, so four or five of the girls perched on one of the empty tables and just sat, huddled like a stranded theatrical troupe. Mr. Larkin turned a deaf ear to our entreaties for the afternoon off. Major Gardner took pity on us, however, and told us to get out. We didn't wait for a second invitation and hurried away lest he change his mind.

January 28: Mr. Larkin asked if I would like to go to New York as his stenographer when he left on February 15. His position isn't certain yet, but it was very probable that he would be able to place me, he said, and it is just what I like to do. I thought it was very kind of Mr. Larkin to consider me, but I suppose he is considering himself as well.

February 3: Received a phone call from the Department of Labor today offering me a job at $1,200, but I turned it down. Mr. Larkin told me I could stay here three months yet if I wished. Dell received some fresh pork tenderloin from home today, also doughnuts, butter and pickles, and with the addition of some bread and grape juice we had a very creditable feast, one that brought tears of envy to the rest of the house when they smelled the meat frying.

February 5: Grace, Martha, Smittie and I went to a dance at the Neighborhood House given for the returned Camouflage Regiment.[3] They were surely an interesting bunch of chaps. Most of them had been in France a year and related some scary adventures. The floor was unmercifully crowded and I received a generous bruise on my left foot. Camouflage costumes were provided for the girls, who looked like rag pickers. I danced most of the evening with a nice tall chap from Arizona, also with the major, the captain and two or three lieutenants, who had condescended to donate their presence to the affair. Two of the camouflage men, McCarty and Conway, came home with us, and we stood on the doorstep until one-thirty, our teeth chattering and our feet and faces freezing while McCarty, who was a civil engineer in private life, told story after story of his experiences in France, some pathetic, some funny, and some horrible. He was in the battles of Chateau-Thierry, Argonne Forest, St. Michel, and one or two others. He has been gassed, gone three months without a change of underwear or a bath, being all the time under constant fire in the front line of the trenches, experienced to the utmost the horrors of Brest, which he called the hell-hole of Europe, and knows all about cooties. He held us spellbound.

February 12: I have a cold and I could eat worms with relish in my present state of mind and spirit. Perhaps if I eat some lunch I might feel better. Another worry is the fact that I haven't any decent clothes and haven't any money with which to get them, so have started to save again. I simply must cut down on my expenses. If my will power isn't strong enough to let alone things I don't need, then I am a poor specimen. Mr. Larkin left today for New York, giving me a fine letter of recommendation, and saying he would let me know if he had any position for me. Grace and I have almost decided to go bumming for a year, starting next fall and traveling around the country, just making enough for our expenses.

February 22: Major Harkness expects to leave next week, after which I will be working for Colonel Davis. I don't know anything about my future plans. I have been here a year and I keep thinking of what I was doing a year ago today. Those first days I was in Washington are very vivid in my memory. The city seems like an old story to me now.

February 25: Was sitting alone in the office this afternoon wishing for something to happen when in strolled a big young man who asked for Colonel Davis. As he was not present, the young man asked to be allowed to sit down, which I cordially granted, and we started to talk. From discussion of office work, we drifted to letter writing, then to love letter writing, then to our families, then to ages (he is twenty six), then to names (his is Charles F. Tieman), then to favorite pastimes, then to kisses, then to drinking (I told him I drank milk when I felt quite devilish), then to other rather advanced subjects. He ended up by trying to bet me a night's lodging that he could sell the colonel some storage cases. I didn't accept the bet. He asked for my telephone number, which I gave him. I'll wager that he thought I was a fast piece of furniture[4] and it is my fault if he did, for I certainly led him on by my remarks. I must have been crazy to say some of the things I did, but I had a devilish impulse. I was sorry afterward, for he is evidently a very likable chap and I hated to have him get a wrong impression of me.

February 26: Went up to the bank at noon and finished paying for my first Liberty Bond. I prepared for my engagement with Charles Francis Tieman with some trepidation, albeit with much care as to my personal appearance. Wore my grey dress and red beads, and Smittie's grey fur neckpiece when I met him in the hall. Grace was plainly alarmed after some of the things I had told her about him, and said that if I weren't back by midnight, she would notify the police. I told her I would be careful and that I wouldn't get into any automobile. He told me I looked like a million dollars, and I had to admit he looked decidedly well himself. He is a fine looking chap. We went out, and there on the terrace was a big seven-passenger Lexington sedan. I swallowed a couple of times, but managed to ask him calmly if that was his car, and he said it was furnished him by the automobile company he represents. It was a wonderful car, and in we hopped. (Curtain on scene one.)

We drove about the city for fifteen or twenty minutes, stopping to get some Martha Washington chocolates, while my escort talked impersonally and entertainingly on various subjects. So far, so good. He asked if I would rather go to a show or for a ride, and I decided on the ride, partly because it wasn't at all cold in the closed car [cars were not equipped with heaters] and the weather was beautiful, and partly because I was curious as to what line of advance he was going to follow. We drove to Georgetown and back, then down the speedway, around the point, and to a place about opposite to the War College. At this point, he asked if I didn't think the engine was tired and needed a rest. He said if he overworked it, it might give out on us, and then we would have to stay all night. I replied that I was a good walker, and was perfectly able to get back to the city. He stopped the car; we got out the candy and started to eat. So far, so good. (Curtain on scene two.)

We had been there an hour, almost, talking like old friends, and I was just ready to think that all my nervousness had been useless, when he gave me a hug and a very "impressing" kiss. I have to hand it to him that his kisses aren't half bad, that is, there is nothing of the sticky, mushy, quality about them that characterized a few I have had. I began to think that something had started. (I was right.) He went on to tell me that he was very outspoken, and generally said right out what he wanted without beating about the bush. He first asked if I didn't believe in going the limit to get a good time. I said that I didn't. I made no pretense at misunderstanding him, seeing that he was so plain in his methods. He asked if I weren't passionate, and I answered him in the negative in that, also. He wanted to know if I would give him permission to go ahead and arouse my passion, saying he would bet anything that he could. I told him that it was useless; I wasn't that kind of girl, although I was rather curious to know what he would do. I think I know, though, as I was told once how it was done and won't ever forget.

All this time he had his arm around me but otherwise did not attempt to touch me or take any privileges whatever, which gave him a credit mark. He next said his hands were cold and wanted to know if he could put them inside my coat. I said he could put them inside my plush cuffs, if necessary, but nix on the other. He asked me if I meant that. I said I did. His next line was to ask me out-and-out if he could feel my silk stockings. He didn't attempt to do a thing before asking me, and I had lost all my nervousness and was bending my efforts to repartee. I convinced him the silk hose idea was out of the question, also, and he looked rather hurt. He next resorted to heavy artillery methods of outspokenness. He asked me point blankly if I wouldn't go up to his room at the hotel with him and I answered him most decidedly that I would not. I decided a little display of temper just at this point might be to my advantage.

His next look was surprise. He thought I was stringing him along. He said he knew I was passionate. I said I was not and never had been. He caught up that last remark and said I might as well tell the truth, he knew practically all girls went the limit. I said that he had met an exception right then and there.

He said, "Do you mean to say that you have never done 'that sort of thing' before and that you don't know anything about it?"

"Exactly," says I, wondering what my mother would think of the conversation could she hear it.

"My God!" he said, "Do you think I would have asked you all those things and tried what I did if I knew you were straight?" He actually seemed to take it as a matter of course that all girls were crooked.

His next remark was that he was Catholic and tried to live up to his religion, and that while he had had a lot to do with women, he had never ruined one. He asked me to forgive him. If I would see him again, he couldn't promise not to get "warmed up," as he put it, but that I needn't be afraid of him. He said it was a girl of my build who invariably worked up a man's passion and I told him I wasn't to blame for my build. He asked my pardon again, said that he was a good loser, took out a cigar and smoked it, and seemed to consider the incident closed. (Curtain on scene three).

We smoked and ate candy for some time; that is, he smoked and I ate the candy, and we reverted back to impersonal subjects, and anyone, to have heard us, would never have guessed the decidedly risqué conversation we had been having only a few minutes before. When I think of it now I have a wild impulse to howl. We started back to town about eleven, went up to the terrace and talked a while in the car. He can be really charming when he wants to. When I said I must go in he said he would call me Friday at seven, escorted me to the door and opened it, bade me a very nice goodnight (in words only) and was gone.

I don't think he kissed me more than three times during the evening. I am resolved that he can't put anything over on me, but admit that he has me interested, although I haven't the least bit of a case on him. He is leaving Washington in two or three weeks and I am not even counting on his calling up again. I shouldn't be surprised if he should start to get funny were I to go out with him again; but at least, he did nothing that I wouldn't allow.

February 28: Charley didn't come until almost nine o'clock, having been halted by a cop for not having a tail light. It was raining, but not hard. He asked me what I wanted to do, and forgetting about playing with fire I chose a ride to Great Falls along the canal road instead of going to a show. The first part of the evening was all right. Charley was as nice as he could possibly be until we were on the road home, and he stopped the car beside the road, and said he was tired of driving. He proceeded to sit down on the back seat, light a cigarette, and asked if I weren't going to be sociable. I hesitated.

He said he didn't think I was going to be afraid of him after the other night when he had promised to reform, so I went back and we sat ourselves down in the back seat. It really was quite comfy with the rain pattering on the roof of the car, and nice and warm inside. We talked and argued on various subjects, we sang a song or two and in general had a nice time until he started to kiss me.

Knowing that that might start something (Oh, I am getting wise and experienced in my old age), I tried to make him stop, and I was right. It was just a repetition of part of the other evening, and I was so angry and disappointed that I almost cried, whereupon he fairly ate the dust and apologized forty-eleven times.

I can't understand how a man can let his baser passions get the best of him. If he only wouldn't do it, I could like him a lot, he has so many charming qualities and is so nice looking. Perhaps I started out wrong by giving him the wrong impression of me at the start. He said when he brought me home that he was going to call me up tonight and have a little long distance chat. He evidently recognizes that he can be much more agree-able at a distance. He tells me that I have no business being so damned enticing to a man. I surely don't mean to be enticing. I cannot understand why he wants to come again. He either wants my friendship in the right way, or else thinks if he keeps coming and ask-ing for the same thing that he will gain what he wants in the end. If he calls me tonight, I think I will tell him that I don't care to see him again. That would be a lie, as I really would, but I can't put up with that sort of thing. Whenever I think that I might weaken and lose my will power while I am around him, I get scared. The sooner it is stopped, the better. I thought I knew everything there was to know in that line through my various little talks with other men, but found out that I am hopelessly ignorant of what he calls life. I prefer ignorance, I think.

As a farm girl my mother knew the nuts and bolts of sex and had "heard how it is done," but it seems obvious that, as curious as she was, she had kept a firm control on her passions and didn't really understand how provocative it was to go into the back seat with Charley. Her dismay with his uncontrolled "baser passions" shows that she didn't understand the sexual relationship between a man and a woman. Although a member of the class of "new woman" — free of family restraint, and facing 20th-century temptations such as automobiles, movies, and dancing — that she considered men's passions "base," harked back to the morality of her 19th-century parents: Nice girls did not "go the limit," nor did they take one step toward it. Automobiles pro-vided privacy and marked the end of the era of the "gentleman caller" in the parlor. Young men like Charley often gained their initial sexual experience from prostitutes, and a great sexual gulf existed between middle-class men and women of the same age. Most women remained virginal and chaste, with desire suppressed well short of sexual intercourse, while many men honored the ideal of abstinence only in theory.

By 1918, the country had entered a new sexual era — un-chaperoned women spent their leisure time with men in public places, movies displayed eroticism, and advertis-ing related sex to leisure. Unmarried women away from home explored a new stan-dard of behavior. A few weeks after her adventures with Charley, for her twenty-first birthday, Martha gave my mother a copy of Havelock Ellis' *Studies in the Psychology of Sex*. Ellis asked his readers "Why should people be afraid of rousing passions which, after all, are the great driving forces of human life?"

NOTES

[1] *When the war began there were 770 civilians and twenty-six officers in the Ordnance Department of the U.S. Army; by the end there were 53,000 civilians and 5,530 officers.*

[2] *Lack of heat in the house was the result of a severe coal shortage. Both the military draft and the flu epidemic had shorthanded the coalmines.*

[3] *The Camoufleurs were a corps of architects, mural and scenic artists, interior decorators, sculptors, scenic designers and stage carpenters who had trained at the American University camp to camouflage anything on a battlefield.*

[4] *Ten years after an excerpt from this book was published in Washington History, I received a letter from Jeff Nelson in Toledo, Ohio. He told me he had played in a rock band in Washington, was a student of history and charmed by my mother's diary. When he moved to Ohio he named his rock band "Fast Piece of Furniture".*

4

SPRING 1919

Entertaining the Wounded At Walter Reed

Jo in the garden at Walter Reed Hospital, 1919.

"I have been filling the time in the usual methods, and have added a new role, that of entertainer to the Walter Reed Hospital boys. Don't be surprised. I know only too well that I only know two pieces on the piano, and that if I started to sing or recite to them, they would shout, 'Let me get back to nice old Chateau-Thierry.'"

My mother volunteered, along with many young women, to "cheer the wounded" at Walter Reed Army Hospital. There she became friendly with Bryan Kane, a soldier who returned from France with a shattered leg, and she went once or twice a week to visit him, and to help entertain the men while they were rehabilitated. The pressure of thousands of horribly mutilated soldiers just returned from the trenches put Walter Reed at the forefront of rehabilitative therapy. The American Red Cross established a convalescent center on the grounds and took a major role to make the public aware of the services needed for severely wounded and shell-shocked men. Those who were mobile or in wheelchairs had specially trained "reconstruction aides" to assist them in the newly developed field of occupational therapy. With a solarium and recreational facilities, the large, homey building was nestled back in the woods, away from the smells and miseries of the hospital wards. The large lounge could be quickly converted to a dance hall, and the hospital had its own twenty-eight-piece band.

March 1: Received a letter from Bryan saying that he had been terribly ill and they had given him up, but that he was better and wants me to come out on Sunday.

March 2: Sunday, and I stayed in bed until eleven-thirty, dressing just in time for dinner and the trip to Walter Reed to see Bryan. I found him back in his private room, looking very thin but full of pep and good spirits, and quite confident that he will be on his feet in a week or two. I don't know whether I want him to come and see me or not when he is well. One thing for which I can be thankful is that Bryan is such a clean boy. I never fear any of the Charles Francis stuff from him. He's too nice for that.

March 12: Another letter from Bryan, which said although he was being wheeled around, he couldn't get downtown for some time yet, and wanted me to come out Sunday. Took an extra quarter hour at noon and went downtown to sell my Liberty Bond so I can buy a new suit. Paid my income tax and went for my suit after work.[1]

March 17: Yesterday was my birthday, but there was nothing exciting about it, as the girls didn't know it, and I almost forgot it myself. Three years ago twenty-one sounded horribly ancient to me, but I don't feel a bit that way now. Mr. Spencer wrote offering me a place on the *Sentinel*. Not if I can help it, do I go back to Ionia.

Sunday afternoon I went out to Walter Reed Hospital to see Bryan and the first thing I saw was him standing up and walking around. He waved his cane at me, and said he was well enough to come downtown and see me Monday night. He was quite embittered because he hadn't had a chance to get a haircut before I came, and because "those darned store-room people had gotten his uniform wrinkled while they had it."

Monday Bryan came rather early, bringing a huge box of candy for my birthday. He was rather "tuckered out" from his exertions in coming downtown, and was glad to sit down and rest when he got to the house. We talked a blue streak and played the Victrola, and the girls came down to see him, so he was quite in the limelight.

March 28: It is just twenty minutes to five o'clock, and as the Secretary of War sent out a notice that all employees now have to work until five o'clock in order to hurry up the closing of activities, I have just that much more time to write in my diary. The Colonel is out of town again (he usually is every other day), so I am "keeping the store," as usual.

The wind is blowing here at the rate of sixty miles an hour, and the automobiles in the streets are being tossed around. It rained all day yesterday and snowed last night, and today is one of the coldest days we have had during the winter. The streetcars were so packed that when I tried to leave I had to push and struggle for four blocks to make my way out. Some Washington. It was too windy to go outside the building for lunch, so I went downstairs to the counter and bought four sandwiches and an apple and lived on that during the day. Tonight is fish night, so I suppose Mrs. Dudley will have some old bony smelly stuff for dinner.

April 7: Major Harkness came back yesterday from his two weeks' leave but left again today with the Colonel to be gone three days, so I am alone again. I spent most of the day writing personal letters and bringing my diary up to date.

Last Saturday night Grace and Martha and I went to Neighborhood House. Reached home late from the dance. It was crowded so sat out much of the evening with a boy from Walter Reed who lost a leg at Chateau-Thierry, and who likes to come to the dances to look on.

April 8: Dear Parents: I have been filling the time in the usual methods, and have added a new role, that of entertainer to the Walter Reed Hospital boys. Don't be surprised. I know only too well that I only know two pieces on the piano, and that if I started to sing or recite to them, they would shout, "Let me get back to nice old Chateau-Thierry."

The boys came from the hospital in automobiles and arrived at Neighborhood House about six o'clock. Fifteen or twenty girls had been there since five o'clock preparing supper and when the boys arrived, formality was dispensed with. Each girl grabbed a soldier and the grand march to the eats started.

A soldier who I helped eat was a tall, rangy, red-haired Kentuckian who had been wounded at Verdun by machine gun fire. He had lain in a shell hole thirty-six hours before a first aid party had reached him. One arm had to be amputated at the shoulder, so close, he said, that an artificial arm would be of no use to him. The other had been broken at the elbow and part of the bone was removed. That was eight months ago, but he still has no use of his one arm, which is in a plaster cast. So, for the first time since the old days when I fed bread and milk to my various young sisters, I fed a person again. I think I was more fussed about it than he was, but then, he has had eight months practice. When it seemed like I was shoveling coal instead of feeding an invalid, he grinned and said, "Ah reckon you'all had bettah stop a bit til Ah ketch up."

He said the pleasure was all his when I spilled coffee and potato salad on his lap, and gave me many valued pointers on the feeding of helpless patients. I admire the spirit that boy had. He took his disability as a matter of course — he had gone over to do his bit and his chief disappointment was that he didn't get another chance to get back and fight.

Another boy had been wounded in the face by a piece of shell at the Argonne. By the marvelous surgical skill of the several operations performed on his face, he will be but slightly disfigured. A little yellow haired fellow down at the end of the table, looking barely old enough to be out of school, was wearing three service stripes, two wound stripes and the French Croix de Guerre. Several of the boys had artificial arms and legs, but no matter what their condition, all were in high spirits. Not one complaint was voiced. Afterward, when some of us danced, the ones who could not join accepted their lots cheerfully.

When I was serving one of the latecomers, I noticed that one of them wasn't eating as much as I thought a hungry man should, and asked him what was the trouble. "Oh, the supper is fine," he assured me, "but some of us ate something before we came. You see," he added half apologetically, half roguishly, "we've been to some of these places before, and we don't take any chances any more on going away hungry." Their precautions were unnecessary this time. It makes one wish to do more and more and still more when one sees the pleasure they get from a simple affair like our supper. It isn't money these boys want, although some of them have mighty little. Most of them don't know a soul in Washington. It is true that they are given theatre parties through the generosity of societies and individuals, but what they really want is the chance to meet some young people and to enter into the spirit of a social time — something to take the place of the church suppers, the strawberry socials, the lodge dances, the college hops, and all such affairs in which they participated back home.

Across the table from me was a boy who had been gassed severely. He hadn't been able to get his spectacles off in time to put on his gas mask, he told us.

In August 1914, when the French fired tear gas grenades against the Germans, they were the first to use chemicals in the war, but the Germans were the first to develop poisonous gas as a large-scale weapon. In April 1918, by the time American forces arrived on the French battlefields, a more efficient type of gas mask with charcoal or antidote chemical filters was in use. A siren warned the men when a gas attack was imminent, but many of the men who worked deep in the trenches took off the awkward masks and couldn't always get them back on fast enough. Mustard gas wasn't an immediate killing agent, but it disabled the enemy and polluted the battlefield. Heavier than air, the gas settled in the bottom of a trench as an oily liquid and remained active for days. If even the smallest amount touched the skin the burns were horrific, and caused internal and external bleeding, attacked the bronchial tubes, and stripped off the mucous membrane. If a man absorbed a lot of gas, his painful death was protracted for weeks. By 1918, the worst of gas warfare was over but still, almost 73,000 doughboys were wounded and 1,400 died from the effects of mustard gas. The Geneva Protocol of 1925 outlawed the use of gas as a weapon of war and the treaty was signed by forty nations.

April 10: Occasionally see a lot of Indians[2] from home down around Fourth Street; they came here from the reservation to see the President, but usually see only his steenth assistant to his steenth assistant.

April 17: The Atlantic fleet is in New York harbor and Washington is full of sailors from the ships. There was an exciting demonstration battle of airplanes over Washington, in which the captured Hun planes took part.

In the fifth and final Liberty Loan drive, the District had a goal of just over $4 million. An aviator, flying 2,600 feet above the crowd, read President Wilson's message to the people with a wireless telephone. The newly invented, horn-shaped, Magnavox sound amplifier was set up on the south steps of the Treasury. Jo was one of several thousand Victory Loan volunteers who participated in the three-week campaign. In various public locations, an official or well-known personality made a patriotic pitch before the film started, and the volunteers, who were set up in a booth in the lobby, sold the bonds.

April 18: The Liberty Loan opened today and Billie Burke spoke on the steps of the Treasury and Admiral Sims and Naval Secretary Franklin Roosevelt were on the steps of the State, War and Navy building.[3] An aviator talked to the crowd from a plane by means of a radiophone. Every night the dome of the Capitol and the Monument are illuminated with a powerful searchlight brought from France that makes them look like molten fire. Oh, it's wonderful.

Went uptown to cash my check. Did some shopping and then had lunch at the Allies Inn, eighty cents. The hundred Belgian veterans of some of the early battles of the war are here in Washington with all the St. Bernard dogs that were used to haul machine guns. Went by the aviation department and saw some French aviators in a big car in front. There are always some interesting men to be seen there.

APRIL 23: Bought a Liberty Bond today, which makes our division go over the top 100 percent in the drive. In the evening a friend of Margaret's came for Dell and me, and we went down to the Garden Theatre in his car to sell Liberty Bonds. We saw part of the movie there, and then went over to the Strand. The speaker didn't appear on the scene there, so we saw the movie all through and then he brought us home in the car.

APRIL 25: Grace, Smittie and I went to a dance at Walter Reed. Arrived at the hospital and Bryan took us through his ward and then to the Red Cross Building, where we found quite the worst crowd I have ever seen at any dance. On the floor were men without arms, blind men, and soldiers otherwise crippled, all seeming to have a good time, however. Toward the end, while the boys were getting us some ice cream and cakes, two soldiers approached, both slightly the worse for something stronger than lemonade, one of them tall and countrified, wearing a little colored knitted cap, and the other very nice looking. They told us first that they came from the "nut" ward, but we finally discovered that they were injured in the legs so could not dance.

APRIL 26: Saw an advertisement for a steno-sock [secretary] in the *Star* by F.G. Carpenter, the writer, and answered it. Grace seemed to think that my stating in my letter that I didn't chew gum, and a few other such remarks, queered my chances, but I don't expect to hear anyway, so don't care.

"In response to your advertisement for a secretary-stenographer, I would request that you consider my application for this position. Although I am but twenty-one years of age, I have had four years of business experience. Upon graduation from a four-year high school course in 1915 I began work as stenographer and office assistant in a newspaper office. I am thoroughly competent in the various branches of office work, including filing, bookkeeping and general business methods. I had been with the newspaper but a short time when I was placed on reporting work, at which I continued until I came to Washington.

"Although the newspaper on which I worked was a comparatively small publication, it was thoroughly modern in every respect and offered a very comprehensive experience in that line. In addition to general reporting I have done special features and articles and was allowed to use my own judgment and discretion in covering many conferences, conventions and political meetings. In several instances, in the absence of both the editor and business manager of the paper, I was placed in complete charge, both in a business and editorial capacity.

"In this position I acquired the speed in typewriting that is essential to newspaper work, and passed the civil service speed examination with a rating of ninety-eight. In every position I have held I have been considered very proficient in both shorthand and machine dictation.

"In February 1918, I received an appointment as stenographer in the Ordnance Department and left my home in Michigan to come to Washington. For three months I was placed on miscellaneous assignments, at the end of which time, a reorganization of the Ordnance Department having just been completed, I received a definite assignment in the shell loading section. Incidentally, during these three months, I was selected from among fifty or more stenographers to take the dictation of Mr. M. V. de Roquelaine, the head of the French military experts in the United States, whose work, because of its technical nature and Mr. de Roquelaine's difficult accent and somewhat imperfect command of English, was very difficult and exacting, it being necessary to put it into correct form without altering its technical meaning.

"I was given general stenographic work in the shell loading section until September 1918, when I was promoted to the position of secretary to the head of one of the branches of that section. In December 1918, I received another promotion when I was made secretary to the chief of the section, Major W. E. Harkness, with whom I was until his discharge from the service a few weeks ago. I am at present one of the only two stenographers who were retained from the large force employed before the signing of the armistice. As the work of this section, created by the war emergency, will soon be over, I am desirous of entering a new field of work now instead of waiting until there is no further need for my services in this department. I will add that I do not have nerves, I do not mind overtime, I do not chew gum, and am generally conceded to know how to spell. Respectfully, Josephine Lehman"

April 28: Reached home to find that I had had a telephone call from a man who sounded like an old man. "Carpenter," thought I, hardly daring to believe that he called me. However, he called later, and it was true. I'll bet the chewing gum did it. He asked me if I could come down to see him tomorrow at nine o'clock, which I did. Dressed in my new suit, borrowed a pair of hose from Martha and wore my long, cerise pettibochers [4] to give me courage.

The house is just next to the Church of the Covenant, I found not only Mr. Carpenter, but Mrs. Carpenter and little boy Jack Carpenter, the latter being about thirty, very nice looking, very businesslike, and living in Chicago. Mr. Carpenter is old and white haired with straggly whiskers.[5] Mrs. Carpenter is large and fat and motherly, and makes about three of him. I was thus taken into the bosom of the family and quizzed, mostly by the son. Mr. Carpenter said the letter I had written was very good, very good, indeed, and said he had selected it from among a hundred others, which made me feel pleased. The job is stenographic and secretarial work assisting him in revising his geographic readers, which I remembered reading back in the grades. Until June first we work in Washington. Then for four months we work at his summer estate near Bluemont, Virginia, about two hours ride from here, the same pay, $130 during the summer. He took me down to his office and gave me some machine dictation. I got it all right, but as the machine was a 1492 model Underwood, I made some mistakes I otherwise wouldn't have done.

May 6: This is my last day at the office, and I've been busy saying goodbye and finishing up loose ends. I hate to leave now, and find it hard to realize that this is really my last day in the government service. I am no longer a war worker, so I think I will start another volume of diary for this new chapter in my life.

May 7: Started my new job today. Mr. Carpenter is very agreeable, and we work at his home.[6] Told me I was a relief from his last secretary who couldn't spell. Mrs. Carpenter is solicitous about my comfort and brought me water with ice. Spent most of the time acknowledging letters from other applicants for the position. They were rich, ranging from one girl who had the "sublime confidence that she was the ideal person," to another who handed Mr. Carpenter enough blarney about his books to keep him for a year. Had a delicious lunch at a tearoom on the street, filled with society people and officers. Came home along N Street, listened to a hurdy-gurdy and strolled through the park. My first day's work included a telephone conversation with the Serbian Prime Minister.

May 16: Miss Simkins, Daddy Carp's library assistant, came today. She seems very pleasant, her age is 26; she was evidently very pretty once.

May 21: Miss Simkins has gone. Couldn't fit the bill.

I have reached that deplorable stage where writing with a pen is a rare event in my life. My activities in that line are limited almost entirely to signing my own name, or impressing new beaus. After I have shown them that I really do know how to write I relapse into my old habits, and use my trusty Underwood. I keep a typewriter of my own in my room — a very trim little machine who answers to the name of Henry. Mr. Carpenter is somewhere about town on business, and went off without providing sufficient work to keep me busy. Before, he went off for a week's trip to his North Carolina property, and during that time I cleaned up all the little odds and ends that are ever present in an office, such as sorting out all his correspondence files, re-arranging all the books in his library, indexing his photographs, cleaning out all the desks and file cases, and a thousand and one other things, so that now when he goes away I lead a rather leisurely life. Mr. C only works from ten to one each day, which leaves me the afternoon for taking care of things all by myself.

I confess that it is a great temptation to do nothing but sit and look out the window. His home is on Connecticut Avenue, which is Washington's equivalent to New York's Fifth Avenue. The upper part is still the fashionable residential part of the city, while the lower part is full of smart shops, dressmakers, studios, beauty parlors, etc. This house is just above the business section of the street, and it is very interesting to watch the people going by on foot, which is a style show in itself. Just across the street is the British embassy, in and out of which silk-hatted diplomats and natty British officers are constantly going. A half block above us is Secretary of State Lansing's home, another half block further the Belgian embassy, around the corner the modest little house where Alice Roosevelt Longworth lives, and just a few doors away is the home of Alexander Graham Bell, the telephone man.

May 29: Calamity to report. Found my first grey hair this morning. Guess maybe I'm growing old. Mr. Carpenter is in New York meeting his daughter Frances and I am in charge of the ship with enough work to keep me busy for four days instead of two, which is all the more reason I should get to work instead of writing this diary.

May 30: Decoration Day, and we all slept late, went down to a fierce breakfast, and then slept some more. I sewed and wrote letters all afternoon and met Martha at five-thirty and went to the Nankin for supper. We then went on a round of the movie houses to find one that neither one of us had seen, and finally decided on "Open Your Eyes," the new propaganda movie against venereal diseases.[7] Wasn't so bad for that kind of thing, and well worth seeing, although I didn't learn anything I didn't already know.

May 31: At dinnertime Bryan came down and we started out shortly after for a walk, I without a hat and Bryan without a coat. Took a car ride to Glen Echo[8], and regardless of the deficiencies in our attire, went in and had two gloriously thrilling rides on the derby racer, then danced out a quarter's worth of tickets, and came home, getting in at something like twelve-thirty.

June 1: Gloriously hot. Didn't do a thing in the morning but loll around, but in the afternoon Martha and I went to Potomac Beach to go bathing. We stayed in the water four hours.[9]

June 2: Got to work fifteen minutes late this morning, with Mr. Carpenter back from New York and already in the office. Met his daughter Frances, just back from France. Received my pay today, and promptly distributed most of it to the girls, who have been keeping me for the past week.

June 4: Hotter than the second coming of hell.

June 6: Oh gollyation! Two weeks from now I will be home in Ionia. Mr. Carpenter dropped a bomb on me by asking if I minded taking a month's vacation with pay to give him a chance to rest up. Mind it indeed! I can hardly wait until the time comes, and can't believe I am really going home so soon.

June 15: Dell, Smittie and Martha went to the train with me. I bade Gracie good-bye at the house and was glad, as I shall miss her most of all.

While she was home, Jo spent a lot of time with her girlfriends and very little time with her family, who complained loudly. I think that this trip got rid of most of her homesickness, and by the first week in July she was back in Washington. Although she wrote home regularly for the rest of her life, she returned to Michigan only occasionally. Except for her oldest brother Leo, who went to Oregon shortly after she was born, my mother was the only one of the ten children to leave the state.

During this spring my mother spent a lot of time with Bryan. He wanted her to "wait for him" to get settled in life, and then they could get married. In her diary she asks herself — throughout many pages — should she or shouldn't she?

"I have been in a whirlpool of thoughts. One minute I resolve one thing, and the next minute something altogether different. I know that in morals and principles, Bryan is head and shoulders above anyone I have met in Washington, and that his wife would never want for anything he could give her. It is true that he hasn't a cent and is only a buck private, but I never seem to think of that. On the other hand are my parents' prejudice against the Catholics and the Irish, and what they would think if I married someone not worth anything, when I might have had Paul, who is now worth several thousands in addition to his farm. I have come to the conclusion that as long as I'm so changeable, I'd better call it off. I never was so wobbly in my life. The only thing that keeps me from telling him that I don't think I can ever marry him is that he is just now starting out with a lot of ambition, and I hate to hurt him in any way." Although she went out with Bryan when she returned from Ionia, by the time she leaves for the summer in Virginia, he disappears from her diary.

NOTES

[1] *In 1914 income tax became a part of American life. After a $1,000 exemption, Jo paid 2 percent of her remaining salary, or $10.80.*

[2] *Members of Michigan's Ottawa and Chippewa tribes lobbied for adjustment and enforcement of 1795 and 1855 treaties, which provided land and money to the tribes. The Ottawa representative said that when the treaties were made, the tribal members could not speak English and "were easily imposed upon." Bills that met the claims were introduced in Congress.*

[3] *Completed in 1887, it is now the Eisenhower Executive Office Building.*

[4] *Pettibochers were an undergarment reaching to the knees, like a petticoat, but pants.*

[5] *In 1918, Frank Carpenter, sixty-four, retired from thirty years of syndicated travel writing to update his geographical readers because of boundary changes brought about by the war.*

[6] *Carpenter's daughter, Frances, described the house in an article she wrote after her father's death: "This house was ideal for his writing. It had been built by a doctor and had well lighted offices upon the ground floor with their own private entrance. These rooms were easily transformed into a commodious working library, so isolated that when a guest entered to pay a visit to the family, he did not know they existed. As with many city homes, the living rooms were to be found on the second floor. There was a large drawing room, a library and a dining room, all well arranged for entertaining."*

[7] *This Public Health Service film produced by Warner Brothers had separate showings for men and women.*

[8] *Glen Echo amusement park was a popular excursion destination two miles north of the District line, with a picnic area, dozens of rides, band concerts and an open-air dance pavilion with a ten-piece orchestra. The trolley shouldered the river's edge, and passengers had a spectacular view of the Potomac. I went to Washington with my senior class in high school and, on my mother's recommendation, went to Glen Echo, which, in 1950, did not have an orchestra, but did have a roller coaster and I glued myself on the seat for sixteen exhilarating rides. It was the high spot of my trip. Looking back on it, I wonder why my mother didn't ask me to visit any of her old haunts.*

[9] *Jo and her friends went swimming in the Tidal Basin of the Potomac River (above). The land has since been filled, reconfigured, and the Jefferson Memorial was built about where they swam.*

5
SUMMER 1919
Bluemont, Virginia

Jo at Frank Carpenter's Bluemont estate, summer 1919

"She goes barefoot until she gets within sight of our house, when she puts on her shoes. She and her husband and all the children, a grandmother and several dogs live in a one-room shanty."

In 1896, Frank Carpenter and his wife, Joanna, built their weekend and summer getaway in the village of Bluemont, Virginia, about 50 miles southwest of Washington. They named the estate Joannasberg — Joanna's Mountain. Just after the Independence Day holiday, my mother boarded the train to join the family and see her new office. I have consolidated her diary and letters to family and friends.

July

I left the station at two o'clock and arrived at Bluemont at five, my apprehension of the night before still with me. Arriving at the station, I looked in vain for the Cadillac eight and resplendent chauffeur the Carpenters had in town. Not a whiff of them. While I was standing desolately trying to decide whether to phone to the house or to cut and run down the mountain back to Washington, a voice said, "Right heah, Miss Lehman," and lo, if it wasn't Arthur, the butler of the town house, dressed in a farmerly looking costume and driving a conveyance that was not a Cadillac, but a horse and buggy. It seems that the car is undergoing repairs.

I piled into the buggy beside Arthur, who is man of all work and family counselor while the family is up here. The Carpenter villa is four miles up from Bluemont — and up is right, as the whole four miles was one winding climb.

Arthur asked if I were afraid of snakes and I smiled superciliously and said, "Oh my, no," thinking of the little garden snakes at home. "You'all ain't," he exclaimed. "Well, I is glad to fin' one young lady what ain't. Ah tell yeh, they ain't no need to be, seeing's how they rattle and warn you anyway."

"R-r-r-rattle," I stuttered, while my garden snake immediately changed to a boa constrictor. "Are there rattlesnakes around here?"

"Lots of 'em," was the answer, "but, shaw now, they ain't half's bad as them air coppah-heads. Now you'all wants to steah clear of them."

Our next conversation started when I exclaimed about the large rocks along the road. "Law, chile," snickered Arthur, "these here ain't rocks. They's just gravel, they be. You'll see some sure nuff rocks up by the house." And sure nuff I did. They're regular wollapalousers of rocks.

As we clip-clopped up the mountain I could get glimpses of the valley below, but still I couldn't see anything to justify the ravings I had heard about the scenery. Halfway up Arthur pointed out the house where it stood on the very peak of the mountain, outlined by the sky, in the highest part of this section of the Blue Ridge. We passed Snicker's Gap, where a marble slab marks the spot of a hard fought battle of the Civil War, and soon we reached the entrance of the Carpenter estate, the gate was a mile from the house. The road continued to ascend, and suddenly we were out of the woods and there. The house isn't especially pretentious looking, but very solid and comfortable in appearance. It is built completely of stone, with two stories and an attic, and a mammoth veranda running around three sides of it, the latter very luxuriously furnished with swings and chairs and covered with flowering vines.

But the veranda faded into insignificance when I turned to look at the view. It is the most glorious panorama I ever saw, I could look into four states — Virginia, West Virginia, Maryland and Pennsylvania. One look and it makes it very easy to believe that it's the most wonderful bit of scenery in the Blue Ridge Mountains. The house is at the very top of the mountain, facing west, and from the veranda I can see fifty miles across the valley, and a north and south sweep of 125 miles up from the Shenandoah Valley. In one direction the valley is a checkerboard of fields and farms, to the north there are forests, far below us is the thin silver line of the Shenandoah, then the low foothills of the west slopes of the Blue Ridge, and far off to the west, the Allegheny range, faintly blue in the distance.

The land down in the valley is owned by the rich old families of Virginia, the kinds who employ hundreds of darkies, educate their children at home with governesses, and all that sort of thing.

The mountaineers interest me more. Hundreds of families of them live in little shacks (one room and a lean-to) immediately below us down the mountainside. Each family has something like sixteen children and a like number of dogs. Evidently, it takes all sixteen to till the acres of garden constituting their cultivated land. The only other thing they do is hunt. Occasionally, Mrs. Carpenter says, on rare occasions, it is possible to get some of them to work on the farms, but in spite of their laziness and illiteracy they have an innate refinement and their cabins are always scrupulously clean. Indeed, some of these mountaineers have the bluest blood of Virginia in them, and most are very honest. More than a few of the Distinguished Service Crosses were awarded to these same mountaineer boys. Mrs. Carpenter told me mountain lore by the yard while she showed me around the place.

As for pluck, one story will illustrate. When they were having a new wall built around the house, she noticed that one of the mountaineers used his hand rather strangely, and asked him what was the matter. He said that he had cut it rather deeply on a stone the day before and showed it to her. She said his hand was cut to the bone from his wrist to the base of his first finger, and that he had gone home and sewed up the wound with an ordinary needle and black thread, and come back to work without a word of complaint.

The Carpenters own the entire top of this mountain. The slope is very precipitous west of the house; and to the east are several cultivated fields, the garden, and a big orchard before the wooded eastern slope begins. The mountaineers call it Carpenter's Hill, but the name it usually goes by is Joanna's Mountain, after Mrs. Carpenter.

The library is another stone building south of the house. The room in which I work is about twenty by forty feet. Windows and glass doors open on all sides of it, with bookshelves filling in the remaining space. There are window seats built in, a stone fireplace big enough to hold a barbecue, raftered ceiling, polished floor, safe, file cases, two large tables and typewriter desk, several leather chairs and a billiard table. Upstairs are two rooms and a bathroom, which are used for overflow company. Downstairs are some more rooms used for old files and books, and at the south is a balcony facing that wonderful valley.

My room isn't large by any means, about the size of an ordinary bedroom, and it only has one window, but that window looks right out on the valley; why complain of a ten by twelve room when it has such an outlook? Also, the bedrooms are used for sleeping only, and not as living rooms as in my dearly beloved Washington. The room is finished in plaster, and the pictures are ones Mr. Carpenter got all over the world, and I have an embroidered panel from Egypt across one side of the room. There is matting on the floor with a rug over it, and I have a bed (all to myself!), a big dresser with three huge drawers with hooks on three sides to spread my wardrobe. The bathroom isn't private but it's right next door.

On the first floor are two big rooms with raftered ceilings and the comfiest kind of cozy furniture. One is used as a combination reception and entrance hall, living and dining room. The other is filled with bookshelves, piano, Victrola, reading table, etc.

I looked forward to my first meal with blissful expectancy. When I was informed that they had dinner at noon and that supper was very light my heart sank for I was awfully hungry, what with the light lunch I had at eleven-thirty, my trip here, and all the running around the top of the mountain I did from five to seven-thirty. Supper is usually at seven. I need not have worried, though, and now I am wondering how if what I had was a light meal, what besides an ox could eat a heavy one. There was a meat pie of some kind, mashed potatoes whipped to a fluff with cream and then browned, peas out of the garden instead of cans, with real cream sauce on them, fruit jelly, home-made pickles, milk or tea to drink, bread with butter made from cows and not coconuts, and huge dishes — dishes, I said — of blackberries, and again some more honest-to-gosh cream. I shamelessly ate until I felt the hooks on my belt tearing off. For breakfast I wore a skirt with a looser belt. We had blackberries again — a big dishful, not four berries, some more cream, cereal, some more cream, bacon and eggs, hot corn bread, preserves and coffee. Both the corn bread and the coffee were second-cousin-twice-removed from what I used to get at Dudleys'.

Reinforced for the day with a breakfast like that, I was feeling fine for my first day's labor: only six and one-half hours do I toil during the summer. I'm all by myself as Mr. Carp went to Washington for the day. I put the library in order, finished unpacking some books and files, cleaned off the tops of the desks, straightened up all the shelves, brought the cash books up to date, fixed the accounts and then, as Mr. Carp had told me to "play around," I took the time to write letters.

Mr. and Mrs. Carpenter and Frances and I spent last evening playing fan-tan. It's a card game I learned when I was a child, while they have been playing it for only a month, so it wasn't any effort to come out the winner. Perhaps it would have been more diplomatic to have let someone else win, but I had to show them I could do something.

Contrary to my expectations, or apprehensions, I have the most peaceful, satisfied feeling I have experienced in a long time. The smell of the pine trees is delicious, the air is so good I swallow big mouthfuls, and I sleep like the dead. I thought I would be lonesome and homesick, but I'm not. I feel as though I could just bury myself here for the summer and be perfectly content.

The Kings, one of the families living on the other mountain overlooking the valley toward Washington, had a tennis tournament last Sunday morning, and nearly all this part of Virginia were there. Frances and I went in the yellow cart, which just matches my yellow beads. Frances put me wise to all the celebrities. One man in particular! Capt. DeVries Larner of the aviation service, and when it came to decorations, he looked like a Christmas tree and Fourth of July parade all in one. He had on his silver flying wings, a Distinguished Service Cross with a palm, which meant he had been recommended twice for it, a Croix de Guerre with another palm, meaning the same thing, and four other citation ribbons for bravery in bringing down German planes. And I mustn't forget his mustache. It was small and tenderly cared for and evidently very cherished to judge from the solicitous manner in which he mothered it. This paragon is only about twenty-three years old in spite of his wonderful record.

In the afternoon we had two or three different sets of guests here at the Carpenters. Among them were Mrs. Moore, the sister of John Fox, Jr., who wrote "The Trail of the Lonesome Pine" and other Blue Ridge stories. When Johnny Fox married Fritzi Schiff, the actress, he bought a big estate just a few miles from here, but Fritzi didn't care for the rustic neighborhood and wouldn't come here to live. They had quite some divorce. Oh, yes, I'm becoming versed in all of the private affairs of the nabobs.

Henry Kirke Bush-Browne, the sculptor of the Lincoln Memorial at Gettysburg, was here for dinner and sat beside me and ate sweet corn off the cob just like other mortals. General Carter came, and Mrs. Morrison, wife of the president of the United States Civil Service Commission, and Dr. Harvey Wiley, the pure food man and his wife.[1]

Late Sunday afternoon I came down to the library to write a letter or two, and had just started when Dr. Plaster, (good name for a doctor, isn't it — now if he'd only marry a Miss Mustard) the leading MD of the Bluemont metropolis, came down and asked me to play billiards. Our motto here is "Six days shalt thou labor and toil, and on the seventh shalt thou play billiards." So play we did, and he beat me too, but I am getting so I can hold my own very well with Mr. Carpenter. Dr. Plaster is about thirty-five and unmarried and one of the nicest men I've ever met. He's here nearly every day as Mrs. Carpenter isn't well. He is the grandson of President Monroe and is related to General Robert E. Lee on the other side of the family. These Virginians fairly ooze family trees. The sad part of it is that he is about six inches shorter than I am, and I haven't a heart to angle for him unless I fill out his height by putting a sign on top of his head telling people who his antecedents were, which might detract attention from his shortness.

However, I am quite resigned to the beauless condition of the neighborhood. Well, not exactly beauless, as there are lots of young people one meets in the neighborhood get-togethers. We spend the evenings playing cards for the most part, but as we don't have dinner until seven-thirty, the evenings are short. Arthur, the coachman, gives nightly concerts on the accordion and guitar for the entertainment of the other servants, with the Carpenters and me uninvited, but none the less delighted, listeners.

Meals are affairs of state — courses, doilies, black-gowned and white-capped maid, perfect service and all that. I suppose by the time I do get used to the amazingly good eats I have here, it will be time to go back to Washington, and I will have forgotten all the scientific details of managing to get enough to eat at the boarding house table. We have a jewel of a cook here. She knows more ways of fixing chicken than anyone ever knew, and when it comes to hot rolls and Virginia ham and corn bread, and peach preserves, and meat pie I seem to lose sight of the fact that my weight is creeping up to the 150 mark.

General and Mrs. Carter, who live on the other side of the mountain with their little grandson and his nurse, were today's company. Very charming people — also very interesting, as they mention the high-and-mighties of Washington off-handedly. They gave a highly astonishing recital of a scandal that happened at a dinner at Alice Roosevelt's home.[2]

Frances went to Washington yesterday, returning to Bluemont on the five o'clock train, and I went with Arthur to get her. It was the first time that I have dressed up since I came, and dressing up mainly consisted in wearing a hat and putting on a clean middy and skirt.

I had to stop at the post office before we went to the station. The post office is at one end of the general store, which, to judge from appearances, is a combination club-room, Mecca for swapping stories and rifle range for tobacco juice for the queer characters of this vicinity. The steps were occupied by three or four such, and it was necessary for me to pause before they got themselves to their feet and let me pass. The same performance was gone through when I came back out, whereupon they sat down again and had first row seats for the spectacle of seeing a goodly display of my leg, as I had to step up into the high old carriage.

Met some interesting characters on our excursion. At the post office was a girl dressed in a khaki shirt and dirty bloomers of the same material, reaching halfway below her knees. It seems she was formerly governess to a rich family on the other side of the mountain, and from the stories she told she had hobnobbed with everyone from Russian nobility to Chinese potentates. While the family was still in Washington, a man whom she introduced as her brother came to see her frequently. Soon after they came up to the mountains, the same man appeared on the scene again and this time she introduced him as her uncle. Her employer then noted that said niece and uncle had a habit of staying out until three in the morning in a manner very un-unclelike. Becoming suspicious, she started to corroborate a few of the girl's stories and references and found they were all as nice a mess of fiction as ever she came across. Then followed the denouement, and the governess left, taking with her the children's nurse, and the two of them, with the "uncle," rented a tumbledown cabin about a mile down the mountain from us. The two girls bobbed their hair and took to wearing bloomers.[3]

Mr. Carpenter was in the library playing billiards with Dr. Plaster, so Frances and I joined them and we all played until seven-thirty, and the dinner bell had to be rung twice. The doctor stayed for dinner, and was generally the life of the party. He's a regular circus. Mrs. Carpenter has him attend her just to hear him tell funny stories. After dinner we started with cards and played steadily until after eleven.

The sun is shining and the breeze is doing the shimmy around the corner of the veranda, and everything is lovely. I am down in the library, from where I can look out to the valley with the Shenandoah River sparkling in the sun and the Allegheny Mountains all hazy in the distance. The atmosphere up here rather tends to make me placid and contented.

Mrs. Carpenter asked me to go with her on a drive and we started out with Mack and the buggy. We clip-clopped past the Carpenters' fifty-acre apple orchard, past a couple of summer camps and boarding houses, then crossed the state line into West Virginia and drove two or three miles along a wild, wooded mountain road to the house of a mountaineer whom Mrs. Carpenter wished to see. I pulled and tugged and hauled to get open a dirty heavy gate and then pulled and again to get it shut and we drove down a long lane covered with rocks until I thought every thump would be our last. Our destination was a little house in the clearing. The grass was green, there was a spring and tiny brook in the yard and the fence was a mass of brilliant flowers. It was as pretty a place as I have seen around here. These people regard Mrs. C with a kind of worship. Every day they bring her presents of fruit and vegetables, rough handiwork, or an occasional skin from a wildcat, and she is the only person I have met who can get more than "yes" or "no" out of the mountaineers that come up to the house.

My job may fall out from under me. Mr. Carpenter is considering a trip to Egypt, Persia, the Balkan states and possibly Panama. If he goes alone, by all rules of propriety he will have to take a male secretary. If he takes the family, he has to take all of them and perhaps a nurse for Mrs. Carpenter, and that would make too big a party of it. However, I'm not worrying. It isn't such hard work to get a job. That New York proposition is still open and there are other things in Washington.

Carpenter had conceived the idea of putting together a lifetime of travel writing in what became the twenty-volume set, *Carpenter's World Travels*. To do this, he went back on the road again. His daughter tried to dissuade him. She later wrote: "I wondered whether his strength would match his determination, for a man of sixty-six, however enthusiastic, cannot have the vitality of one thirty years younger."

August

One of the mountaineer women came up the mountain the other morning bringing some blackberries to Mrs. Carpenter. She has eight children, and is only thirty years old but looks fifty. She told me that she goes barefoot until she gets within sight of our house, when she puts on her shoes. She and her husband and all the children, a grandmother and several dogs all live in a one-room shanty.

Mr. and Mrs. Carpenter and I had a very interesting ride to Round Hill, Virginia. We could see the battleground of Bull Run, and passed several ruins of stone houses and barns that were left as souvenirs by the "damnyankees," as several Virginians still call them. Indeed, I am told that there are some Virginians who still think that damnyankee is one word. When we reached home Mrs. C and I started a card-playing contest, the winner of the first fifty-one games to be taken to the theater. Frances is going to teach me to play bridge.

I took a solitary walk yesterday afternoon. I set out calm and serene, taking my camera and snapping at any bits of scenery that I happened to fancy. I had got as far as Snickers Gap, which is about a mile below Carpenters, and didn't know whether to go up the other mountain to Bear's Den first, or to Bluemont. I was decided by a bunch of facetiously inclined young men lounging on the store steps at the gap, not mountaineers, but evidently from Washington. They had just finished purchasing ginger ale and the like, and were starting down to Bluemont, so I decided not to go that way, but started up the other mountain.

I had understood Frances to say that the Bear's Den was only a quarter of a mile, but I walked and walked, and then walked some more, all the time up a good respectable grade, and I was darned if it wasn't the longest quarter of a mile I ever saw. I found out later that I had misunderstood her, and that it was a mile-and-a-quarter.

When I had gone about what I thought was the height of four Pike's Peaks with a Mt. McKinley thrown in, I came to a gate and little house and a sign that gave me encouragement. Still, there were two paths from there and I didn't know which one to take, and I hadn't passed a house in all that way, and there were woods all around, and I started to sort of wish I weren't by myself, or that I would see someone else. Just then a man came around the corner of the little house — an ordinary sort of man smoking a pipe and needing a shave, and I asked the way to the Bear's Den.

"To the right," was the answer, and in my nervousness I thought he looked at me rather searchingly. "You aren't all alone, are you?"

"No-n-no, not exactly," I managed to bring out, and cast about wildly for something to say, couldn't think of anything, so thanked him and started to move on, but he interrupted again.

"Oh, were you with a party?" (Aha, I thought, he furnishes the idea himself.)

"Yes," I said, "I'll just go right on and see if they're down on the rocks."

"How big a party?" he next asked.

"S-s-s-six," I stuttered, thinking there was at least safety in numbers. If he had any intentions of carrying me off, that would make him hesitate, no doubt, but I felt the conversation was getting too complicated, and again started to move on.

"Oh, a party of six just went through," he informed me, "Right down there."

This was getting worse and worse. Here the man was falling right into my own manufactured plans. "Those aren't the ones," I said gently but firmly, "I'll just go and look farther down."

"Only party of six that's gone in these gates this afternoon," he said. Then followed some more questions as to how I missed them, and this and that and the other thing, and I told him I was from the other mountain, while "my friends" were from Washington. I could see that he was a perfectly nice man and apparently harmless, and could also see that there were several more people down through the rocks and trees, and was mentally kicking myself for having gotten so mixed up.

When I told him I was from the other mountain, he said he knew all the people up there and asked where I was staying. When I told him, he was still more talkative, asked about all the family, and said to give Dr. Lawson's regards to Mr. Carpenter. When I found out that he was Dr. Huron Lawson of Washington, I was ready to howl, for all his looks he might have been a tramp or a rough mountaineer or anybody — that is, until I started to talk to him. I finally got extricated, went down to Bear's Den and then home.

I remembered afterward that a sign had said ten cents admission, but I failed entirely to heed it, and anyway the doctor told me to come up any time I liked, seeing I was a friend of the Carpenters.

Got back to the house without seeing anyone and in five minutes was luxuriously wiggling my toes in a warm bath. By the time I was bathed and dressed, I felt as spry as ever, and when I told the Carpenters of the seven miles I had walked they made me feel quite a pedestrian and said I must be dead, which I denied and said I didn't feel at all tired — and I didn't. All in all, it was a great walk.

I went down to Washington Saturday afternoon and Grace and I went to a fortune-teller, a very black, very fat, very shiny, very soiled specimen of the African race. Said Maisie lives in a little house on Sixteenth Street, also very soiled. Frances Carpenter had told me about her; it seems that all of Frances' fashionable friends have taken her up as a fad. In prophesying Frances' future and telling her past, the seeress wasn't so bad. She evidently was lucky in hitting on the right things. When it came to me, she fell flat. Her fortune telling was like my tennis playing — a hundred wild shots with perhaps one correct one. According to her I'm going to be the mother of a wonderful son in 18 months. There was also a middle-aged man who meant quite a lot to me, but he was married. I took that to mean Mr. Carpenter — he means thirty dollars a week to me. All things considered, I am inclined to believe Maisie a fraud, but I got my dollar's worth in amusement.

Received a parcel from Sears Roebuck the other day. I got three cakes of Woodbury's soap for fifty-four cents, thereby paying only four cents for the third cake, and also bought six bars of Ivory. Started sewing my new dress. We played bridge until the clock said it was the Sabbath, when Mrs. C called a halt.

As I had the previous Monday off, like a little lamb I started back to the library to work Saturday afternoon. Mr. Carpenter headed me off and said to go and amuse myself — he guessed the manuscript wasn't pressing enough to make it necessary for me to work Saturday afternoon — all that after growling at me when I asked for the Monday off, but I have learned by this time that his growl is much worse than his bite. I didn't press the point, and spent most of the afternoon sewing on that wonderful dress of mine.

"Our son Jack" arrived at six o'clock, an extra delicious and heaping dinner being served in his honor. After dinner Frances, Mrs. C, Jack and I played bridge until midnight, when Mrs. Carpenter made us quit exactly on the stroke of the clock. Jack made her look very thoughtful by saying that if she was as religious as all that, she should have quit at eleven, as she was going by the new daylight saving law instead of the Bible. I wish he hadn't said that, for I believe she will really call the halt at eleven on Saturday nights.

The little doctor was here for Sunday dinner, and we spent from three until seven shooting pool in spite of Mrs. C's protests. The doctor left then, and Mrs. Carpenter and Frances leisurely started to get out some cold things for supper as every one of the servants had been given the afternoon off. I was upstairs when a frenzied call from Frances brought me back down. Dr. and Mrs. Wiley and a guest had just arrived, and it behooved us to step lively to get supper for three more. Therefore, while Frances frantically peeled tomatoes I peeled peaches, and I made a wild search for a bread knife while Frances turned the cook's immaculate cupboard upside down trying to find where she kept the corkscrew for the olives.

We finally turned out a very presentable supper with enough for all, and it's lucky we did, as that man Wiley surely does eat. We cleared off the table and stacked up the dishes, but decided not to wash them, leaving them for the servants when they got home.

All Monday morning I spent in the employ of son Jack, who gave me two long legal documents about patent cases. The first was on some mechanical appliance. He told me that the next was about a bust confiner and wanted to know if it would embarrass me to take the dictation about it. I informed him that I had once been a newspaper reporter and nothing embarrassed me any more. I might also have said that I had been a war worker for over a year, but not having been a war worker himself and probably not knowing just what things occur in a war worker's career, he wouldn't have got the connection.

Dr. Plaster came over again Monday evening for dinner and afterwards the four of us got into a highly exciting game, something like poker. It was really tense. Nobody could win anything, and all that money went into the bank, and not one of us would give up until the bank could be broken. At frequent intervals Mrs. Carpenter would ask if we weren't almost through. Her interruptions were received with savage looks. Finally I was lucky enough to break into the bank and get half the money and about two hours later Jack made a grand swoop and won the rest and we all trooped off to bed at one o'clock.

The doctor stayed and slept with Jack. Mrs. Carpenter told him that he'd find pajamas in the dresser drawer, and if both pieces weren't there she would look elsewhere. Jack then had the bright idea that as Dr. Plaster was so short anyway, if the trouser weren't in the drawer the coat would be long on him anyway that he could wear it alone and make believe it was a nightshirt. There followed several choked giggles on Frances' and my part, and a rosy blush of embarrassment on the cherubic features of the doctor.

He's such a dear. He has the perfect manners of a Southerner and lives a life of sacrifice and devotion for these mountaineers. He's always being roused up in the middle of the night to go off about twelve miles or so and bring small mountaineers into the world and then whistle up the valley for his money. He has been offered big opportunities in cities, but instead remains up here with his aged parents. He broke loose from duty last night, however, by suggesting that the Carpenters turn down the switch on their phone. He said if anyone called here for him he would have to go, but if he didn't get the call there wouldn't be anyone on his conscience.

September

I don't feel especially active today due to the party yesterday. This was the annual affair that Mrs. Carpenter gives to the mountaineer families who live just below us. We had about forty children here with their mothers, and in some cases their grandmothers and great-grandmothers. The party was scheduled at two and no one was late — one little girl said she had been counting the days for two weeks.

This party is the only fun of this kind that they have all year. The children don't go to school, none of them can read and write, they rarely see outsiders, Christmas is never observed, a birthday present is an unknown article, and the poor little kiddies have no pleasures whatever except those they manufacture themselves.

The fathers of the families work a little when the notion strikes them, but mostly hunt and lie around, and their food consists of cornmeal, pork, and coffee. One of the women had a two-months old baby and when asked what she fed it, she said that "there wasn't much milk since the keow went dry, but the bebby et pork and cawnpone right smart lively."

The women get married at seventeen, do their bit for the prolongation of the race by having a baby a year, and that's about all there is to their life. One woman had eight children going down in steps to the tiniest in her arms. They were all red-haired chunky little youngsters except one little girl of about eight. She was a tiny little thing with pretty dark hair and big blue eyes and the oldest, brightest little face. She'll be a beauty when she grows up and it seems a shame that she'll never have any advantages of any kind.

The people arrived in all shapes and sizes and costumes. We started games for the children while Mrs. Carpenter gossiped with the old ladies on the porch. I dropped the handkerchief frantically and repeatedly, went to Jerusalem and directed peanut races and the like. Frances and I were recreation leaders, as it were.[4]

After we had gone through the program of games, prizes generously given for each one, pinning the tail on the donkey was the next stunt. Frances and I held up the sheet with the donkey on it and most of the tails were pinned on us, the donkey only getting two. When we were through, tails dangled on all conceivable places of my attire, much to the hilarity of the assembled company. The toothless old ladies fairly cackled with glee.

Next came the eats, spelled with a capital E, no, I mean E-A-T-S! Once a year those children have all the ice cream and cake they can eat and the quantities they were able to stow away were surprising and wonderful. They ate, and ate, and then ate some more — wiggled around to settle it — ate some more, and finally with deep reluctance gave up their plates. I can positively swear that a mite of a thing about four years old had over a pint.

After the feed each child was presented with a little gift and when they started out they got a big apple and about a pound of mixed nuts and candy to take home with them. Such a beatific and thoroughly contented lot of youngsters I never saw. And it wasn't only the youngsters. One old lady shook hands with me in parting and said that if I had had as good a time as she, then I wouldn't "fergit it never."

One of the little girls took home something for her sister, who was "sick to her stummick." Mrs. C asked her if the child vomited, and Virgie said "No, but she threwed up a powerful lot." You should see the way those children fairly worship Mrs. Carpenter. She is fairy godmother and Santa Claus all in one.

Frances went to Washington on Sunday, and on Monday Mr. Carpenter left for New York to see his brother Reid sail for Scotland. Mrs. Carpenter then asked if I wanted to go to the city to see the big parade with Pershing and the First Division, which I did, and she said Mr. Carpenter wouldn't care if I went. I came to Washington the night before the parade and found the city crowded and running over, grandstands erected at every corner, and a general bustle in the atmosphere. Across the Avenue in front of the Treasury at Fifteenth Street was the huge arch of victory.

A crowd estimated at 400,000 honored the 24,000 veterans of the First Division in a parade that took five hours to pass any given point. The *Post* expressed Washington's feelings: "All Washington looked on amazed at the splendid pageant that is war moving in the paths of peace. It was the spirit of war, and they also marched who sleep in France."

In the morning several of the girls stood out on Highland Terrace and watched a part of the parade go down Massachusetts Avenue. It kept going for over an hour. Six of us started downtown to see the parade together, but Mabel and I lost the others. We had just congratulated ourselves on getting a good seat in front of the Treasury when a policeman came along and evicted us, whereupon we spent the rest of the afternoon strolling from one place to another, getting ever more miserable and hot. I carried some chocolate bars with me until they turned into liquid and melted on my skirt.

I spent about an hour trying to locate my brother John, who had just returned from being posted in Germany with the Army of Occupation, but to no avail. I actually did see John marching but couldn't get close enough even to yell to him. I hauled Mabel up to Twenty-first Street in an effort to intercept him there, but s.o.l.[5] Everyone with whom I talked followed the good old army habit of passing the buck and by the time it was passed a dozen times or so I desisted.

I worked Friday from four to six in the apple crop and put in a full half day Saturday from one to six and pulled down the munificent salary of one dollar fifty. The Carpenter's orchard is about a mile from the house and I had to walk out alone through the tall grass. Every time a cricket buzzed or a harmless little locust sang his solo I jumped — either mentally or physically — several feet from the ground and wished that I had about four more eyes to watch for rattlesnakes.

Considering that I have added twenty pounds to my weight this summer, I didn't consider myself sylphlike enough to get up into the trees and pick; and considering the size of my legs I always avoid any occupation that might bring them into prominence. My work, therefore, was at the grading bench — perfect apples in one box, not so perfect ones in another, and so on down to the rotten ones, which I threw away, but some of the others, not being so polite, used them as articles of assault and battery.

Besides Frances and me, there were about twenty or more mountaineers and their conversation was a constant source of amazement, delight, and pleasure. The talk turned to books, and one girl proudly stated the fact that "she read a book clear through onct." When I asked what the name of the book was she didn't remember, "but it was a right good book, purty red cover, and everything." Another girl had written a story and informed me that she had "wrote a whole tableful. She woulda made it longer, but her paper give out and she had to end it kinda suddint."

I enjoy the unique distinction of being known as "The Sekkiterry." I overheard one girl telling another that I "write Mr. Carpenter's books." I grasped her meaning and she is right as far as the mechanical part goes, otherwise I have to refuse the honor.

I am negotiating for a box of beauties from Mrs. C. The only objection is that they won't ripen for eating until January or February and I don't know whether there is a cool enough place to keep them at 1415. I think I shall chance it. There are also some fall apples that are good for eating now and I think I shall have some of those to stow away under my bed. In addition to all the money I earned in the apples, I won twenty-seven cents Sunday shooting pool with Dr. Plaster and Mr. Carpenter. Heathenish, yes, but twenty-seven cents is twenty-seven cents.

After the Carpenters bought the property in 1897, they planted an orchard of 5,000 peach and apple trees. The fruit was expected to carry the expenses of running the estate. In the years before the war, with Frank Carpenter away so often, Mrs. Carpenter became "orchard manager." She studied methods of spraying and pruning, picking and packing, and according to Frances, she handled the shipments "as well as any man." The mountaineers thought this was all backwards. Frances said it gave her parents a good laugh when they heard their neighbors say that they didn't see why "Mr. C did not stay at home and tend to his business, instead of gallivantin' around and letting his wife do it for him."

My Mother's Applesauce

For one batch use six to eight apples, perhaps three varieties depending on what's in season, but always a granny smith. Peel, or if the apples are organic, partially peel; the skins add color and nutrients. Chop into large and smaller pieces and toss into large saucepan. Pour about a cup of water, or apple cider if it's in season, depending on how many apples, into the pot. Add the zest of one lemon — I use a sharp knife rather than a zester — and a few tablespoons of sugar. Sprinkle with nutmeg and cinnamon — or a quarter stick of cinnamon. Add a handful of raisins, unless you don't like raisins. Sometimes I use dried cranberries. Bring to a boil and simmer on medium-low heat until apples are soft. The timing depends on the freshness of the apples; check the pot every 10 minutes. I like my applesauce lumpy, more like compote. If you want a fine sauce, do not add raisins and cook longer.

My mother devoured apples; a brother, and later a nephew, had an apple orchard in Ionia, and at Christmas for most of her life, wherever she was, a box of apples arrived from Michigan. Her apple pie and applesauce were memorable. I don't bake, but I make her applesauce regularly — just the making of it, let alone the eating, is a comfort. Like most of her recipes, the proportions were challengingly vague.

NOTES

[1] *The seventy-four-year-old Wiley was the crusader who initiated* Good Housekeeping's *advertising "seal of approval" and was the driving force behind the 1906 Pure Food and Drug Act. His much-younger wife was a militant suffragist.*

[2] *At one of her parties, President Theodore Roosevelt's daughter Alice discovered her husband, Nicholas, Speaker of the House, having sexual relations with her good friend Cissy Patterson on the bathroom floor. My mother didn't record the details in her diary, but I found the story in the newspaper.*

[3] *Although this attitude was changing, girls who "bobbed" (cut) their hair and wore bloomers — baggy pants that came to just below the knee — were considered "fast."*

[4] *Drop the Handkerchief is a 19th-century circle game; we know Going to Jerusalem as Musical Chairs.*

[5] *The modern meaning of "s.o.l." is shit out of luck, but that vulgarity is so out of character for my mother perhaps ninety years ago it meant "same old luck."*

6

FALL AND WINTER 1919

Washington, D.C.

Jo in her new suit on the banks of the Potomac River.

"It is cold here now and there is ice-skating on the Potomac, which doesn't happen often in Washington. Our house has been quite cold, and Grace and I have to go to a movie or to bed to keep warm, but cold weather never lasts here … Mrs. Carpenter gave me a box of sugar to help out if Mrs. Dudley's runs short. She also says she will take me to live with them if Mrs. Dudley's coal runs out."

October

Came back to the city; didn't want to, but had to make the move. Had a bedbug scare one night. I woke up and killed twenty. I was so stirred up by the slaughter that I sat down and wrote a poem at three o'clock in the morning.

Frances returned yesterday from New York. She showed me her new clothes and I wanted to go in a corner and die after I had viewed them all. Why wasn't I born rich? Finished my made-over purple dress and wore it to work, Mr. and Mrs. C said it was lovely.

The King and Queen of Belgium are coming to Washington tomorrow and I hope I get a chance to see them. They will be entertained at the home of the former Ambassador to Belgium, Breckinridge Long. I am enjoying my work very much these days. Connecticut Avenue is really a wonderful place to be. From my window I see big limousines going by, and I get lots of style ideas just from watching the women who go past. Mr. Carpenter is nice as ever, and sends me home in the car when it is raining, and I can use the chauffeur and car when I go downtown on a business errand or to the bank. Mrs. Carpenter is a dear and comes to talk to me a lot. She has to take me to the theatre as a result of a bet she lost, and she has also invited me to go driving with her.

I have a season ticket for five concerts, and have bought tickets for two more, Galli-Curci and Jascha Heifitz. I don't regret my fourteen dollars in the least for the season ticket, although I was left with something like two dollars and ninety-some cents to last until payday, still eight long days away. Fortunate, isn't it, that I have a prosperous roommate. I may be reckless to spend all my money like that, but I always feel as though I could die contented when I am listening to a good violinist. A violin always touches some chord in me that makes the most delicious little thrills have relay races up and down my back. Personally, I can play about two pieces on the piano, and that is the sum total of my musical accomplishments, but my father is one of those persons who can listen to a piece and then play it by ear in a way to make you look for a secluded corner to wipe the tears away, but I seemed to have been forgotten when it came to passing on the musical talent.[1]

My seat is down in the orchestra among the nabobs and Grace said that I might get chummy with the woman next to me and see if I couldn't coax a loan on her ticket for the Kreisler, but I ask you, how is one to get chummy with a woman who looks at your year-before-last coat through a diamond studded platinum lorgnette? The Farrar[2] concert was very good, although Geraldine was a bit off tune, she was as usual very exposé in dress, but it was a pretty dress, no-back, gold straps. She sang one of my favorite songs, "Mammy's Coal Black Rose," and played her own accompaniment, which brought down the house.

After we left the theatre and were on our way home we saw a big crowd out in front of the Willard Hotel, so we stopped to see what the comosh was. We heard that the King and Queen were going in to attend the ball given there, but they didn't. We did see General Pershing go in, and Mrs. Cornelius Vanderbilt of New York, and several other bejeweled people.

Sunday I prepared for a quiet evening, but about seven-thirty remembered that the King and Queen of Belgium were dining just a couple of blocks up the avenue, so Grace and I raced up the street. We got to the corner just as the advance guard of motorcyclists were rounding the corner and thought we were going to be late, but an obliging streetcar blocked their path and while the limousine was being held up we got to the house of

Secretary Lansing. I fervently thanked whoever was responsible that I was made long, as I could see over the heads of everyone in front of me. The King is very tall and good looking, and the Crown Prince is a mighty nice-looking boy. Looks as if he would like to cast off some of the dignity and pomp he is obliged to maintain and flirt with a girl.

More than 100,000 people gathered at Union Station to cheer the arrival of the popular King Albert and Queen Elizabeth. Vice President Marshall, cabinet officials and the full diplomatic corps in frock coats and silk top hats, led the official reception, along with the Marine Band, a cavalry troop and the 500 voices of the War Camp Community Chorus. After the Germans invaded Belgium, the Queen worked as a nurse and her husband fought as a soldier; they captured the public imagination on both sides of the Atlantic.

November

Mr. Carpenter is at present writing two books. We work on Europe a while until we want a change of climate, then make a rapid journey down to South America and worry that a bit. His publishers are rushing him to get one of the manuscripts to them in double quick time, and my job is to get it copied. Mr. Carpenter's daughter, therefore, has come down to do my research while I devote my entire time to typing. By the time I get fifteen thousand words written a day I rather wish that fingers and Underwoods and speed and a few other things were not invented. But the agony will soon be over.

I like my work immensely (exclusive of the typing) and my employer to the utmost. He is a mixture of sarcasm, ill-temper, bushy hair, scraggly whiskers, wit, humor, good nature, generosity, and the most general contrariness I ever saw. Mrs. Carpenter was a mother to me all summer out in the mountains, and I think, as their butler does when he was telling me about something she did for him: "Ah tells yo', Miss Lehman, right dar's a woman what's gwina live by her good deeds after she dies."[3]

Washington is very changed from what it was in 1918. Thousands of war workers have left, the soldiers are gone, all that hurry and rush is lessening, and it is even possible at times to get waited on in a store or to get a meal after waiting not more than a half hour in a restaurant. I haven't done much rushing around since I came back from the mountains. Rather got out of the habit and feel rather content to live the quiet and simple life.

The Neighborhood House still has dances and I was there once since coming back, but as we no longer feel it our duty (Ha!) to entertain poor lonesome soldiers; none of the girls go as often. I never used to give a thought about going to community centers and the like and dancing the entire evening with perfectly strange men, but somehow it is different when the men aren't in uniform. I was telling my mother when I was home this summer of the places to which I went, she seemed slightly puzzled, slightly shocked, and said, "You don't mean *public* dances?"

I shut up like the proverbial clam and reflected that as long as she hadn't known wartime Washington she couldn't appreciate the fact that given a city, several thousand soldiers, and ditto girls — community centers like the Neighborhood House filled a big need.

Grace and I had supper in our room last night instead of going out — the family treasury is in a state of perilous lowness. Grace has a trifle more than I have and I have told her that it is up to her to keep me alive until payday. I am really saving money these days. The minute I get my check I walk it to the bank and deposit a certain amount before I have time to spend it — then I get along until the next payday as best I can.

Jessie Phillips arrived from Ionia and stayed all night Saturday and you should have seen the way we looked three in bed. Jessie and I slept as one is supposed to sleep in bed — with our heads at the head of the bed — but Grace decided it wouldn't make it so crowded up at the head if she would reverse, which she did, and her feet graced the space between our two pillows. I offered to sleep at the foot but Grace vetoed that — said her feet were so much smaller they wouldn't be noticed if she happened to land one of them in our faces during a bad dream on her part — but she absolutely refused to take any chance on having one of my "canalboats" (yep, that's what she calls them) demolish her features. All in all, I can say that I have spent worse nights.

Armistice Day, and just a year ago from the time Smittie and I did the crazy dance on Ninth Street. Didn't celebrate during the day as it was raining, but in the evening Grace and I went up to Eighteenth Street to see the Prince of Wales as he went to the Lansing home for dinner. He was dressed in evening clothes and looked merely like a very nice yellow-haired boy.[4]

Payday, and I decided to shop during the afternoon, but as I couldn't get my check cashed, I spent some time listening to Victrola records, finally buying one, and then went home. [5]

Grace is talking about marriage, but if she does I shall be lost. She sets me a good example by showing me will power and giving up candy and getting up to early church and all that, and she's the only girl I know that can do darn fool things and still have some sense — I mean that we can go off on a spree and do crazy things, yet keep our heads. I asked her if she would rather get married, scrub, wash, cook, sew, mend, make beds, sweep floors, spank babies, and when she wanted some money say, "Oh, please Jimmy or Georgie can I have a quarter, I have to pay the coal man," or be her own boss and haul in $55 every two weeks? Maybe if I cared enough for one of these darling men I would be perfectly willing to do all that for him and wouldn't kick, but I refuse to consider it when I don't even like them a lot. So just for the present, I'm still answering to the name of Lehman. Grace tells me that some day I am going to fall head over heels in love with some poor simp who doesn't amount to a cent. Well, maybe I will in time. As yet, I haven't been able to fall in love with anybody. That's me all over, Mabel.[6]

December

Mr. Carpenter said something today about taking up newspaper work and foreign correspondence again, and asked me how I'd like to travel, and believe me, if there's a chance for me to do some globe trotting — think what a wasted opportunity it would be to throw that away.

Thanksgiving afternoon Grace and I saw Constance Talmadge in "The Virtuous

Vamp"; it's the funniest thing I have seen in a long time. Movies now cost forty cents to get a good seat. Speaking of high finance, I lost a nickel to Mrs. Carpenter playing bridge the other night.

No dates for a long time but I do have a man who calls me regularly on the telephone. If you could hear the excuses I concoct for not seeing him you would know that I have imagination if nothing else. This man is one of these fellows about whom the best can be said is, "He'll make a good husband for some poor girl." And he will. He is well educated, he did his bit over in France, has traveled all over the United States, he writes a very clever letter, and he is witty and a good conversationalist, but when it comes to looks he is somewhere else entirely. His hair is a nondescript yellow and will stand up everywhere except where he wants it to. His face has freckles that make mine look beautiful in comparison, and his nose is the most aspiring thing I have yet seen. And his clothes. I don't know where he gets them. Bow ties? Black and white checked caps? Knitted mittens? Oh, yes, all those and more. There are two kinds of men — those whose pant legs won't shake down when they stand up, and those whose will. He is the first kind — very much so.

I really did "bust" out in society last week — the Carpenters had me to dinner. I pressed the doorbell, gave a long swallow, and determined to do or die. If Arthur the butler had answered the door I might have taken heart as he is a good friend of mine, but it was the maid, instead, and she took my wraps and set me down in the library until the family came down. It went off all right, even if we did have five courses, four spoons, three forks, and two knives, to say nothing of finger bowls and coffee demitasse. I had three months practice last summer using all those things, and I hadn't forgotten after all. After dinner we went to the theatre, Mrs. Carpenter, Frances and I, *à la* limousine, arriving fashionably late. We sat among all the "powers wot is" and when Mrs. Carpenter smiled and bowed to some old blokes, they were Samuel Gompers or Alexander Graham Bell or somebody like that. Margaret Wilson[7] sat two seats from me. I always wondered why she never married. After having sat for two and a half hours where I could get a good look at her I no longer wonder. The play was Otis Skinner[8] in a new production and was very good, indeed. Afterward, I was dropped at my door and hiked myself to my third story room and went to bed — turned the pillow case so the ragged side wouldn't show, put my coat on the bed to help out the skimpy bedclothes, wondered if we'd have stewed prunes and fish for breakfast and dreamed that I was a millionaire too, but felt poor and forlorn.

I was bossless all last week when Mr. C went hunting down on his North Carolina estate. I made use of his absence to fix up the office, index his books, sort the files, catalog all of the information, and clean out his two desks, in one of which I found letters that dated back as far as 1896. I thought afterwards that if it hadn't been cleaned out in that long it must have been because he didn't want it to be, and trembled in my boots for fear that I had done something that I shouldn't, but he didn't seem to mind and called me his "Able P.S." which is commendation to the nth degree.

A real snowfall today, the first one I have seen in Washington. There is even sleighing, and I yearn for an honest-to-gosh coasting party. Mrs. C invited me up to lunch. I accepted.

Christmas has come and gone. Our room still looks like Christmas, as we had a little Christmas tree and had the room trimmed with holly and red and green crepe paper. Jessie came over and stayed with us Christmas day. We had a very good dinner at the house, but someone stole one of the turkeys the night before, so none of us could ask for a second helping. We had roast turkey with dressing, sweet potatoes, peas, cranberry jelly, fruit salad, bread and butter, plum pudding, oranges, bananas, apples and grapes and candy and nuts.

Washington had an airplane Christmas, that is, Santa Claus came in an airplane and landed down in one of the parks and all the poor children were invited to come and get a present. After Santa had given them all out, he went up in the airplane again and flew away.

It is cold here now and there is ice-skating on the Potomac, which doesn't happen often in Washington. Our house has been quite cold, and Grace and I have to go to a movie or to bed to keep warm, but cold weather never lasts here. We tried sitting on the radiator to warm up a bit, then Grace brought out her little old pint bottle of port from the bottom of her trunk. It helped but little. Mrs. Carpenter gave me a box of sugar to help out if Mrs. Dudley's runs short. She also says she will take me to live with them if Mrs. Dudley's coal runs out.

We had some real excitement when the house next to Mrs. Dudley's caught fire about seven thirty in the morning. We were roused by the landlady who said to get into our clothes and prepare for the worst, but it was such a confoundedly cold morning that we didn't much care whether the house caught fire or not if that would make us any warmer. When I finally worked up enough enthusiasm to get partly dressed to go outside, it was announced the fire was out. The street in front of the house was filled with people wearing kimonos and sleepy looks, but they finally trooped back to bed and I did likewise.[9]

The Carpenters have been unusually nice to me of late. Mr. Carpenter remarked to me today that I was a nice girl. Apropos of what, I don't know. Sometimes I just stand still and pinch myself and ask if I am dreaming or if it is really I, Josephine Matilda Lehman (middle name despised but owned nevertheless), aged twenty-one, sound of mind (I hope so at least), who has fallen into such a fine place. The summer I spent in the Blue Ridge Mountains was the most wonderful summer I have ever known. I have read of life at big country estates with millionaires before, but I never thought I would land in one myself.

January

Grace and I were invited to a reception at Carpenters' on New Years Day in honor of son Jack and his wife, who were visiting from Chicago. We went with fear and trembling lest we should look like the country cousin in last year's suits, but I think we got away with it all right. We saw several people who looked shoddier than we did, which cheered us considerably, but Grace remembered that a "somebody" can look shoddy and get away

71

with it, but not a government clerk.

A group of young people in Frances' set were there — just oodles of young million-aires and debutantes and Army and Naval officers, to say nothing of a few senators and congressmen — and punch with a stick in it![10] Grace wanted to meet Mr. Carpenter, who finally put in his appearance. She has raved about him ever since, he really is very charm-ing and I don't blame her, only I'm so used to him that I have passed the raving point. We had a delightful time and the only misfortune was that we both forgot our handbags, and when we reached Carpenters' didn't have our calling cards,[11] but I slipped past the card tray under cover of talking to Pauline, the maid. Grace suggested that I take our cards and slip them in the tray the next morning at work when nobody was looking. A very bright suggestion but as the cards were all removed by the next morning ours would have looked a trifle lonesome, so the only thing to do was forget it.

Mrs. Carpenter came into the office today to have me write a couple of little notes for her, and then tendered an invitation to dinner and the theater. I went to a concert after work and came home late — it was Jascha Heifetz and his violin, and I'm telling you, that boy can fiddle.[12]

Nothing much is happening in Washington now; as one of the girls at the house said, "Peace may have advantages, but give me war any old time." All of which meant that during war there was something doing every minute of the time, with plenty of excite-ment and enough to spare. It is very different now but I enjoy myself — I would take nothing for my two years here, and especially my experiences in wartime Washington. The rush and mystery of the Ordnance Department is a thing of the past, the crowds are going home, and I realize the war is really over.

I used to work in a building with 26,000 others and run my days by clock-work, now I am by myself in an office and have pretty much my own schedule, seeing my boss only about three hours a day. Where I used to do a lot of routine work, take dictation ga-lore on technical letters, and be used to seeing colonels and majors and occasional generals popping in and out of the office, now I browse around in a luxurious library and arrange my work to suit myself and see hardly anyone else besides a little skinny old man with straggly whiskers and a sarcastic tongue and a warm heart. My boss is one of the most interesting men I ever met.

Sometimes, however, I long for a job where I will be eternally rushing around and know that I can't sit back and rock if I want to: for instance, being back on the *Sentinel* with a Chautauqua program morning, afternoon and night, and then to have someone commit suicide and have a couple of deaths, besides writing up a wedding where it is like pulling teeth to get information, to say nothing of meeting four trains and waiting on customers and answering telephones in between times, while an impatient composi-tor points a menacing finger at the clock and says in all caps, "NO COPY SET AFTER THREE O'CLOCK." That was what I called a full day.

I wrote some crazy verse to Mrs. Carpenter on a Christmas card, and it made such a hit with the family that this morning Mr. Carpenter broached the subject of collaborating with me on a book of jingles for children to teach geography. I was all interest, but if that man writes all the books he has already contracted for, he won't have any time left for jingles, so I'm not counting on the prospect to the extent of retiring from work.

February

Eight new girls have come to the house during the past week. Two of them are in the room next to mine and one of them has a ukulele and one has a jazz horn. They started to give a free concert the other evening while Grace and I were reading. Concentration was out of the question when such a medley of sound in the next room was proclaiming the fact that "Everything is lovely in that land of jaaaaaaaazzzz." So I became enthusiastic and gathered up a comb and tissue paper and added my contribution to the ensemble. We kept it up until I wasn't sure if Grace was going to throw a fit or a club, but I judged by the gleam in her eye that she didn't like our music, so we desisted. Another one of the new girls has a canary. We might have added that to the orchestra, but the poor bird is so behind the times that he doesn't know how to sing jazz yet.

A bunch of us went to the Neighborhood House last Saturday and it was just like old times. We all had a very good time and a man from Georgia by the name of Bradshaw danced nearly every dance with me. He is with a shipbuilding company here and expects to go to Panama soon, so I had best get my innings in early. We all went to Child's restaurant at one o'clock in the morning and had griddlecakes and syrup. The next morning I was flat on my back with the grippe, and the Carpenters called the doctor. He happened to be Dr. Lawson, the man I met up at Bluemont last summer one Saturday afternoon when I lost my way in the mountains, so I was rather glad I was sick just for the sake of being able to talk Bluemont with somebody.

The next morning I got up and went to work, but about eleven o'clock the desks and bookshelves and chairs all started to do the shimmy, and the floor started to biff me in the face, so my boss said that I had better go home and stay there until I got my land legs again. He sent for the car which delivered me at my door, so home I stayed — at least until the next afternoon, when I had a ticket to hear Galli-Curci and I was bound to hear her if they had to carry me there in an ambulance.

She was very wonderful, but I would have enjoyed it more had it not been for the conversation of a man and woman behind me. They were these people who know it all so they started to air their knowledge of musical technique. When they were tired of that (a feeling also experienced by everyone within earshot of them) they started discussing Galli-Curci's recent divorce.

Luigi Curci had denied his wife Amelia Galli-Curci's allegations that he squandered her money, and of indiscretions with chorus women and hotel maids, and countered with accusations of infidelity with her accompanist, specifying hotels and sleeping cars between Washington and Chicago. He also attempted to keep her by pleading they were Italian citizens, and married under an agreement never to divorce. The story was front-page news.

Frances Carpenter gave Grace and me tickets for four plays being given by the Arts Club players. Frances was in two of them. I enjoyed the audience almost as much as the plays, as it consisted of everybody who was somebody. Grace and I were a small expanse of nobodies entirely surrounded by somebodies. Talk about ermine evening wraps and platinum combs and ostrich fans and uncovered buzzums and general haughtiness!!!

Saturday evening Jessie and Grace and I went to the Neighborhood House. I danced with Mr. Bradshaw several times, and we talked on the subject of hoboism, which career he seems to have followed for several years, although one would never know it to look at him. He seems to have been all over a great part of the world. I was further startled to have him tell me that he had once been a dancing instructor.

A working class, hobo subculture of young, unmarried, English-speaking laborers who migrated with the crops arose a generation earlier. Hoboing spread to the middle class and became for many young men a youthful rite of passage, an adventurous interlude between high school or college and settling down to work. The fashion passed by the late twenties.

Grace and I went to the Garrick to see Lowell Thomas, hear him, rather, in his lecture "The Last of the Crusaders in Arabia and Palestine," for which Mr. Carpenter had given me tickets.

Thomas was an adventurer and journalist who embarked for Europe just after the United States entered the war; he filmed Americans at the front for the Committee on Public Information. He and his crew traveled from France to the Balkan front, then Italy, and Palestine and Arabia, where he met T. E. Lawrence. After the armistice he finagled his way across Germany's closed border, the only American to report from there. The series of shows based on these experiences — a combination of talk, special lighting effects, still and moving pictures, the Power-Point of the era —were hits in England and the United States. A show about the Holy Land, featuring Lawrence, whom Thomas promoted as Lawrence of Arabia, was the most popular, and made T. E. Lawrence a household word. It laid the groundwork for Lowell's career as a filmmaker, lecturer, author, news commentator, and world famous personality. My mother could not have imagined that in less than a decade she would be one of Lowell Thomas' ghostwriters.

I have finally moved. We are living at the Longfellow Inn, where Connecticut Avenue, M Street and Eighteenth come together at Longfellow Park, just a block south of Dupont Circle. This house overlooks one of those little parks that are as thick here as mules are in Missouri. It's a little three-cornered affair with a statue of Longfellow in the center. We are located in the midst of the combined residential and shopping section, although I never patronize the shops in this district. The people who do, roll up in their seven-passenger Pierce Arrows, but the only thing I could roll up in would be a wheelbarrow or bicycle. An advantage of its situation is that it is almost directly across the street from the Carpenter residence. I like that fact in the morning, but I rather miss a bit of the walk in the afternoon. Martha and Grace and I have a big front room on the third floor. The room itself isn't so pretty as the one Grace and I had together at Dudleys', but the room is WARM, and my poor typewriter has been sadly neglected of late, but now that I am settled in a room where I don't have to sit on my fingers to keep them warm, I hope to get to work again.

They mop up the floor and dust the room every day; our towels are furnished three times a week; our dresser scarves are furnished and frequently one can get more than a pint of hot water at a time. The bed linens, especially the spreads, are spotless; we have clean napkins every day; we have our choice of foods and we have service. The latter includes not only service at the table, but someone who comes to our door and calls us when we have a telephone call or a caller, instead of bellowing up four flights of stairs that we "have company." It's the very antithesis of our other place.

Grace calls our place the Coney Island Maze. We go in at the door of 1202, go halfway down a long hall, turn to our left, ascend a winding staircase with only four turns in it, then turn to our right, go up two steps, turn to our left and through a cross-hall into 1204, turn to our right again, go up another winding staircase, turn to our left, and go to the last door.[13] Three of us in one room make it cheaper for each of us, although it is still quite steep, but it is such a decided improvement on the Dudley mansion that we don't mind the extra price. We get real eats now, just as we once did at the Dudleys' before it went from bad to worse. Dinner is served in three courses, and breakfast brings us all the bacon and eggs we can eat. About fifty people are living here, all shapes, sizes and assortments. Our landlady is a woman about thirty-five. We have a Major and his wife and two children, two or three middle-aged couples and about six old ladies who wear loads of diamonds and old-fashioned dew-daddies and who look like moveable antique shops. There are about a dozen or more girls, most of whom, as Grace says, look like the last row of the Follies. They all seem out of the same pattern — exaggerated pompadours, pulled eyebrows, enameled complexions, bored expressions. Several others are just common everyday folks, and one is an ex-Russian countess. She has long animated conversations over the phone in French and Russian.

After dinner, the entire company retires to the parlor, where one of the girls seats herself at the piano and goes through her repertoire of classical music. The other girls arrange themselves artistically about the best-looking young man and pay assiduous court to him, while the old ladies sit primly on the various chairs and sofas and nod their heads in time to the music until some particularly rending crash occurs on the keys. After this is over, another girl takes her place, and the music is now ragtime for a while. Then the younger folks take their departure, and the older ones play cards — I don't know how long, for I never waited to find out. We have learned all about this procedure by being able to cast wistful glances into the parlor while waiting to use the telephone. Even if we were courageous enough to go in and sit down without an invitation there would be no place to sit. Perhaps we are on probation for a certain time and if at the end of that time we are not classified as undesirables, we shall be invited into the inner sanctum.

Mr. Carpenter is away today, and for that matter, he might be away every day for all the work we have accomplished this week. His daughter is to be married in a month to Chapin Huntington, the commercial attaché at the American embassy in Paris, and they sail for France immediately after the wedding.

Ever since she told me, I have been feeling as though someone had died. She has been working for her father all winter and has been in the same office with me. She is a jolly good sort, and now when I think of myself all alone in the office when she goes, and when I think of how lonesome it will be up in the Blue Ridge Mountains next summer with just Mr. and Mrs. Carpenter, I feel as if I could point my nose at the moon and bellow. Mr. and Mrs. C said they would try to import some young people for me. They are so good to me that I can hardly believe it. When I started work for Mr. Carpenter I told him I would not get married for a year and leave him in a lurch, and now he is trying to figure out if I am going to extend that promise another year, as he has so much work to do.

The whole house has been transformed into a ways and means committee, and far more lingerie, trousseau, announcements, invitations, and so on, are discussed in the office than problems of geography. I will take up some of the work that Frances has been doing in collaboration with her father, and Mr. Carpenter will get another secretary to take my place.

I have lost twenty-five pounds since last fall. I think as soon as I get out in the country with lots of butter and eggs and cream I shall pick up and break the scales again. I am getting thin as a pancake, but I try to take things easy. I was going to ask my boss for a vacation, but now that his daughter is getting married they are awfully busy and I hate to do it.

NOTES

[1] *I never met my grandfather Lehman, but when I was a child and wanted piano lessons my mother told me how beautifully her father played. She described his long, graceful fingers. My grandmother Lehman was short and plump and her husband was tall, with an elegant carriage. Before she died, my mother revealed to me that late in his life her father told her that he was the illegitimate son of a Prussian nobleman. Perhaps he thought that she had seen enough of the world not to be shocked by this. My mother said this background was responsible for his innate grace. When I asked various cousins in Michigan, no one else had heard the story.*

[2] *Geraldine Farrar was the Metropolitan Opera Company's original Madame Butterfly and a prima donna there for sixteen years. Teenage girls were so crazy about Farrar that they formed a fan club called "Gerryflappers."*

[3] *My mother often mentions that the Carpenters treat her like one of the family, but a rigid social division was firmly in place. As friendly as she was with Frances in the less formal summer atmosphere, Jo could never be in her "set," with its millionaires, officers, and debutantes. Frances' letter thanking Jo for her wedding present began, "My Dear Miss Lehman." It's obvious, however, that the Carpenters and Jo had real affection for each other, and the social lessons she learned with them served her well in her next job.*

[4] *Jo took a snapshot of the Duke and pasted it in her album. In 1936, the twenty-five-year-old Prince Edward abdicated the English throne in order to marry Wallis Simpson, a divorced commoner, and became the Duke of Windsor. In the window seat, I found a copy of the* New York Herald Tribune *from December 11, 1936, with a*

*three-deck banner headline proclaiming, "**Edward VIII, as David Windsor, to Broadcast Farewell Message to British Empire Today After Duke of York Becomes King George VI.**" The present Queen Elizabeth is George VI's daughter.*

⁵ Listening booths in record stores were the only way customers could hear music before they bought it. The first radio station broadcast the 1920 election results on November 2nd, and wireless receiving sets went on sale to the public that year, but it was not until 1925 that radios became all electric, eliminating large numbers of batteries and earphones, and music-lovers could easily receive the music "in the air."

⁶ "That's Me All Over, Mabel" was the title of a popular book by John Edward Hazard. Jo was partial to Mabel, and throughout her diary addresses many comments to her. Mabel could also refer to the chorus girls whose dialogue song became common slang: "The way folks talk about us, too / For the smallest thing we do / 'nuff to make a girl feel blue, / Ain't it awful, Mabel?"

⁷ Margaret Wilson was the President's daughter.

⁸ Otis Skinner was an actor famous from the 1870s until the 1930s.

⁹ The Star *reported that, "Scores of scantily clad occupants sought safety in flight and two young girls were taken down a ladder by firemen... but they suffered more from the bitter cold than from fire."*

¹⁰ A "stick" meant the punch was spiked with alcohol.

¹¹ A visitor left a card engraved with her name on a small, square, silver tray on an entrance hall table. The subtleties of calling card etiquette were intricate, but relaxed somewhat in the chaotic wartime society. Although the cards were often associated with the upper classes, Jo, her friends, and the men they met, had and exchanged them. My mother has pages of them in her photo and memory albums.

¹² Three years earlier, the sixteen-year-old violinist Jascha Heifetz debuted at Carnegie Hall.

¹³ In 1995, when I explored my mother's Washington, a large office building filled half the block, but Longfellow was still in his spot in the tiny triangular park.

7

SPRING 1920

Jo Gets a Raise;
A Society Wedding

Jo lived near Thomas Circle, seen here just before World War 1.

"The regime here at the house has been considerably changed in the past few weeks and I have had a promotion, have my own office, and am now being paid $140. With Frances' leaving, Mr. Carpenter has decided to put me on her work. I am writing a book on clothing and how it is made."

My mother was having trouble making ends meet. She had to sell her Liberty Bond to get enough money to buy clothes for the wedding and a present for Frances. Since the end of the war, inflation had reduced the buying power of the dollar by thirty-two percent, and in mid-1920 the economy dropped into a sharp recession. The government put price controls on bread, coal, milk, and rent, but a buyer's strike erupted. Men took old shirts to tailors to have them "turned," and women resisted fashion mandates and wore last year's hats and dresses. Wearing old clothes became almost a style in reverse; even President Wilson's son-in-law displayed elbow patches on his jacket. The "overalls movement" was the silliest expression of discontent over inflation — men substituted cotton overalls for suits and wore them in offices, schools, brokerage houses, banks, and even in Congress. By the end of the year prices had dropped somewhat, but the recession lasted until 1922.

March

I thought I was going to save a lot of money this payday, but I have to pay out so much for income tax and so much for living that I'm no better off than before. Prices in Washington are sky high now. I had to pay fourteen dollars for a plain pair of black slippers, and five dollars for gloves, four-fifty for some good black hose, and two dollars for a veil the other day. That was almost thirty dollars gone, and it wasn't even enough to cover me unless I stretched the veil. Many of the men in the government departments here are wearing overalls. I see men with brown oxfords and silk socks and funny old blue overalls. Even some of the senators are wearing them.

One thing that has become very popular here is taffeta dresses of all colors, or figured veils trimmed with little taffeta ruffles. All the best stores are featuring them for spring. Another is the accordion or knife pleated skirt of plaid or stripes and worn with one of the new sport coats. The spring coats are all sport models, mostly tan, and I see a lot of "shimmy" dresses of poplin and linen. They are the little one-piece dresses made with long waists and short sleeves, and slip over the head. All the waists are long and worn over the skirt. Oh yes, you must have big ribbon bows on your pumps to be up to the minute and many of the new hats are made of ribbon with little or no straw. My hat is black straw, very chic, and very now. I have some new pumps, hose, veils, gloves and ideas, but not much more. If we go to the mountains early I won't need any fussy clothes, but I do have to throw something together for the Carpenter wedding. I might have to put a new feather on my hat and a new expression on my face and try to make them do.

My birthday dawned calmly and peacefully, with no one to catch me unaware and give the accredited number of thumps, with several extras to aid me in growing, as is the custom. I flattered myself that nobody in the house knew the importance of March sixteenth, but it did seem strange that they couldn't see I was a whole year older. I had previously gotten a few things through the mail, but as I always see the mail before my roommates do, the parcels went into my bureau and nobody was the wiser.

Received a little bonus of five dollars today from Father Carp for my work on his income tax. I went down to the bank this morning and transacted some business for the firm. As it was raining and sloppy, I sent around for the car to take me. Spent some more time helping Frances with her wedding lists.

The wedding is on April sixth at four-thirty, and will be comparatively small. The reception that follows will be at five o'clock, and will include about 500 people. Secretary of Navy and Mrs. Daniels are coming, Secretary and Mrs. Lansing, Professor Alexander

Graham Bell, Dr. Harvey Wiley, Secretary Houston of the Treasury, Edwin Sweet of Grand Rapids, who is Assistant Secretary of Commerce, and just oodles of others whom I hope to meet. Just to get an introduction to them will mean something. Frances and her husband sail for his post at Paris three days after the wedding on the *Imperator*, the next to the biggest ship afloat.

I envy her the trip. I envy her the man she is going to marry, too. He is about six feet tall, dark and very good-looking, and his eight years in the consular service have made him very polished, indeed. Even his bow is an accomplishment in itself, but he isn't at all stiff. When he gets unwound and starts entertaining, he is as good as any vaudeville show. He speaks five languages, has lived much in England, Germany, and Russia. Frances has known him barely two months, but it seems to be a case of love at first sight and getting worse every day.

I came back to my room from the Carpenters' and found it vacated. The only clue I have as to Grace's disappearance are two amputated sleeves from her black velvet dress, so I surmise that she has transformed said dress into an evening affair and gone off to a dance.

Mr. Carpenter has been sick for three days with ptomaine poisoning, and son Jack is here for a visit. I might go to Paris if the Carpenters go over to visit Frances.

Jessie and Grace and I went to the Neighborhood House. Danced several times with a tall Marine from Detroit. He was so tall that my head came right on his shoulder, and I naturally rested it there, whereupon Mr. Fraser pointed his finger at me.[1]

Mr. Carpenter is slowly getting up and around, and we went out for a little walk around the block. He was out in front talking with Secretary of State Lansing and telling him he was glad to hear he was out of office, and the Secretary echoed that statement.[2] Mr. Carpenter told me about what happened at a dinner party when Mrs. George Barnet told Postmaster General Burleson apropos of some slighting remarks he made on women's work during the war, that if he didn't know any more about females than he did about the mail, then she didn't think much of his opinion. Payday, and a beautiful spring day, too. Mr. Carpenter told me I could take my foot in hand and go out for a walk at noon, so I walked down to the bank and cashed my check and then strolled home.

April

Again I say that when I get married I am going to clutch my little $2.50 in my moist and trembling hand and wistfully offer it to some justice of the peace. For the past week I haven't done much in the line of secretarial duties, literary work, or geographical research. I have been helping Frances with her invitations and receptions, checking in presents as they come and helping to write notes of acknowledgment, receiving and signing for packages and gifts all day long, acting as social secretary to Mrs. Carpenter, and between times paying a bit of attention to the Boss, who has been wandering about the house like something lost. Between having the house turned upside down with wedding preparations, losing his only daughter, and having his working hours broken into and his office help abducted, the poor man didn't know where he was.

Monday was a constant flurry of packing and doing last minute things. It rained all day, but everyone hoped and prayed that Tuesday would be fair. Monday night every trunk was out of the house, the offices and library had been cleared to be used as cloak-rooms, and the furniture had been moved out of the drawing rooms so that all would be ready for the decorators and caterers in the morning. And then what did Mrs. Carpenter do the very morning of the wedding but fall down and break her hip. Frances got up early to go to communion with her to-be and went off singing to think that everything was ready and the day was beautiful. When she came back an hour later, it was to find her mother upstairs with three specialists and two nurses. It was terrible for her. Mrs. Carpenter absolutely refused to let the wedding be postponed, however, so while the doctors were working over her most of the day, Frances had to "carry on" and get things ready. Her injury is not dangerous, but it means that Mrs. Carpenter will be flat on her back for months.[3]

For the rest of the day, yours truly was the original little busy bod. Did I hurry from pillar to post? No, I jumped, hopped, and slid. There was telephoning to do, telegrams to send, bells to answer, while between times I slipped in a prod at the decorators, musicians, and caterers, none of whom got there on time. The reporters were calling up constantly, and at least six photographers wanted to come up and take the bridal pictures. About noon I switched off twenty minutes to eat some lunch, then was on the job again until two, when I came across to my room and changed into my fancy scenery. It wasn't so fancy, after all, but it did very nicely. I wore my finest dress, which went forth as new after being tenderly brushed up, and invested in a handmade lace collar, new black pumps, long white kid gloves, and big black hat. I didn't look so bad if I do say so myself. Then I went back over to the Carpenters', pitched my hat and gloves into a corner, and made myself useful until the guests started to arrive, when I put them back on and tried to look like a lady of leisure.

By this time the decorators were finished and the results were beautiful. One end of the drawing room had been banked with palms, in front of which were tall jardinières of white roses and white snapdragons, with a little altar of white satin. The other parts of the rooms were decorated with colored flowers. A string orchestra was hidden behind a geranium in the library upstairs and exuded soft music, and it was my duty to stand where I could see both the procession and them and to give the signal to start the wedding march, when to start the soft music for the ceremony, and when to stop for the prayer. I tried valiantly, but not having seven eyes, it almost got the best of me.

There were two clergymen, both dressed in their robes. After them came the maid of honor, then the groom with his best man, and the bride on the arm of her father. Her gown was exquisite, made of chiffon over satin and embroidered in pearls, with the waist of some old lace that had been in the family for centuries. Her veil formed the long train and she made a stunning picture as she stood in front of the altar. Only a small company were there for the ceremony, but about a half an hour later the reception guests started to come, and come — and come. I got my little old orchestra started on their music again, and then slowly fought my way into the dining room, where with a few chosen snake-like movements I wormed my way under someone's arm and got something to eat. The salads were the most delicious things I have ever eaten, and the cakes were heaven. There seemed no end of good things to eat, but I was too tired to enjoy them. Oh, yes, there was punch, too.

All this time Frances was still in the reception line, getting kissed and fussed over, while she was just dying to get upstairs to her mother.[4] I didn't kiss the groom, but he surely was good material. He looked like a combination of a Greek god and the man in the Arrow collar advertisement. There were notables galore at the reception — the Russian ambassador, several of the cabinet members and their wives and scores of others. I think I should have been wildly excited over it all had I not been so tired, but as it was I saw there was nothing more I could do, so quietly snuck out the side door and came home.

Today was a letdown from all the excitement, and I generally fussed around and saw that the offices and library were put back into shape. A specialist came over from Baltimore, and there are two nurses on duty with Mrs. Carpenter, so everything is being done for her that possibly can be. The presents continued to come all day for Frances, and I suppose it will be a week before things settle down again.

Frances gave me a big picture of herself, and a beautiful little bar pin with sapphires and pearls, which I thought was very sweet of her. She gave a pin just like mine to the maid of honor. Really, they are the sweetest family and treat me as if I belonged there instead of just being an accessory. Mrs. Carpenter's accident will change a lot of plans for the summer, it will be a long, long time before she can be moved, so instead of going to the Blue Ridge Mountains early, it will be midsummer when we go, if then. They had planned to go to Europe in August to visit Frances, but that will be changed now, so I don't know what to plan on.

I spent a great part of Friday interviewing typists to help in the office. They were of all kinds, but the choice has narrowed down to a Miss Surls and a Miss Ford, with the betting on Miss Ford, who is kind of a rough diamond, but I think I shall like her if she comes. She has immense possibilities.

PAYDAY. It deserves capital letters, as I had gotten as low as one car ticket by noon, when I went downtown to cash my check. Mr. Carpenter told me that starting next month my salary was raised ten dollars a month. Not bad, not bad.

May

The regime here at the house has been considerably changed in the past few weeks and I have had a promotion, have my own office, and am now being paid $140. With Frances' leaving, Mr. Carpenter has decided to put me on her work.

I am writing a book on clothing and how it is made. It tells about everything from which we make clothing — all about cotton, wool, silk, straw, leather, flax, fur, jewelry, and so on. Whenever I get a chapter done I let Mr. Carpenter look over it and he offers suggestions, but for the most part I plug along by myself. It is great fun, but hard work, and I have to dream about it at night to get any ideas. I have been going to Washington schools this week to read my book to the children and see if they like it and can understand it. If they don't take to it, then it means something is wrong and I have to write it over.[5]

After several and varied experiences interviewing typists, we have decided on Miss Ethel Ford, who is one of the best "key hitters" I have ever seen, in spite of the fact she has bobbed hair. She is coming Friday and she is going to get the same salary as I do with my raise — which isn't at all satisfactory to me, as I feel that having been here a year I am worth more to Mr. Carpenter than she is, coming in new and inexperienced in the work. Miss Ford is a Washington girl, and is very nice. Mr. Carpenter expects to take her to Bluemont with him this summer, and says he is going to give us the whole third floor of the house.

Last Saturday afternoon I clutched my little salary and sallied forth to buy clothes, but it took only a few sad and disillusioning moments to convince me that sixty dollars will buy very few clothes. I had dreamed of a dress, but their prices showed me that I should buy some cloth and make one, so I bought some blue and tan goods to make an accordion pleated skirt. I wanted a hat, too, and the only one I could find to suit me was a flaming cerise, one at Jellefs costing twenty dollars, so again I was reckless and bought it on a charge account.

I have been doing library work every Monday night for the past month at the Neighborhood House. Grace and I volunteer there every Monday until nine o'clock. I stamp the books and put them away on the shelves and help the children and grown people hunt for any books they want. Hundreds of children come, and they range from Yiddish to the sons and daughters of Ireland. Some little girl about eight years old will say, "My ma wants four love stories, and my pa wants a detective story," so I hunt around and give the youngster the four juiciest love stories I can find — the more hugs and kisses the better they like them — and then find an exciting story for pa, and the child goes away happy. Sweet young things of sixteen with rouged cheeks and hair combed with an eggbeater ask for "a real romantic story," and I pick out something that fairly drips with lovemaking and send them off satisfied.

Mrs. Carpenter surprised me the other day by sending for me to come upstairs and giving me a beautiful rose colored taffeta and georgette dinner dress. It is embroidered in rose and blue and silver, and has a handmade lace collar on it. It made Frances look sallow, so she didn't take it with her. Mrs. Carpenter said that even if I couldn't wear the dress that the collar would be worth using, and it is, as it is just like the ones they sell in stores for twelve-fifty. I could wear the dress all right, it fit as if it had been made for me. She hoped I wouldn't be offended. Offended? What she should have said was overjoyed. I have passed the point where I get offended when some nice lady offers me an equally nice dress. It is suitable for dinner and informal dress.

My new book hopes eventually to develop into a series of readers for school use on food, clothing, shelter — textbooks nicely disguised with fairy stories and baby talk — sort of a sugar coated pill for the children. I get the material and lasso some ideas, then put it into shape and the boss gives it the once-over and criticizes, and then I go to work again. The new typist is very clever and good-natured, and we get along splendidly. I am glad she has come, for it isn't so lonesome. I don't see her much as she is in Mr. Carpenter's office where he can give dictation, but when he is away she slips in and we gossip until we hear his footsteps.

The other Sunday a man Grace knows was coming to take her to a ball game, and he telephoned and said that a friend of his had dropped in on him, and would I go along to make a party of four. I obligingly said yes, waiting with curious interest to see the escort of the afternoon. You should have seen him. I should judge he was fifty years old. He had little hair — mostly a place where it used to be. He was inclined to be stoutish, yes, fat. His blue serge suit was fairly well cut and pressed, but he was inclined to a bright green and white striped shirt and light tan shoes. As the song says, however, "the worst is yet to come." Stuck into his tie was a huge tooth set into a pin. I suppose it was an Elk insignia or something of that kind, but nevertheless it made me feel creepy but I couldn't take my eyes off it. I would look back at something else and then feel my fascinated glance going back to that tooth. Draped across his waistcoat was a huge watch and as a charm he wore an enormous blue and white cross of some kind. He said it was a German war cross he had gotten when he was in the war. Judging by its size and brilliancy it must have been meant for von Hindenburg at the very least. Between its glitter and the ghastly tooth above it, I spent a rather uncomfortable afternoon. As far as the ball game was concerned, I enjoyed it. Washington and Philadelphia played, and Walter Johnson pitched for Washington. It was a real game and exciting. About 2,000 people were there to see it. Washington won five to four. [6]

Washington had a big time yesterday up in the air. The Arlington Amphitheatre was being dedicated. The first international airplane field meet was held and more exciting things are happening in the air than I have seen in years. The champion altitude flyer is here, and General Billy Mitchell himself of the Air Corps flew. One machine can make 210 miles an hour. There were races around the Capitol Dome, all kinds of stunts, and demonstrations of the wireless telephone from the air. All the government departments got off for the afternoon so I met Grace at one-thirty. We went to the United Cafeteria for lunch, then strolled about the streets a bit. This is one of the things, fortunately, for which one doesn't have to pay three dollars per seat — plus war tax.

Standing in for the sick President, Secretaries Baker and Daniels dedicated the Arlington Memorial amphitheater. The newspaper rapturously reported the upside-down flying and "reverse turns, loops, barrel rolls, tail spins and long falls" performed by the planes out of Bolling field. The war had increased America's fascination with heavier-than-air flight and the men piloting the wooden frame and fabric bi-wing airplanes were heroes, called sky-jazzers by the adoring public.

Martha and I went to Child's for something to eat. Nothing exciting seemed due to happen there, so we wearily wended our way homeward. Just as we turned the corner from Fifteenth to F Street by the Washington Hotel, up drove a big car with three Marine officers in the back seat. They called out something to us, and when I looked around I recognized one of them as Lieutenant St. George, whom we had heard being introduced at Child's about two weeks before. He was so attractive and good-looking that I couldn't help remembering him. The car stopped and out he popped, running up to us and taking hold of each of us by an arm. "Good evening, girls," he said, "What's the hurry?"

It was plain that he had just a wee nippie too much. Martha carried off the situation beautifully, though. "Good evening, Mr. St. George," she said calmly. "How are you tonight?" He became nearly sober at that. "My God," he exclaimed with a grin, "I'm discovered." We had to laugh at that, and then he called his two companions and introduced us all around inventing names for Martha and me with a surprising ingenuity. They all wanted to take us for a ride, but we refused and tried to walk on. St. George, however, kept us detained by a firm hold. The other two men left finally when they saw we meant what we said, calling out that they would see St. G at the Capitol Park Hotel. He remained and devilishly invited us to go somewhere and all get drunk. We murmured that he had reached that stage already, but he said he was good for a lot more. Then he invited us to go into the hotel and meet Raymond Hitchcock and Cecil DeMille, but we refused that also. He said he was getting out of the service July first and was going to fly in the movies for Mr. DeMille. He really thought that Martha had met him, and she told him that it was at a dance in Quantico. We finally bid him goodnight and continued on our way home.

Martha, Grace and I took a river excursion on the steamer line down the Potomac on Decoration Day. The weather was perfect, and we remained on deck until long after sunset and stayed until the moon came up. I doubt if there are many more interesting river trips anywhere in the country than down the Potomac from Washington. We steamed past the U.S. War College and the Potomac Barracks Camp that has now been vacated by the battalion of infantry; the buildings will be torn down and the site used for playgrounds and park space. We passed the Bolling Flying Field, the scene of the big aerial meet a few weeks ago, and then down the river past one historic point after another. The old town of Alexandria is just below Washington, but the view we had of it seemed very modern, with the huge shipbuilding yards along the riverfront. High up on the bluff on the other side is Fort Foote, and farther down the river are Fort Washington and Camp Humphreys. They looked much different than they did during the war — then they were crowded and busy, but now all we could see moving were a few indolent soldiers out for an evening stroll.

June

Martha left tonight. It was hard to see her go, as we have had such wonderful times together while she was with us, and I feel that we shall never all be together again.

One awful night. Grace had made plans to go out to dinner with a man from New York, so I went to dinner at the Ebbitt with Jessie and Frances. Afterwards, we left for Glen Echo. We first went into the Derby Racer, where two soldiers had attached themselves to our party, mostly to Jessie and Frances, and took us for another ride, then for some rides on the Gravity and the Whip. We then went up to the dancing pavilion and Frances danced with one of the soldiers, while Jessie and I stood and stood and stood. Just opposite us were the Marines, one of them tall and splendid looking. I just upped and smiled at the tall one and he responded nobly. He popped up in front of me, bowed, took off his hat, and said he couldn't resist that smile a moment longer, and would I dance? I would, and he was a dream on his feet.

After that dance he took me into the Derby for a couple of rides, and then through the old mill. The old mill was as dark as pitch, and I feared he would develop spooniness, but not so. He was as nice as they make 'em. We then went back to the dancing floor and danced until it closed, or nearly that late, and he took me home. When we reached the house I remembered that I had forgotten my key, and I thought that as long as I had to ring anyway, I might as well stay out there a while longer. I did, and therein things started.

This boy, whose name is Fred Wellman, was one of the nicest chaps I had met in ages. We sat on the porch and started to talk, and he told me all about himself. He is twenty-one and comes from South Dakota. It seems that his father is well off, at least they have two automobiles, and his brothers have gone to college, but he would not go to school and got into scrapes and finally had a fuss with his dad and left home and enlisted seven months ago. He is stationed on the *U.S.S. Minnesota*, and is with the fleet at Annapolis. He bemoaned the fact that the fleet was sailing Saturday morning, and he was on duty Friday and so could not see me anymore, but wanted to try to go A.W.O.L. and come the next night. I wouldn't hear of that so he said he would be back this way in September and would look me up then.

While I imagine he can be just about as devilish as the rest of them, he was as sweet as he could be, and I liked him immensely and was as sorry as he was that he had to leave Washington so soon. He really seemed to fall for me, and he didn't attempt to get objectionable. He complimented me on my black hair, said my smile was bewitching, admired my waist and clothes, kissed my hands, and rifled my handbag for a memento. He finally got off with my powder puff and a streetcar ticket. Perhaps it was all a blind for him to get some carfare. At any rate, he was either very finished in the art of saying pretty nothings, or else was merely ingenuous. He told me that I was a nice girl and that he liked me and was going to write to me.

Several times during our conversation I came to sufficiently to remind him that he had better leave, but he always said he would pretty soon, but to have a heart, this was his last day, or rather night. Finally he got up and said he didn't dare keep me out any longer, for my landlady would be sore at me. Just about that time a milk wagon rumbled past and I came to the awful realization that it must be at least three a.m. and I also realized then and there that I didn't have the nerve to ring the doorbell at that time in the morning. When this boy left he said something about would I have any trouble getting in and I said, "Oh, no indeed," whereupon he took a lingering departure. He asked me to kiss him good-bye and I said I didn't give kisses. He said, "Well, I do," and did, and left.

And there I stood, not knowing where in the devil I was going to spend the rest of the night. The only thing I could think of was to go down to the Union Station and sit up for the rest of the night, but another car wouldn't be along for nearly an hour, so I went down the stairs to the servant's entrance and sat down on the bottom step. I must have started to doze, for I suddenly came to when something furry rubbed against my leg. I gave one awful jump and then saw that it was the cat! I was so nervous I couldn't stay down there another minute, not even if I perched in a tree for the rest of the night, so started up the stairs. Again Fate was agin me. The milk wagon was stopping just in front of the house and a man got out with some bottles. I made a rapid and hasty retreat back under the porch and prayed that he would put the bottles on the steps and not down by the kitchen door. Whether it was in answer to my prayer, or just his regular custom I have no way of knowing, but praise be, he sat the bottles down on the steps and was off. I stood there and waited, getting nervouser and nervouser. I kept feeling that it was all a dream and that I would wake up soon, and between times I giggled to myself, to think of the awful humor of the situation.

Finally I heard a car coming and gave one wild dash across the park and hopped on. Two men looked at me curiously, but I maintained an air of dignity and reserve and thanked my lucky stars I didn't know them. I had to pull down the shade by my seat going past the Baltimore Station, as I knew Wellman would be sitting in there waiting for his early train to Annapolis and I couldn't risk his seeing me. I arrived at Union Station at four-twenty and went into the woman's waiting room. All the benches were taken by sleeping forms of all shapes, sizes and degrees of snoring, so I found a chair and sat and sat and sat. When it was about six-thirty I caught a car home and luckily found the door unlocked and nobody saw me come in. I was nearly dead the next day at work and came home that afternoon and slept fifteen hours.

They have closed the dining room here at Longfellow Inn, and Grace is moving to the government dormitories July first, while I suppose it will be another week after that before I go to the mountains. Mrs. Carpenter gets well slowly, and her best nurse has been called away. The new nurse declares she will not go to the country, and everything is in turmoil over there.

NOTES

[1] All War Community Centers required "a daylight zone between partners," although "head dancing," or cheek-to-cheek, was accepted in supper clubs. The shocking new style was illustrated in Life.

[2] After continuing disagreement on foreign policy, especially concerning the League of Nations, President Wilson requested Secretary of State Lansing's resignation.

[3] Treatments for a broken hip were either to put the patient in a cast, or under the stress of traction, or just bed rest. The patient was fortunate not to die within several months of blood clots caused by the immobility. It wasn't until the early 1930s that operations to set the break were attempted, and not until after World War II that orthopedics became a specialty.

[4] *The society section of the* Washington Post *reported the wedding with emphasis on the women's clothing, and included what Mrs. Carpenter wore as she stood in the receiving line. The story must have been written well in advance, as Mrs. C was upstairs in bed.*

[5] *My mother received no credit in the acknowledgments of* How the World Is Clothed, *which was published after Frank Carpenter died. Frances was listed as author, even though she was living in France when my mother wrote it. Jo was credited as associate editor for her work in the revisions of the twenty-volume edition of* Carpenter's World Travels *and* Carpenter's New Geographical Readers, Europe and South America. *Her boss inscribed the South America volume "To my dear friend Josephine Lehman with my best wishes I give this book which she has assisted materially in making."*

[6] *Only on Wednesdays could "ladies" go to the game without a male escort; women were not charged on that day, although they had to enter through a designated turnstile to pay the ten cents war tax. The one "ladies retiring room" was under the supervision of a maid. Box seats were $1.27 and bleacher seats 45 cents. The program, pasted in my mother's album, had a photo of Clarke Griffith, president of the Washington club, and future Hall-of-Famer Johnson, and explained the new electric scoreboard.*

8
SUMMER 1920
A Sad Summer at Bluemont

Jo and Ethel Ford walked through the woods to the rock outcropping at Bear's Den.

"Later Gertrude went out to the barn and got a rifle with nine shells in it, and came back in an altogether unfriendly mood to argue with Pauline on the sins of stealing her beau, emphasizing her argument with meaningful gestures of the gun."

By the end of June, my mother's typewritten diary had dwindled to one-line reminders; when she went to Bluemont in July, copies of long letters to friends and family replaced diary entries. Jo wrote her sister Marian that they came to Bluemont "in great style;" she shipped her trunk in advance and carried nothing but her traveling bag and umbrella. Mr. Carpenter told Jo, "All you have to do is pick up your foot in your little hand" and get to the train station. But Jo didn't walk because she'd saved eight cents for carfare. The family took Mrs. Carpenter to the station in an ambulance and moved her into a private car in the train.

July

About twelve of us were in the car, including three nurses, the doctor, Mr. and Mrs. Carpenter, three servants, and Miss Ford and I. Dr. Plaster sat with us most of the way up. The car left at ten o'clock, and at about noon Gertrude came out with a whopping big basket, and said, "All food hounds to the front," or words to that effect, and we dug in. I hadn't taken the time to eat any breakfast that morning, so told Miss Ford to give me a little poke if I seemed to lose control of myself, as I wanted to keep a few manners.

A private car is something of a great happening on the Bluemont railroad, for in every little town we passed, the people thought it was the regular train and came running to catch it. One man chased us half a block, yelling all the time at the engineer that he wanted to catch the car, and the engineer finally yelled back, "Aw, whatsa matter witcha? This here's a private car."

We got to Bluemont at twelve-thirty and the procession up the mountain would have made a street parade for Ionia. First came Mrs. Carpenter in her bed on a truck with one of the nurses, then a car with the other nurses and Miss Ford and I, then Dr. Plaster and Dr. Hall with Mr. Carpenter, then a car with the servants, then a truck with the baggage, and lastly another truck from Washington with the things they brought up from the town house.

We are settled in now at the library, and everyone who views our quarters tells us we have the best rooms on the place. The library has two stories and a basement like a barn, as it is built into the side of the mountain. The basement floor, looking off across the west slope of the mountains, is my office where I work on my clothing book, but for now I have been helping Mr. Carpenter, whose private library takes up the whole first floor.

Miss Ford and I have the two upstairs rooms and they surely are the prettiest little rooms I have ever seen. I have a small window opening to the east and overlooking the Loudoun valley, a large window with French doors facing the house, and another large window facing the south and the mountains, with just a bit of the Shenandoah Valley, if I stretch my ostrich-like neck. Miss Ford's room is on the west side of the library. The bathroom is all white with white tiled floor, and it is just for Miss Ford and me.

There is just one little drawback — There is no hot water here, and we had visions of carrying a washtub down from the main house whenever we wanted to get a hot bath, or else dressing in a bathrobe and dodging through the trees to the house and taking a bath, and then dodging back again. However, we have discovered what a good cold bath really is, and like it. It's mighty chilly to leap into a tub of icy cold mountain water the first thing in the morning. We have to make some kind of noise, though, so when I hear Miss Ford singing to beat the band I know she is getting up enough courage to get into the tub. I tried the same stunt and it works fine. If the water isn't too cold I can get along with humming "Sweet and Low" or something like that, with "Everybody Shimmy Now" for a little colder water, but when sounds of grand opera start to come forth from the bathroom, you know that water is pretty darn cold.

Dear Grace: Things up at the house are not going smoothly. Mrs. Carpenter is in the library, the piano has been moved into the living room, all the trunks are not yet un-packed and Arthur ran a nail through his hand. One of the nurses has gone now and just two are left. Mrs. Carpenter was so tired out by the trip she hasn't been able to sit up since, so I go talk to her and jolly her a bit. I surely do feel sorry for her. She doesn't like the new nurses she has, and neither do I, to be perfectly frank. One of them has just graduated and does nothing else but tee-hee and say, "Oh, my gosh." The other is short and fat and given to telling rather appetite-losing stories at the table. I always thought I was a good eater, but when I watch her I feel like a canary. The food is just as good as it was last summer.

Miss Ford and I are developing into quite some athletes. The second day we were here we unpacked seven trunks, which held Mr. Carpenter's books and papers he had brought up for work. We wanted to get the library all cleaned up that morning and settled, but none of the men had time to carry away the trunks, so we picked them up and carried them to the basement ourselves — I have three black and blue marks on my knee to prove it. If we have all the muscle by fall we think we are going to have, we shall have to get a job as baggage smashers or trunk hefters to use up our pep. We have two pairs of boxing gloves, and we are going to have a try at spoiling each other's beauty, and we are going to mark the tennis court as soon as the weather clears off. In addition, there is a big contraption downstairs known as an "All Round Exerciser." It has a pair of rowing things to develop the arm muscles, another thing to expand one's chest, and another to develop the legs. Needless to say, I don't even go near the last one for fear just the sight of it might increase the size of my lower extremities.

Dear Grace: How the World is Clothed goes well. I am having a heavenly time, and the weather is so deliciously cool that I am full of pep, yet I can't get rid of that wish-Gracie-were-here feeling. Miss Ford is a splendid pal, but you know how it is — please write soon, Gracie. My friendship will stand a lot, but it must have letters — nice fat ones telling me all about how you went to the Washington last night and that you are going to the Powhatan Roof tomorrow, and where you are going on that auto tour Sunday, and how many men you have refused since I last saw you.

Dr. Plaster and Dr. Hall were here for dinner, so I dressed all pretty-like in my satin skirt and georgette smock, and then I spilled coffee on my blouse at dinner, dripped candy on it and was beaten at pool three times. I just beat Miss Ford two games, however, which cheers me up a bit. Dinner was in great style today, five courses, ended with demitasse. Oh, I sit at the head of the Carpenter table in Mrs. Carpenter's place. Daddy C said he "guessed he would like to look at me across from him."

Miss Ford and I went for a long walk Friday afternoon through the woods, trying to find the ledge of rock overlooking the valley. We went through almost two miles of underbrush, looking for a snake at every step, and not enjoying the scenery at all. We finally found the rocks. A long ledge stretches for some distance around the side of the mountain, with a sheer drop of about seventy-five feet into the valley. Some people say it is the setting used by John Fox for his "Trail of the Lonesome Pine." Coming back we got an acute attack of the chiggers, and had to rub ourselves with salt that night.

I am getting to the point now where I take two cold baths a day instead of one, and like it more and more. Miss Ford and I put on the boxing gloves Friday night, and at present we are artistic studies in black and blue and purple with shadings of pale lavender about the edges of our bruises. Great fun, but rather rough. I keep busy up here all the time, even to eleven-thirty at night, what with boxing, walking, knitting, sewing, writing letters, working, and talking with Mrs. Carpenter.

Dear Smittie: Ethel Ford and I were strolling around the grounds one night when we came upon a little two-wheeled pushcart like the kind banana peddlers use. We thought it would be good fun to wheel each other about in it — being skittish, you know, to make believe we were still young and kittenish.

We took turns pushing each other to the top of the hill, and when we turned around I offered to push Ethel down the slope of the mountain back to the barn. It started out beautifully, but the cart started to gain speed on its own account — so much so that I had hard work keeping up with it, and when I stepped on a loose stone my ankle did a hairpin curve and doubled up on itself, and for a while everything was so mixed up that I didn't know which was Ethel, which was myself, and which was the cart.

When we found ourselves at last, the cart was still intact, Ethel's only damage was to her dress and her feelings, but my ankle was so touchy that she put me in the cart and wheeled me to the house. One of the nurses said to soak it in hot water in something that was big enough to get my whole foot in it, so I had Arthur get a wash-boiler as an article of suitable size, and just soaked and soaked. Ethel rubbed me with liniment and we kept the whole thing on the quiet, so as not to worry Mrs. Carpenter, who has been very sick.

The next morning, however, my pedal extremity had turned a lovely shade of bluish black, and humped itself up into a queer shape, so I had the doctor look at it, and he muttered something about torn ligaments and strained tendons, and strapped it up so tightly that I know just how a high-born Chinese lady feels. As Mrs. Carpenter had broken her hip, we had crutches right in the family, and for the next few days I went thumping around.

On Saturday my foot felt entirely well, and I felt so joyful that I took the bandages off, and nearly died that night. So the next day the doctor tied me all up again and added insult to injury by saying something about the patience doctors have to have to put up with such pigheaded people.

The other day a bunch of us went on a long motor trip to Winchester. We went through the gap in the mountains, and slowly downward until we passed over the Shenandoah River, three miles below us. From there we were on the Virginia Pike, and we fairly whizzed along the valley, stopping only to pay toll, which is still done in Virginia. We passed splendid big estates built before the Civil War. Some of the hardest fighting of that war took place in that valley. I saw both a Confederate and a Federal cemetery.

The residential part of Winchester reminds me of the old-fashioned stories of the South — wide shady streets with beautiful old houses — everything quiet and dignified, and lacking the busy spirit of the West and North. There was a difference in the stores, too. The clerks act more as though you were paying a social call, and if it is too much trouble to make change they tell you to pay as near as you can and never mind the rest. We did a lot of shopping, and brought back candy and souvenirs for the servants and Mrs. Carpenter. She has been so sick that Frances is coming home from Paris for a visit. Indications point to a "little Huntington" on the way.

Dear Marian: I don't know when I shall get home. I mentioned vacation last week to the boss, but he didn't take to it kindly. He is so everlastingly busy trying to get his books to the publishers on time and worrying about Mrs. Carpenter, that he hates to let me go, but I shall get there sooner or later. The wind is whistling in the trees, the owls are hooting, the dogs are barking down the mountainside, and I'm feeling lonesome.

On August 8th, Mrs. Carpenter died as a result of complications from the broken hip. My mother told me how fond she was of Mrs. C, how she made her feel "like family" and what a loss it was when she died. In a 1925 three-part article about her father, Frances wrote: "I cannot write about the life and work of my father without speaking of my mother. From the day they were married her chief thought was of him and how she could help him. She had a keen mind and my father considered her his most valuable critic. During her lifetime no article was ever published over his signature which had not passed her censorship."

Dear Gracie: Mrs. Carpenter died Sunday morning about seven-thirty and I have been left in charge of things. Frances was here only a few days before her mother died. Their son came from Chicago the night before.

The two nurses left Sunday night, and Mr. Carpenter and his children left early Monday morning with the body, taking it for burial in Ohio, where Mrs. Carpenter lived when she was a girl. They won't get back until Thursday night or Friday morning, so Miss Ford and I are left here with the servants. We feel lost in this big house all by ourselves.

I just can't make it seem possible. Mrs. Carpenter had always been so bright and cheerful, and always doing something for someone else; it is hard to realize she is gone. The whole mountainside feels that it has lost a friend, and the servants especially. Monday after they had gone we all turned out to get the house straightened and remove all trace of Mrs. Carpenter's sickness. The men carted up the wheelchair and fixed the room as it was last summer. We finally got the house in order.

I am looking after Mr. Carpenter's affairs, so I have had hardly a moment to turn around. Frances is going to stay here until the middle of September, but she has to leave then and go back to her home in Paris, or the stork will beat her to it, and I don't know what Mr. Carpenter is going to do after that. I shouldn't be surprised if he would go to Paris to live with her, and I may be walking around Washington soon with a big sign on my back, "Wanted, a Job."

Dear Smittie: I went down to Washington on a hurry trip to go to the bank and get some of Mrs. Carpenter's private papers out of the safe deposit vault. Ever since I came back things have been in a fuss.

It all started when the bathtub stopper was shut and I forgot to turn off the water tightly, so that when morning came the bathroom was flooded, and the water had run down into the library and that floor was flooded. It had not dripped on any of the desks, but the pool table was soaked, and I was terrified for fear it was ruined. When I saw the looks of that library I was ready to leave the country. However, I ran back upstairs to where Ethel was mopping up the bathroom floor. She had taken off the trousers of her pajamas, and was trotting around with only the top part on and not even a piece of tulle below. I told her about the condition downstairs and we made a beeline armed with bath towels. We worked so rapidly, sweeping out water and soaking it up into towels for over a half hour, that we didn't have time to be modest, but heaven help us if someone had come down to the library. There simply would have been no place to hide without making a sprint across the whole length of that room. We finally got the water out and the puddles wiped up, and I buried the pool table in blotting paper, and then we devoted the rest of our efforts to praying that it would dry before Mr. Carpenter came back.

Gertrude came hotfooting it down to the library. She was full of some tale about going upstairs and finding the butler and the maid having (please don't laugh) "a date on Miss Frances' bed. I tole 'em Ah'd tell you all, and now I has," she said, and then went back to the house.

Ethel and I hardly digested that fact when down came Pauline and Arthur, mad as hatters, demanding to know what Gertrude had told us. We hesitated at telling them, as I was under the impression that so-called "dates on beds" were not mentioned in mixed company. We tried to be tactful and at the same time stifle our wild desire to howl, while Pauline and Arthur assured us that they had merely been in the attic putting away Mrs. Carpenter's bed, and that Gertrude had been so madly jealous that she made up the story. She had already told Pauline that she "was going to run her off this mountain if she had to kick her off," and I guess she started as soon as the family went. We finally told Arthur and Pauline to forget the whole matter and not to have anything to do with Gertrude until Mrs. Huntington came back.

Evidently Gertrude wanted more action, however, for when Pauline got back to the house she slammed into her with both fists and almost beat the poor girl up. She would have if Arthur hadn't interfered. When we got there we found Pauline barricaded in her room packing her trunk to go. We went up to talk to her, but we really couldn't see any reason for keeping her, for we didn't know what Gertrude would do if she got any madder. Pauline was crying all the time, and Gertrude was downstairs in the kitchen raving at Arthur like a madwoman. The language she used fairly turned the atmosphere purple. I was afraid to go into the kitchen, as she doesn't care where a frying pan hits you when she is in that mood, and she doesn't care who she hits.

Later Gertrude went out to the barn and got a rifle with nine shells in it, and came back in an altogether unfriendly mood to argue with Pauline on the sins of stealing her beau, emphasizing her argument with meaningful gestures of the gun. One cannot blame

Pauline for taking to her heels, and just about that time Ethel and I arrived on the scene. We were brave, at least Ethel was, and took the gun off the table where Gertrude had put it, while I tried to tell both of them to stop, without much success. They were all talking at the same time, and of all the picturesque language I have ever heard, Gertrude's was the worst. We thought we had finally calmed them down, and took the gun across a quarter mile of plowed field to have the hired man take out the shells.

Pauline phoned for a taxi to take her to the station, and they told her that the last car had gone down. When she heard that, she almost howled, and cried so that we were at our wits ends. She was afraid to stay all night in that house with Gertrude, so we told her she could sleep down in the library with us, as there is a big lounge downstairs. That rather calmed her, and she got our supper while Gertrude raved.

We woke her at five this morning to get the early train. We didn't know whether to expect any breakfast or not, but luckily Gertrude made the usual excellent breakfast, and we thought that she was over her fit. Not so. Her jealousy had been merely simmering. With Pauline out of the house, Gertrude was afraid to sleep up there by herself, so forced herself into Arthur's little house and sat in a rocking chair the whole night. This morning after breakfast she started raving at Arthur again, but he wouldn't speak to her. After dinner she packed her trunk, too, and said she was going to Washington until Miss Frances got back. Arthur asked her how Miss Lehman and Miss Ford were going to get their meals and she retorted that she "didn't give a damn how anybody got their meals — she was going." And go she did, so now Ethel and Arthur and I are holding the fort. Arthur got our supper for us tonight, and an excellent one it was, too.

I shall be so thankful when Mr. C and Frances get back that I shall fall on their necks. How they will take the news that their cook and maid are gone is more than I can imagine, although I think Gertrude will come back. All this happening on top of Mrs. Carpenter's death is enough to set a person wild.

Dr. Plaster came around Wednesday evening and played pool with Ethel and me. He stayed for supper and taught us how to play poker, and then took us for a ride with him while he visited several patients. Ethel drove the car, and we all sat on the front seat.

Friday afternoon our kitchen angel of the fiery temper came back in order to be here to get dinner for Mr. C and his daughter. She waylaid them in Washington to tell her side of the story, very highly embellished by virtue of her fertile imagination, and to spread the story among her circle about Pauline and Arthur. Therefore, Ethel and I had to tell our side of the affair to Mr. C and Frances, which we did fully, omitting only the details about the "date on the bed," having some consideration for Mr. Carpenter's years.

The next morning Pauline came back after her trunk, and Frances talked her most tactful to all of them, with the result that they would all stay until we go back to the city, at least. A further inducement was the fact that they are each to get a certain sum from Mrs. Carpenter. Hence, peace reigneth, but Gertrude takes her meals by herself and there is not much conversation going on in the rear portions of the house.

Everywhere we feel the absence of Mrs. Carpenter. Mr. Carpenter and Frances don't waste any time in weeping and wailing, but make everything as cheerful as possible, which is the only sensible thing to do. We play pool, bridge and poker.

September

Dear Grace: Ethel and I took a walk on Sunday, but when we had gone down this mountain and half way up the other we lost all our fresh enthusiasm for the plan. It's not so much fun climbing steep mountains on a sunny day as it is to read about it. However, along came a big car driven by a boy who often takes us to the station, and he gave us a ride up to the top, telling us that if we weren't too long we could ride back with him too. So we paid our fifteen cents admission and strolled down to the rocks that overhang the valley. It is a beautiful spot, and we skipped about from rock to rock, enjoying the scenery, and then started back thinking about the ride we were going to have.

Just then we saw a sign saying, "Spring, 440 yards down the mountain," and decided to have a drink, that distance not sounding especially far. We walked down and down, until I thought sure we would reach the Shenandoah River soon, and we thought we had lost our way, as there was no spring, nothing but a narrow path through the woods, and it was so steep that if we had slipped we wouldn't have stopped until we had hit Berryville in the valley. We finally found the spring, but it seemed more like 440 rods than yards, and when we started the climb back up we were willing to take an oath that miles would have best expressed it.

We were so tired before we had got half way back up that we wanted to leave this earth, and there was no place to sit down. If any hungry rattler had poked his head at me I wouldn't have had the energy to even say, "Come on, old boy, you're welcome to what is left of me." We finally made the top and saw with joy that our car was still there, and the boy ready to give us a ride back. We had only gone a little way when along came Dr. Plaster in his car looking for us, so he took us home, where we finished the afternoon in a good Christian-like manner — playing pool.

Dear Marian: Dr. Plaster came over yesterday and took Miss Ford and me for another long ride. We drove down out of the mountains into the Shenandoah Valley and about twenty miles or so south through some Virginia villages, Dr. Plaster pointing out the scenes of interest. That locality is where General McClellan's Union army laid everything flat during the Civil War, and the people around there are still loyal to the old South. It surprises me to learn of the feeling still existing against the North. We passed the little cabin where the old darky who was General Lee's personal servant during the war still lives. Dr. Plaster then took us up to his home where we met his mother, a delightful lady of nearly eighty years, and then home. He stayed for supper and blarneyed us into playing poker afterward. I'm glad he did, for I celebrated the evening by winning ninety-six cents.

Dr. Plaster came again last night and played pool and stayed to supper. We played fan-tan afterward at one-third of a cent a chip, and I won considerable. Poker has been our main diversion of late, and poor Ethel has lost sixty-five cents at it. Our doctor has been coming up quite frequently, all spruced up, but he is old enough to be a father to either of us, and probably thinks Ethel with her bobbed hair and smaller stature is more "childlike" than I am. Just the same, if that man were only six inches taller, age or no age, I should find him frightfully attractive, even though he is homely.

Frances sails from New York Tuesday and Mr. C will be back to Washington Wednesday, so I want to get the offices settled Monday and Tuesday, if possible, so we can start in on business when he is back. I have been working almost every Sunday and holiday in the service of the company. I hate like the Devil to leave. I have such affection for this place, and I hope I can come up again next summer.

The next year, my mother returned to Bluemont for only a few days. In 1922, Carpenter advertised the property with 437 acres in the *Washington Post* for rent or sale as a "Gentleman's Country Home." In 1940, Frances and her brother Jack sold the estate. Joannasberg has been saved within the Bear's Den Rural Historic District, an honorary historic district that encompasses about 1,855 acres, listed in the Virginia Landmarks Register.

A narrow, blacktop road has replaced the path that my mother walked to Bears Den, where the Washington physician, Dr. Huron Lawson, startled her. In 1933, his "shack" became a large, stone, turreted summer home and since 1983 is a lodge for hikers on the Appalachian Trail. When I visited Bluemont, I climbed out onto the rock ledge where my mother overlooked the valley and came home with chiggers; the view was not altered.

My mother was very fond of Dr. Henry Garnett Plaster, but we hear no more about him. Dr. Plaster's son, Henry G. Plaster, Jr., invited me to the family farm, where he spends part of each year, and where the doctor took Ethel Ford and Jo. Over cocktails, and with good humor, Henry told me that his father was not "homely," had married in 1925, when he was forty-one, and practiced medicine in Washington. Dr. Plaster died in 1949. Henry drove me around town, and we explored the now vacant general store, where the annoying boys who oogled my mother hung out on the steps. The Bluemont residents got into the spirit of my exploration, and enhanced my appreciation of my mother's life there.

9
1920 TO 1926
Hard Work Pays Off

Jo on her 24th birthday, March 16, 1922.

"I have now finished and sent off the book on which I was working and am taking things rather easy until I start the next one. Only two more and the set will be finished. The next one I tackle will be Central America and the West Indies, and the last about England, Ireland, Scotland and Wales. After that I go to the poorhouse, I suppose."

Jo hated to leave Bluemont, she said, but society would have frowned if Mr. Carpenter and his two young office assistants remained in the house without Mrs. Carpenter as a chaperon. By mid-September she was back in Washington. Smittie eloped with a man she met at Neighborhood House and Grace, who worked in the

Department of Commerce, moved to the government dormitories. Jo was forced to move to a single room, and she is not happy with it. She wrote to Smittie: "My room is next door to the bathroom, but it has the kind of wallpaper that is calculated to drive one insane. I am sure that the person who selected it is the same one who chooses Queen Mary of England's hats. It has a dresser that is too high when I sit before it, but when I stand the mirror is too low, and I have to assume the semi-crouching attitude with bended knees that I affect when I go out with a short man and try not to appear so giraffic beside him."

Mr. Carpenter was remodeling his home and by the end of the month they were still not settled. Work was difficult. Jo recorded, "A regiment of plasterers, paperhangers, painters, varnishers, electricians, plumbers, decorators, and carpenters are fixing over the place, and in between poundings and paint smells Mr. Carpenter tries to get inspirations and I try to catch them, but so far with no appreciable success."

October

Dear Parents: I am sitting in my chilly room trying to compose a letter, but my fingers are like sticks. We are still not settled at the office and I suppose it will be nearly Christmas before we are. Tomorrow I have to run all over the city — Mrs. Carpenter was paying the premiums on three insurance policies for her old cook, and since Mrs. C has died we cannot find the policies. Therefore I have to locate the cook and find out what she knows about them, and if she does not have them I have to visit each insurance office and have them make out a new policy.

The matter of rooms is still discouraging. The government hotels raised the rent five dollars a week and every landlady in the city immediately tacked five dollars to her price. The room I have is not all that pretty, and I have to speak gently to the furniture lest it fall apart, yet for room and board I am now paying seventy dollars a month. That sounds like an awful lot, yet it is almost impossible to get it for less unless I go farther out of the business center, and that means carfare and spending half one's time riding back and forth. It is an awful problem, but everyone has to meet it.

Prices are higher than during the War. I thought of buying a new coat for winter, but the girl in the room next to me bought one and had to pay $210,[1] so I have decided to wear my fall coat a while yet. I was going to send home my winter coat, but it's the only thing I have to keep me warm at night. Boarding houses never give us enough bed clothing.

I never see Daddy Carp much anymore as I work in a different office in the morning, and he isn't here in the afternoon. I'm broke, and if I don't get another raise soon I shall never get home. Don't know where my money goes, but it does, so the other night when I started to do a little arithmetic I found that if I bought Christmas presents I wouldn't have any money left to buy a heavy suit, and if I didn't have a heavy suit I couldn't go home to Michigan weather, and if I did buy a suit I wouldn't have any money left to go home. By the time I spend seventy dollars a month on board and room, ten for my Spanish lessons, fifteen for lunches, four for typewriter rent, two for magazines and newspapers, three for laundry, to say nothing of clothes, I don't have very many pennies left. As for putting money in the bank, I have almost forgotten where my bank book is, I use it so seldom. Perhaps the boss will be moved by the Christmas spirit and peel off a hundred from his fat roll, and say, "Here, my trusty secretary, take this spondulix and take a trip home to see your family."

To add to my hard luck, the landlady is giving up this house November first, which is something like five days notice. I don't know where I shall go but if I buy a cot and camp in the park it will surely save room rent, so maybe her moving is a financial blessing in disguise. I am trying to get into a girls' boarding house near here where the charge is only forty dollars a month, but it is hard to get in.

Dear Martha: I have been living such a quiet life since coming back from Bluemont that I hardly know myself. Somebody still thinks of me though, in one day I got three letters from three men in different parts of the United States. Walter Damme in Montana says he will come to Washington or Michigan, whichever I say, if I will go back with him. I suppose he wants to get all mixed up with a preacher and a wedding license and that sort of thing. I haven't answered him yet, but when I do I shall tell him that traveling is very expensive and he had best save his money and stay in Montana. Chester Williams is in New York and this poor afflicted man says he has been unable to forget me since leaving Washington last spring, and that if I promise to care for him he will come back to Washington. The third letter was from Bryan Kane in Pennsylvania — but I'm not going to write what he said. To think that three such letters came all in one day struck me as so funny that I didn't need to go to vaudeville for a week. I think I'll shake three slips in a hat and draw one and act accordingly. The trouble is that there is something the matter with all of them — one stutters, one is smaller than I am, and one is poor.

Ethel Ford and I have been having some hilarious times. She lives in Washington, and I often stay all night at her apartment. The other night we started out to have a regular old time. The other girl, Cherry, is the recreational supervisor at the telephone girls' apartment house. Those girls are howling millionaires compared to me. In the short time we were there waiting for Cherry, I saw more gorgeous dresses floating down the stairs and out the door into the tonneaus of Pierce Arrows and Rolls Royces than I ever thought possible. They have a beautiful place to live, with charming reception rooms and parlors, and a big ballroom where they have dances. I am thinking seriously of becoming a telephone girl.[2]

Last week I went to see Pavlova, the Russian dancer.[3] She had a company of about twenty-five with her, all of whom were wonderful dancers. A dozen of them performed an old-fashioned Polish dance, and it was the funniest thing I have seen for a long time.

November 1920

Dear Marian: I have moved again — not to a different house but only to a different floor of the same house, and am more satisfied than I have been for months and months of boarding house life. I am rooming with Margaret Black,[4] whom I have known since

100

I first came to Washington. She lived at 1415 Mass. Avenue for the two years that I was there, comes from Philadelphia, works in the Navy Department, and is small and pretty. She left Mrs. Dudley's and went to the dormitories, but did not like it. We have a large room together; the new landlady in the house has given us an entirely new outfit of furniture.

My boss snorts every time I talk vacation. He is the workingest man I ever saw. There is no more getting a day off every week or so, as I did when I was in the government. On January first he will finish his present contract with his publishers, and then I think he will slow up and possibly he will not keep Miss Ford any longer. Just at present I am editing some of his newspaper articles and putting them into book form while he and Miss Ford are working on his geographical reader on North America, which has to be sent in before Christmas.

Carpenter once wrote: "Hard work is a disease, I think. It is something like the love of drink or the slavery of tobacco or opium. It becomes ingrained in a man ... It is a labor wholly unconnected with financial circumstances. I have seen newspaper men stricken with this disease. They are diggers and delvers with never a letup until they actually drop dead from exhaustion."

Dear Smittie: I went down to the Ordnance Department several weeks ago. My old division had moved to B Building, so thither I wended my wistful steps and was accosted by a sign saying "Aircraft Department." I went in anyway and asked everyone I met where Ordnance was, and was invariably met by a blank stare. I kept looking and finally, way up on the third floor of the sixth wing, I found the handful of people who were once our proud and illustrious family. Of all the workers who were in those four buildings over two years ago, only a half of one floor of one wing remains. D Building houses the Census Bureau, E building part of the A.G.O., A Building has Military Intelligence and some of the War Risk, and C Building has Quartermaster and Construction.

Only half a dozen people whom I had known are left. Ada Howell, that pretty girl who used to work for Colonel Burns, left a year ago to join "The Passing Show."[5] She is now playing either Youth or Beauty in the play "Experience."

I had a forlorn feeling as I left. All those people with whom I lived and worked so intensely are scattered all over the country now, and soon the Production Division will be history and nothing else. Martha and I would sit side by side rattling out those damned old shipping orders that we hated so, and whenever Larkin was out of the room we tried to work on some personal letter writing. Then an officer would come over from the other side of the room to give dictation and we would pretend that we were loaded up with enough work to keep us clicking the ivories until the Call of Judgment. Later we would wander down the hall and enamel our faces a bit and stop to jolly Lieutenant Maher on the way. Then Mr. Jennings would come along and tease us a bit, and we would no sooner get back to our desks but in would come a spiffy shavetail and all the weary stenogs would take on new life and arrange themselves in assorted positions of more or less flirtatious grace. Then recess, and out we would throng to the old Center Market and five minutes later everyone would be eating something, no matter whether it was a cinnamon bun or a sour pickle.

I feel sad when I think of it. I worked my head off those few months before the Armistice, but I did enjoy the comradeship and good nature among the Loading Section. I often wish the old times back. Was that the life? Oh, man, you said it!

For another five years, Josephine stayed in Washington, working at a frenzied pace with longer and longer hours as Frank Carpenter pushed hard to meet his publisher's deadline for the revised *World Travels* series. World War I had so altered the world's political divisions that he was determined to update twenty volumes before he died. Jo wrote her parents in April 1921 that her weight had dropped to 132 from her usual 150 and that the doctor said she had "nervous dyspepsia combined with a general overworked condition." Carpenter sent her to Bluemont for a week's rest, and when she returned they started a health regime: "I drink a quart of milk a day to pad my bones. Every morning at 11 o'clock the boss has the butler bring in a pint of milk each for him and me and we have a little party."

Carpenter spent most of his life trying to gain weight, but the diminutive man could never get above 125 pounds. Jo had the opposite problem, keeping it off. Although in early photos she is quite slim, my memories are of a tall, not fat, but sturdy mother wearing size fourteen dresses. The financial pressure let up somewhat that summer when Carpenter went to Europe and left Jo in charge. She wrote her youngest sister, Lillian: "When he left, Mr. C. deposited a thousand dollars to my name for incidental expenses, to keep the business running through the summer. What a lot of money!"

A year later Carpenter had his tonsils removed and again Jo reported "keeping the store." He was recuperating in his apartment at the Cosmos Club, where he moved after his wife died. Both secretaries quit and Jo had to find replacements. Her sister Marian wanted to come to Washington and Jo wrote her: "If you are very good you could get a job here for about twenty-five dollars a week, or maybe thirty. All that I want is someone who is bright enough to do as they are told, and that is hard to find. My life was made miserable for two weeks interviewing girls for the position, and for the past week it has been almost as miserable correcting their mistakes. Then, too, Washington in general has changed its working hours from nine to four-thirty, to eight to three-thirty. At least, that is what it was supposed to mean. What it really meant, though, for me, was working from eight until six. Along with the others in the office, I rebelled, and we have gone back to the old starting time, although the quitting time still stays somewhere around six. Mr. Carpenter has always been very fine to me, however, even if he does work me like thunder. I spent several days at Bluemont resting up. Margaret Black went with me and we had the run of the place. I did nothing but eat and sleep and bake myself in the sunshine with the result that I came away feeling much better."

In June 1922, Jo went to New York to see her boss off on the *Majestic*. Carpenter had told her she couldn't go, as convention required that he take a male secretary. However, "as a present for working so hard," he booked her a room at the Waldorf Astoria and paid all expenses. Carp was off with cameras, trunks full of material and his typewriter to discover the new world after the war. He returned the next summer for a few months to supervise and work with what was now a staff of editors at his Washington office. In late 1923 he was in Eastern Europe, where he couldn't shake a dose of dysentery. When he arrived in Paris to recover with his daughter he was almost a skeleton, weighing just over 100 pounds. After six weeks' rest he recovered and planned a trip to Asia.

By 1923, in addition to editing *Carpenter's World Travels*, Jo was cranking out promotional material and newsletters. Journalist Dudley Harmon was hired as editor and office manager; Marian came east and joined the staff as a stenographer, and the sisters moved into an apartment on Dupont Circle. If Jo felt slighted that, as the employee with the most seniority, she had not been put in charge, there is no indication of it in any of her correspondence. Although throughout my life she always told me to assume that I could have any job a man could, I think she thought it was in the natural order of things that a man got the top job. Carpenter acknowledged her as an associate editor.

Carpenter offered Jo $500 if she would "get up the material" for a new book while he was in China during the summer of 1924. He reported from Shanghai that he was "active and full of joy," but in Nanking he was stricken with a kidney infection. His indomitable spirit could not pull him through this illness and on June 24, after a three-week struggle, he died. My mother told me that he'd always wanted to die "in harness," and she stayed on with Harmon to finish the revisions. Her well-thumbed set of *World Travels*, is still in my library. These books have hundreds of photographs in each volume and are a priceless record of life around the world 100 years ago. The original photographs are in the Library of Congress.

Two years later, the story was the same; Jo wrote home: "Since Christmas I've hardly taken time to rest. I never seem to have a moment to myself, but I have now finished and sent off the book on which I was working and am taking things rather easy until I start the next one. Only two more and the set will be finished. The next one I tackle will be Central America and the West Indies, and the last about England, Ireland, Scotland and Wales. After that I go to the poorhouse, I suppose."

NOTES

¹ *I thought at first that $210 for a coat might have been a typo, but newspaper ads corroborated the inflated price. My mother would have paid a month's salary for a good winter coat.*

² *A telephone operator was a new job opportunity for young women.*

³ *Anna Pavlova was the most well-known Russian ballerina of the first two decades of the 20th century. She was famous for creating the role of "The Dying Swan" and the first ballerina to tour around the world with her own dance company. She died of pneumonia in 1931, before she was fifty.*

⁴ *When Jo left Washington she lost track of Margaret Black, but in 1956, her daughter Annette and husband Matt Rue bought a summer home four doors down the street from our house in Harvey Cedars, and through a chance conversation on the street — my mother was taking out the trash — she spoke to Annette's daughter Margaret and made the connection. When Annette called her mother to tell her Josephine Lehman was living nearby, Margaret burst into tears of joy. The roommates got together once before my mother died. Annette still summers in that house and our children grew up together. Even my grandchildren got to know Annette's grandchildren.*

⁵ *"The Passing Show" was a Broadway musical revue by the Shubert brothers. In 1928, Ada and Jo would meet by chance in London, where Ada was living with a very rich husband, and the two old friends would share some good times.*

10
1926 TO 1929
In London and Germany

Jo at Lowell Thomas's Pawling home, where she lived from 1927-30.

"There was a tiny windshield up in front of us, but I had only to lean my head over to one side to almost have it torn from my shoulders. It seemed to be getting foggier and foggier, especially after we left the Channel, but the pilot seemed not to be worried."

By the end of 1926 Josephine had completed the revisions to *Carpenter's World Travels,* but she was not on the way to the poorhouse. Dudley Harmon arranged an interview for her with Lowell Thomas, who had landed a contract to write six books. In his 1975 autobiography, Thomas wrote, "None had been researched or even outlined... I figured I needed help." Help came in the form of Prosper Buranelli,[1] a feature writer who left the *New York World* to head up what Thomas called his book mill, and Josephine, who in 1927 was hired as a researcher and ghost writer.

Jo was even more excited about this job than she had been when she left Ionia for Washington nine years earlier; it would give her what she'd been yearning for most, foreign travel. When not in Europe, she would live and work at Clover Brook Farm, Thomas' new home in Pawling, New York, seventy-five miles north of Manhattan. Jo would no longer think of herself as just a "poor working girl"; she was now being paid well enough to send money to her family when they needed it. (Using the Consumer Price Index, the $1,200 for salary and expenses that she deposited when she returned from the second trip to Europe in the summer of 1929 is the equivalent of a little over $15,000 in 2011 dollars, and that for a trip of eight weeks.)

During the next six years Jo worked on seven of Thomas' books: *The Sea Devil's Fo'c'sle; Woodfill of the Regulars; Raiders of the Deep; Old Gimlet Eye: Adventures of Smedley D. Butler; Sir Hubert Wilkins: His World of Adventure; Born to Raise Hell: The Life Story of Tex O'Reilly; Soldier of Fortune* and *This Side of Hell: Dan Edwards, Adventurer.* Unlike Frank Carpenter, Lowell Thomas did not acknowledge his researchers or ghost writers, although Jo's involvement can be found in his inscriptions. The English journal *Yorkshire Post* credited Thomas' biography, *Woodfill of the Regulars*, "the finest thing yet written on the war." Thomas' inscription to his ghostwriter repeats this sentiment, and continues, "If so, then you ought to be acclaimed the greatest authoress of the age." Woodfill, a professional soldier whom General Pershing called America's most outstanding soldier, was invited to stay at Clover Brook Farm for as long as it took to get the material needed for the book.

Jo's first assignment in Europe was to track down English and German submarine commanders and interview them. The stories resulting from this seven-month stint became one of Thomas' best-selling books, *Raiders of the Deep.* Jo pasted autographs and inscriptions of all the U-boat commanders she interviewed on the inside cover and facing page of her copy.

In the fall of 1927, with a sheaf of letters-of-introduction and her green Royal portable typewriter in hand, she boarded the *Carmania*, en route to London. Her first crossing was a stormy one, and she described the crossing and her weeks in London in letters home.

October

Dear Far Away But Not Forgotten: We had two days of very rough weather and if this boat had not been so steady I think everyone would have been the worse for it. I woke in the middle of the night to hear my suitcases sliding off the sofa with a crack upon the floor, and my shoes sliding from one end of the room to the other. Then there was a terrific roll, and I could hear a crash from the dining room. I thought every dish had been broken, but we still seem to have enough. The ship rolled all night, and I would first hit one side of my bed, and then the railing on the outside.

In the morning the air was thick with fog and the horn was going every minute. The sea was lashing about like a wild animal, with great waves sweeping over the deck. From where I stood on the top deck the ocean looked like mountains and valleys, and the wind was blowing eighty miles an hour. I came down into the social hall to read, but the book jumped about so it was too hard on my eyes. We tried to play cards, but they slid off the table, and suddenly table, chairs, and players were hurled into a corner of the room. After that I hung on to a railing and just sat and hoped for the best. It became so bad everyone was forbidden to go on deck. The boat was still pitching when we went to bed, but this morning the sea is calm again and the sun is shining. We are due to go up the Thames tomorrow afternoon and reach London about five o'clock.

We saw few ships on the crossing. The *Leviathan* passed us one day, pitching and rolling about much worse than we were. Their captain sent our captain a wireless asking how we were getting along. "A smooth crossing," replied our captain, whereupon the *Leviathan* sent back one word only, "Liar."

Dear Marian: When I arrived, a drizzly rain was falling, but the weather was mild. I was glad of that, for the most diligent search has failed to reveal anything in my room that might be construed as heating apparatus. The advertising booklet about the hotel boasts of central heating. Evidently that is just what it is, but my room must be far, very far from the center.

I stopped at the office of the Imperial Airways, to present my compliments and ask for a pass, about which Mr. Thomas had already written them. I also got my passport visa for Germany. "Vy didn't you get it in the United States?" growled the man at the German consulate, looking much like Hindenberg about to go into battle. I told him when I left I wasn't certain I was going to Germany, which was a lie, but he accepted it and banged down his stamp on the passport. After scaring me like that, he didn't charge a cent, and I had expected to have to pay ten dollars.

Thursday I was back in the British Museum, not even going out for lunch. It continued to rain, and I didn't feel hungry. At four-thirty I packed up my things and started looking for the place where tea was being served. I bungled about here and there, through one huge wing after another. I found myself once in the Egyptian mummy section and another time in Greek sculptures with the frieze from the Parthenon. I hadn't noticed where I was, and suddenly was surrounded by these lovely, lovely figures, the most beautiful poetry in stone. It was the first time I ever got a thrill from statues and stone figures.

Friday I started out bright and early for the Admiralty, and this time I saw my man, or rather, several of them. This nice fat man I had met in the Intelligence Department became very friendly, asking me how old I was and why I was not married. He wanted to know if there were many lady journalists in America, and when I asked him if he didn't come across many in England, he said only two, and they were frights.

In the afternoon I had expected to go to Southampton to see another officer, but he was in France. I finally had a long talk with Captain Geoffrey Layton at the Admiralty, who had a few experiences in a submarine and told me all about them. Then in came Captain Max Horton, who had refused to see me only a little while before, as he didn't want to answer any more questions. He rose to the occasion nobly, however, and talked and talked.[2]

All week I have been cooling my heels waiting for people, and I have chilblains on my feet as it is. It is terribly cold and damp. My heavy coat, which was always too heavy for walking in Washington, feels like so much tissue paper here, and I am bundled up in sweaters and woolen stockings. I shall write again when I am settled in Germany.

November 15: Cologne, Germany: This is the end, not of a perfect day, but of a decidedly full one. I have eaten breakfast in London, lunch in Brussels, and dinner in Cologne, and in an hour or two shall be on the sleeper for Berlin.

I awoke in London this morning to a rather misty day, and before making any further plans telephoned to the Imperial Airways office, to find out if the planes were flying in such doubtful weather. The reply was that one plane had taken off already and that the others would "if the fog got no worse." I had a wild scramble to get breakfast, to attend to all the little things, and be at the London starting place at eight-thirty. The first thing was to weigh my baggage and myself. Flying is one way in which the skinny person can save money. Too late I bemoaned the fact that I hadn't cut down a bit on my food since I came over. Ten pounds less in weight might have saved enough money to allow me another day in Europe. All together, I had to pay ten dollars for excess baggage, but as my fare cost me nothing I couldn't exactly complain about this.

A few moments later I was off for the aerodrome at Croydon. The Airways company takes one there, not in a bus, but in a luxurious limousine with a liveried chauffeur, and I was the only occupant. I appreciated the idea of all that magnificence for myself alone, but just the same would have liked a bit of evidence that other people beside myself were flying.

Croydon is about forty-five minutes from downtown London by automobile, and we dashed through the suburbs and beside the Thames, where hundreds of white doves were taking free rides on the boats and barges. At the aerodrome, I knew the worst. The official who escorted me over the muddy field to the airplane assured me I would have plenty of room. "Is nobody else going?" I gasped.

"Only you and the freight," he answered.

If I could have thought of any plausible excuse for turning back I should have done so. I didn't like making my first airplane journey without someone else to share the thrills — and other sensations. The plane was a giant Handley-Page[3] and when I climbed up into the cabin I had sixteen seats to choose from, except that the porter with my bags told me to sit near the center to preserve the balance. Then in came the pilot and the mechanic in their fur-lined flying suits and boots, and climbed through the tiny door at the front of the cabin to their places out in front of the nose. The door was shut, and after that all

I could see of them was the right ear of one and the left ear of the other as they sat just in front of the little window.

There I was in solitary state, with fifteen empty chairs for company. I was frightfully keen about taking my first flight. The motor began to roar with such a terrific noise that I thought my ears would burst, and then we started bumping across the flying field. In a few seconds the bumping ceased and I could see out of my window that the ground was a few feet below. This was my last chance to jump, and I hadn't taken it.

Up and up we went, and in a surprisingly short time we were over the housetops and the church steeples. Have you ever noticed what a very sharp thing a church spire is? Then we were off across the country, and the pilot, a very good-looking one, too, was turning about and making motions with his lips to ask if I was all right. Mentally I wasn't, but I managed to nod my head and put on what I hoped was a smile, although it must have been a very frozen one. As I looked down, we seemed to be no more than creeping along, but the speedometer said ninety miles, and going up steadily to a hundred. When I passed a train below, it seemed to be even more snail-like. I was surprised to get no more sensation of speed. The planes are heated somewhat as an automobile is, but I began to feel chilly, probably from nervousness as much as from cold, but I didn't dare move from my chair to get a sweater from my bag. I remembered what the porter had said about preserving the balance and clutched desperately to the arms of my chair.

The altimeter now showed that we were a thousand feet up in the air, and as we went over the country at a steady speed, I began to look about me a little, inside the plane. Just above my head was a packet marked "Life belt, pull only in case of emergency," but I'm blessed if I knew what one did after one pulled, provided the emergency arose. And just what was an emergency, anyway? Every second seemed like one hour to me. Up above was a sort of canvas insert in the top of the cabin, with a ring in it, which another sign said was likewise to be pulled in case of emergency. Evidently that was where I was to crawl out if we took a ducking in the channel. Following the same line of reasoning, I presumed that after that one adjusted the life belt, then struck out for shore.

I wished desperately for someone to share my apprehensions. Another passenger who knew even a little more than I did about airplanes might be expected to be a bit nervous also, but I knew I could look for no sympathy from the pilot, to whom a trip like this was probably of no more consequence than a jaunt to the corner grocery store. Again, I thought it did not seem quite fair that they should make the flight just on my account, when I was riding free anyway, but I was told afterwards that they flew every day with the fast express and the mails, even if there were no passengers at all. It didn't seem more than half an hour before we were over the Dover cliffs and then out over the Channel. I have heard people say that they feel easier flying over water than over land, but I could notice no diminishing of my fears and wild imaginings. My swimming ability is limited to about three strokes at the most, and I could see little chance for me in that respect. My admiration for Ruth Elder[4] rose higher even than the altimeter in front of me. Surely if she could wangle through 2,000 miles of this, I should not be floored by a few miles. It was rather a relief to get over the water, though, for I settled back in my chair and didn't feel that I needed to look out of the window to be sure not to miss anything. After a while, all the countryside looks the same, anyway. The great height seems to flatten out the hills and hollows, and everything looked like a great patchwork quilt. The grass is still surprisingly green in England.

I realized that even if there had been other passengers, the terrific roar of the motors wouldn't have permitted any conversation except sign language, and I shall undoubtedly have quite enough opportunity to practice that when I reach France. My French is on a par with my swimming.

Just then the mechanic came crawling back through the tiny door and asked, by putting his lips at my ear and shouting, if I should like to ride outside with the pilot, at the same time holding out his fur helmet to me. What a corking opportunity! He fastened the helmet under my chin and helped me tuck in my hair, and then literally boosted me up and out through the door. A folding leather seat came down from the side of the cockpit, and there I was tucked in beside the pilot.

I had nothing to complain of now in the matter of speed. There was a tiny windshield up in front of us, but I had only to lean my head over to one side to almost have it torn from my shoulders. It seemed to be getting foggier and foggier, especially after we left the Channel, but the pilot seemed not to be worried, so I pretended not to be. Sitting out there, with the wind tearing the words from our mouths, we yet managed to carry quite a comprehensive conversation. Shout as loudly as I could, I couldn't hear my voice make a sound, but by signs, lip reading, and yelling in our respective ears, the pilot learned where I was going, and I learned where we were, when we would arrive, and how long he had been piloting. I was glad he said twelve years, and not two. Between yells at me, he was talking to London all this time by wireless telephone through his little headpiece, and getting instructions and information in return. At certain intervals he would report his position and the weather, while the London airfield would give him reports on the weather ahead of him.

As the fog got thicker and the altimeter registered lower, I returned to the relatively enclosed safety of the cabin. We descended nearer and nearer to the ground. Suddenly a hillside seemed to rise up out of nowhere and be about to slam at one of our wings, and as I looked at the altimeter it was registering nothing at all. Then a tip as the plane swerved, while I grabbed harder than ever at the helpful chair in front of me and sat ready to leap goodness knows where. Just then the pilot turned about and nodded reassuringly at me through the window, and I let go my frantic clutch again. Evidently this was some maneuver quite in order with flying, but I must say I didn't like it.

The fog lifted for a while then, and I continued to be all eyes out the windows, looking at the Belgian canals and windmills, and the white washings spread out on the grass. Then we hit the fog again, and for a long time followed the coastline of Belgium. I wondered if this were the regular course, or if the smooth white beach were chosen as a possible landing place. We continued to fly so low that we were just over the roofs of the houses, later leaving the coastline and following a railway track. All this time the fog became thicker and thicker, but the pilot continued to look back every few moments and reassure me. At first this was helpful, but later I began to wonder why he thought of reassuring me in case there was nothing to worry about. It was an instance of "Methinks the gentleman protesteth too much."

Then I ceased to worry about the affairs of air navigation. I had come through four days of stormy weather on the Atlantic without a bit of seasickness, but there was no question now that I was thoroughly and miserably airsick. There was only one consolation about it. I didn't care now whether we crashed in the fog or not. In fact, I shouldn't have minded. Nothing could make me feel worse than I was. I knew I must have been looking a frightful pea-green in the face, and the pilot must have noticed it too, for he held up his five fingers and formed the words, only five minutes yet. Those five minutes were my undoing. Suddenly I was violently and horribly ill, and the little receptacles placed suggestively beside each chair justified their existence.

Almost at the same time, we were at the aerodrome at Brussels, and I felt better after my disgrace. That was the only time during my trip when I was glad I was a lone passenger. It was raining by now, I walked across the muddy landing field to a little café where I drank hot tea, and more hot tea, but nothing else. I thawed in front of the fire for a half hour, and felt considerably better when we were ready to start on for Cologne. I found that I had not been so wrong in my fears, as the pilot told me he had intended to stop at Ostend because of the fog, but went on, thinking it might not be so bad ahead. That is when he began to follow the seacoast. He also told me not to mention my riding outside, as that was an infringement of the rules. That also cheered me a trifle.

The fog became worse and worse between Brussels and Cologne. When it became so bad that the land a hundred feet below us was nothing but a blur, I resigned myself to the fact that worrying wouldn't help matters and actually began to enjoy the trip. The pilot told me in Brussels that by means of his wireless it is possible to land safely in the thickest fog. This part of the trip lasted only an hour and a half, and although it was then only half past two, it was almost as dark as night. Suddenly I saw rockets flashing up into the air ahead of us, and realized we were at the landing field. The fog was so thick we couldn't see the buildings beneath us, but by means of the signals and flares of different colored lights, the pilot circled around and around and landed softly and smoothly.

Here at Cologne the customs man met me at the aerodrome and took a look at my bags, but not at all thoroughly. I had written ahead to the German airline that runs from Cologne to Berlin, and their representative met me, telling me that none of their airplanes would fly tomorrow because of the fog, and that none of them had flown today, either. He said they had not expected the British plane, and that he could hear the sound of our engines for a half hour before we came down and that is why they set off the rockets to guide us to the right place. I was glad I knew all this after it was over. Therefore, instead of waiting here at Cologne until the weather is good enough for flying, I am taking a ten o'clock train out tonight, and shall arrive in Berlin tomorrow morning at eight.

I am frightfully tired, but anxious to reach Berlin and be settled again for a while. With affection to all, Josie.

Josephine registered at Berlin's elegant Kaiserhof Hotel, and then set out for the Admiralty to make her appointments. Her first destination was Wilhelmshaven, the wartime submarine fleet headquarters on the North Sea. In a letter to Lowell Thomas, she wrote: "Wilhelmshaven is a sleepy town, half deserted. It is still a naval station, but the German fleet is but a handful of boats. The great barracks that during the war were filled to overflowing are nearly empty. The U-boats are no more. German sea power is a vanished dream."

But, perhaps anticipating the day when U-boats might again represent the country's power, Germany kept a skeleton crew of the officer corps and its most commanding figure was Commander Lothar von Arnauld de la Perière,[5] who welcomed Jo. The Commander wore his uniform, resplendent with gold braid, medals and decorations. A sword clanked at his side and the Pour le Merité was at his throat. He was a tall, slender man in his early forties, with brown hair and the keenest possible brown eyes, a good-looking chap whose jaw and chin were exceedingly firm and in contrast to a fine, friendly smile. His home was filled with U-boat memorabilia, where the maple doors, moldings and panels were made of wood ripped out of his submarine before he turned it over to the Allies."

My obliging host displayed typical German thoroughness in seeing that the American who wanted to tell the story of the U-boats got plenty to tell. He showed me his diary and photographs, related his adventures, and arranged for me to meet other commanders. Nor did he neglect to have me see the sights. The chaplain of the post, a genial, baldheaded gentleman who, I found, was a fan of Jack London and Upton Sinclair, took me to the garrison church and the naval cemetery. Commander von Arnauld himself took me to the Naval Officer's Club, where there was much clicking of heels and saluting. No better setting could be devised for the telling of U-boat stories. After a characteristic German dinner in a private room — the pièce de resistance was roast hare — the company adjourned to the submarine room. There we sat, the three officers in glittering naval uniform and myself. I listened to wild tales of periscope and torpedo. We talked till long past midnight.

In the port city of Hamburg, Jo stayed at the Atlantic Hotel and interviewed Commander Robert Moraht[6] over tea. She wrote her boss:

"Moraht spoke like a cultured Englishman except for his habit of throwing in American slang. He makes a serious effort to master its latest jazz forms and really has a finer command of our language than the average American, but when I talked with him he constantly swung into American slang."

His interview in *Raiders of the Deep* is peppered with the jazzy language of the roaring twenties: cat's pajamas, tough luck, loony, greenhorn, pipe dream, cock-eyed, hot dog, jiminy Christmas, funk, and hot stuff.

If Jo needed to interview a U-boat commander who had died, she searched out his second officer.

"I interviewed Lieutenant Rudolph Zentner, the officer who had served under the commander who sank the *Lusitania*, on a snowy windswept day in his office in the ancient Hanseatic city of Lubeck. Most of the submarine commanders look young, but he looked even younger — a slender, pleasantly smiling chap with fiery red hair. His mother was born in New York and he spoke excellent English. Zentner ran one hand through his hair, tucked a monocle under one bushy brow, and leaned back in his swivel chair to tell his story."

Next on Jo's list was Commander Otto Hersing[7] in Rastede, a tiny town on the flat North German plain, thirty miles from the North Sea. She described a "rare time" in the days she was there:

"The cottages are quaint and old-fashioned, surrounded by gardens and fruit trees. The church spire, covered with ivy, dates back to the fourteenth century. Nearby is the great estate of the Grand Duke of Oldenberg — a splendid castle — and around it some 7,000 acres laid out as an English park and stocked with deer, game birds, and other quarry for the hunter. The gamekeepers wear green jaegers' uniforms that vaguely remind one of Robin Hood and his merry men. They dropped in very frequently for beer at the little inn where I was the only foreign guest. I met Commander Hersing there. He is a tall, dark, slender man, with all the dignified and hospitable courtesy of the German rural gentry. When I asked him what he was doing now he replied, 'I grow fine potatoes.' He was the only officer I met who gave any aching expression of grief and bitterness over Germany's present lot. The others seemed to take it as a matter of course, the natural attitude of active men who accept hard facts without useless repining. "Commander Hersing and his wife plied me with cordial hospitality, with food and excellent beer, and with the stories of warfare under the sea for which I had come. In the evening they took me back to the inn and we sat and talked U-boats until midnight."

Back in Berlin, Jo negotiated with the officers who had already published their memoirs in German, and reported to her boss:

"One of the men in the Admiralty says Walter Forstmann is a keen business man and drives a hard bargain; he would not listen to a cent a word. To save time, I made him the two-cent a word offer. I shall get on as soon as possible to Rome and Paris, and think I can work through our naval attachés there. Here in Berlin I am almost buried under a last minute avalanche of odds and ends, and this Teutonic deliberation and red tape make me almost frantic. An errand that in New York could be completed in ten minutes, takes anywhere from one to two hours here."

Lowell Thomas did not give Josephine a list of men to interview — just a general outline of the book and how many U-boat commanders he wanted. She would find one and he would lead her to others. She wrote to her boss: "I have made arrrangements to see three men and have heard from two more still in service, who are willing to see me as soon as they get permisson from their superiors Then there are three others who wish first to hear the sound of coin..."

Forstmann suggested she go to Austria and interview Georg von Trapp. She flew to Vienna then took the train to Salzburg, where she searched out von Trapp. She wrote Thomas:

"I knew only that he lived somewhere near Salzburg. At the hotel I was told the only way to reach his place was by automobile. With a driver, I left the city, winding about over quaint bridges and through equally quaint squares and market places, on into the open country, always with those magnificent mountains as a background. Those snow-capped peaks look entirely too theatrical to be real. Several miles out was the Villa Trapp, an enormous establishment, but it needed to be, as I found out later.

"Commander von Trapp was laid up with an infected foot, and I found him reclining on a sofa in his room, nattily garbed in striped pink and blue pajamas. One foot was swathed in bandages; with the other, quite bare, he squirmed about on the couch. Every few minutes my mind would be distracted from submarines by the sight of that bare foot hanging over the side of the couch or sticking out from under the blanket. It was most diverting.

"We made good progress for two or three hours, with the Commander referring now and then to his albums and his notes. When he wanted anything, he blew on the boatswain's whistle beside him — a relic from his submarine. We had a very English tea in front of the fire, tea with milk and buttered toast and jam, such as I had not tasted since I left England. A bit later a very fresh-looking radiant young woman came in and asked how we were getting on. She was introduced as his wife, although she didn't look any more than twenty-two or so. After she went out the Commander made a remark about his family and I asked if he had any children. 'Seven' was the answer. He must have noticed that my eyes widened, as he hastened to add that this was his second wife."

Josephine's typewritten letter continues on for forty pages, in which she has transcribed von Trapp's vivid experiences in his submarine during the war.[8] She then went on to Prague, Rome, and Paris. By the end of March she was back in England, with more Naval officers to interview, and where, quite by chance, she ran into a friend from the early Washington years.

She wrote Marian from London: "Ada Howell, who used to be one of the stenographers in Washington, married Knowlton Ames, an enormously wealthy man from Chicago, and now lives the life of Reilly. I ran smack into her in London on the street one day, and we did all the expensive lunching places in town. Her husband was wrapped up in business, so the two of us jazzed around together. They had hired a Rolls-Royce limousine with a most beautiful chauffeur in dark green livery, and in this we rolled up sumptuously to our lunching places. After that, as I had to do a lick of work, Ada would go back to her hotel for a nap and tell me to keep the car as long as I wanted, whereupon I would be delivered in state to the various places where I had meetings. It made a great impression. I'm sure that all the results I got were due solely to that car and chauffeur."

Just before the Easter holidays, Josephine traveled north to Lowestoft, on the track of the skipper of a fishing smack who, in one day, battled five German submarines. My mother had arranged an interview with W. S. Wharton, who wrote her: "I have got my log from the Great War, which amounts to about 30 or 40 pages. I have had several offers to sell it, but it has never been in print." Afterwards, in her London Hotel, she wrote a long letter to Marian:

"Lowestoft is a fishing town on the North Sea, and I didn't expect anything wonderful in the way of a hotel. I asked the taxi driver to take me to the best one there. It was off on the edge of town, overlooking the sea. My room was as cold as Labrador, but I didn't tarry there long. I snatched some dinner in the very nice dining room and took off to look up the man I had come to see.

"Skipper Wharton was a typical North Sea fisherman, a little roly-poly man with a thatch of grey hair, and the pinkest cheeks you ever saw; he looked exactly like an apple dumpling. He had a shrew of a wife and I wished for a nice dose of chloroform to give her before the evening was over. Nothing her husband said was right and she continued to interrupt his story and correct him until I could have bound and gagged her. When I came back to the hotel, my room seemed colder than before and the only redeeming feature was the jug of hot water I found in my bed. Six jugs would have been more to the point, but I curled around it so it would touch as much of my anatomy as possible, and then dropped off into a frozen stupor.

"The next morning the sun was shining brilliantly, and a bracing wind came off the sea, out where I could see the white sails of the fishing boats, and the surf lashing up on the beach. Just the sight of it gave me an enormous appetite, and I ate a huge breakfast, then settled down in the lounge in front of a blazing open fire to sort over the notes I had got the evening before. In the middle of the morning I had a telephone call from a friend of Skipper Wharton's, one Captain Atkinson, who asked if I would like to go down to the harbor and go on board one of the fishing schooners. Would I? I dashed off at once to meet him at his office, just at the edge of the docks, and as we sat there talking he spotted walking along the sea wall another of the skippers who had had fights with submarines during the war. He called in this fellow, who was at first embarrassed at being introduced to a strange lady from across the Atlantic. He was so shy I thought he would tear his cap to pieces, he was twisting it so much. After a while, however, he saw I wouldn't bite, and then he was in his element, telling me stories about his wartime adventures. I could have listened to him all day.

"I walked along the sea wall back to the hotel where I ate everything on the menu for lunch. After lunch it began to rain — it does that every day about this time in England — and I took a taxi to the town library where a timid little librarian showed me the wartime relics. Then back to the hotel for tea in front of that gorgeous open fire. I went back that evening to get the rest of Skipper Wharton's story and the next morning caught the first train back to London. It was crowded to the roof with people going away for the Easter holiday, which is much more important in England than it is with us. At one time, in a compartment that is comfortably full with six people, there were eleven of us, including three obstreperous children. All the mothers were dressed in obviously new Easter hats and cheap finery, and the children cried and ate sticky cookies, so the new finery got spotted and the children cried some more and I was glad when we reached London.

"I was not certain if I had to change trains or not, so asked at one station, and then at the next I asked the station guard again, to make certain. 'That's right, deary,' said an old lady next to me, 'we have to be careful when we ain't used to traveling, don't we?'"

"So, that was Good Friday. I had expected to accomplish all sorts of things on Saturday, but nearly everything in the city was closed until Tuesday morning, so I stayed close to my room and typed my notes.

"Wednesday morning Captain Max Horton came around to my hotel to see me. Last autumn he almost refused to tell me anything about himself, as he is so confoundedly modest, but this time he has been much better. I had run into him at the Admiralty once or twice, and one day he took me to lunch at the Naval Military Club on Half Moon Street. That was a lot of fun. Before the lunch was over there were two other naval officers at our table; I tell you, your sister may be an old maid,[9] but she has been having a good time. And they were all good looking men. It must be the new hats I bought in Paris. I look very wicked in them. Captain Horton was buying a new Chrysler car, so we talked cars for a while, although I don't know a piston from a spark plug. Very few girls in Europe drive their own cars. He's a very nice man and spoken of as one of the most eligible bachelors in the British Navy.

"That evening I had an engagement with Major Francis Yeats-Brown,[10] the assistant editor of the *London Spectator*, to go a nightclub called the Gargoyle. He is a friend of LT's and has been very helpful. But he rang up and said one of his best friends was leaving the next day for India and had asked him to dine. When YB told him he had an engagement, the other man said to bring the engagement too, which was quite all right with me. So I put on the invaluable black dress and used some purple powder on my face to make my skin white, and if I do say so myself, I did look passable. Antiquated, you know, but passable.

"YB suggested that, as dinner didn't start until nine, I come around to his flat and have a cocktail first, and when I got there, there was his aunt to chaperone us — the Duchess of Westminster, by golly. He said he thought I might be timid about being in a man's flat, although it was quite all right in London. I looked over all his books and autographed photographs of famous men, drank my martini, and sat in front of the fire gossiping with his aunt, a very skittish lady of about sixty-five, I should say, with the bob of a sixteen-year-old.

"Then we left for dinner. It was the first time that I have ever gone out with a high silk hat and a monocle. I have been in company with the stovepipe hat before, and I met several officers who wore monocles in Germany, but this was the first time I had stepped forth with the two combined. We walked up the Strand and hailed a taxi, and in a half-minute were at Prince's, a rather hoity-toity place on Piccadilly. The other members of the party were Major Atkinson, a typical good-looking Englishman, about forty-two, with a short clipped mustache. His wife was lovely in a gold lamé dress and white ermine evening wrap, while your sister Josie checked her old coat at the door and went in with her new flame colored silk shawl over her black dress.

"We sat in the lounge drinking more cocktails — everybody does it — then went into dinner. And what a gorgeous dinner. We started with a fruit compote, the soup, then fillet of sole, then guinea hen with vegetables, then mushrooms on toast, then a salad, then an ice called coupe Jacques, then coffee, and there were three kinds of wine. Between courses we danced or watched cabaret acts. We left at twelve. Oh, it was so much fun.

"Thursday I was as busy as six people all day, getting in at eleven, ready to drop. I did drop, right into bed. Friday I had all the last minute things to attend to, had to make another flying trip to the War Museum library, spent two hours going through the files of the *London Illustrated News* looking for an elusive article about Max Horton published during the war, and then, in the afternoon, although I was so busy, I realized that I couldn't leave England without going to Westminster Abbey, perhaps the finest building in the country. I stayed for the three o'clock service, and spent a half hour just sitting in the quiet sunny cloister and listening to the music. It is ancient and beautiful and impressive and I stayed the whole afternoon. I was particularly intrigued with the effigies of past kings and queens, particularly that of Charles I, or was it Charles II? Anyway, the nose had been broken off and had been pasted back on again, giving him a very devilish appearance."

Josephine spent her last evening in England going full bore. Ada came round in the Rolls and they went to a French restaurant in Soho, then to see "Gentleman Prefer Blonds," and then to a cafe on Piccadilly Square. Even though she said she was "half dead," she packed, got up at seven the next morning, got her trunk and baggage to the station and caught the eight-twenty for Liverpool.

Shortly before Jo left she wrote her boss: "I have a mass of half-finished material and notes that I have been struggling with ever since I left Germany. I can hardly believe that I am actually on my way home at last. Almost seven months! And they have shot by like seven weeks."

On May 8th Jo was back at Clover Brook Farm. She wrote Marian:

"I have been alone here at Pawling since I returned. I think I must have typed about 100,000 words of notes, and I still haven't reached the end. I thought it would be frightfully lonely after the gay life I had in Europe, but I don't mind it. In the evening I work or

117

sew on my clothes and listen to the radio, and before I know it, midnight is here."

By the end of the month, she was on her way back to Germany for final *Raiders of the Deep* research. This time she traveled first class on the *Leviathan,* the largest and fastest ship afloat. She wrote Lillian: "This ship is as big as all Ionia put together, almost, and filled with famous people — Samuel Goldwyn and opera prima donna Rosa Ponselle — and many lovely young flappers with equally lovely clothes."

In Berlin, Jo boarded at a small guesthouse to improve her German.[11] She worked most days in Potsdam, but it was not all work and no play. She went to the North Sea beaches, and on a yachting party with Commander Max Valentiner, an officer whom she interviewed about the sinking of the *Lusitania.* (Valentiner was named a war criminal by the Allies for the 1915 sinking of the *Persia,* a British passenger liner, but not the *Lusitania.*) Jo formed a special attachment to his wife and children, with whom she spent many weekends. Then, after only seven more weeks of work, Lowell Thomas cabled Josephine to come home; he had another project.

NOTES

[1] *Buranelli devised a crossword puzzle for the* New York World *in 1919 and edited* The Crossword Puzzle Book *for Dick Simon and Max Schuster in 1924, which established the two young men's publishing career.*

[2] *Layton was promoted to rear admiral in 1935. Horton, who in 1914 sank the first German warship, had been promoted to Admiral by 1939. In a Life magazine article in August 1943, the 60-year-old Horton was credited with "winning the battle of the North Atlantic."*

[3] *The Handley-Page was the two-engine W10 model.*

[4] *The story of his 1939 escape from the Nazis was the basis of the Rodgers and Hammerstein musical "The Sound of Music."*

[5] *In October, Ruth Elder attempted a transatlantic flight, but wrecked near the Azores and became not only the first woman to make the effort, but the first to be rescued from a plane.*

[6] *During World War II, von Arnauld was recalled to active duty as a Vice Admiral; he died in a plane crash near Paris in 1941.*

[7] *Moraht was elected to the Reichstag in 1932, but by the late 1930s had rejoined the Navy. He survived 1945 to 1948 in a Soviet prisoner of war camp, and died in 1956.*

[8] *Hersing rejoined the Navy in 1939 and lived until 1960.*

[9] *Jo was now thirty-one; most of her contemporaries were married.*

[10] *Yeats-Brown left the Spectator the next year and wrote a memoir, Bengal Lancer, which became a bestseller. By 1939, he was involved in right-wing politics and became an apologist for Hitler. He died in 1944.*

[11] *When my mother was a child, her mother spoke German at home, so she had a basic knowledge of the language when she first went abroad; but she used a translator for many of her interviews.*

11

Caribbean Cruise

Jo and Count Felix von Luckner (center) on his schooner, 1929.

"This cruise is a whirling maze of wild impossibilities — of cliques, scandals, gossip, too much drinking — as well as of tropic nights so lovely that one hurts, and falls in love with whomever has the nearest deck chair."

Lowell Thomas wanted his star researcher on a working Caribbean cruise on Count Felix von Luckner's four-masted schooner, *Vaterland*. Luckner had been a fearless naval raider during the war, and a sequel to *Raiders of the Deep* was in the works. My mother would interview him on board. So, after three weeks in London and five in Berlin, totally exhausted, Jo steamed home on the *George Washington*. Back in Pawling, she didn't want to go on the cruise, but allowed herself to be talked into it. She wrote: "LT made me feel as though I would be letting him down if I backed out at that late date, and spinelessly as usual, I came along."

Host Burt Massee, a onetime Milwaukee newsboy-turned-multi-millionaire, chartered Von Luckner's 209-foot windjammer for his honeymoon cruise and ordered the ship stocked with enormous quantities of luxurious food and drink — 200 Westphalian hams, 3,000 bottles of Mosel and Rhine wines, 10,000 bottles of French champagne and 10,000 bottles of Munich beer. She never regretted going, she told me; the cruise was an unforgettable experience that Thomas described as, "One of the zaniest episodes of the zany 1920s. It was the era of wonderful nonsense, a time when the dizzying spiral of prosperity was supposed to last forever." The host and guests rode the very end of this prosperity; as they sailed off in early August, the spiral turned downward, and the recession that started that month would climax in late October.

Between trying to work and having fun at sea, my mother typed dozens of long letters to friends, which I have combined here.

Bermuda

If you will drink about umteen cocktails, mix them up with all the champagne at some of those publishing parties, and then take a few shots in the arm and let your imagination run wild, you still can't make it as hectic and wild as this jamboree is.

We got to Hamilton Monday forenoon, with most of the party at the dock to meet the boat. The *Vaterland* was laying out in the harbor, looking very big and imposing. My cold was better, and I decided that perhaps I was glad I came after all. My sweet, innocent pleasure was short lived. Part of the crowd — those I didn't know — was introduced, and the icicles began to form. "Oh, hello," says Mrs. Massee without bothering to offer her hand, and goes on talking to a beautifully dressed woman, who eyes me superciliously and also hardly bothers to acknowledge the introduction. It seems that the Massee party and the Thomas party have set up feudal warfare, probably because Mrs. Massee thought LT horned in with too many people. The lack of cordiality didn't stop with me — it extended distinctly to Frances Thomas, although she apparently doesn't get it. But somebody told me that Mrs. M wanted to know whose party this was — Massee's or Lowell Thomas's.

It's an interesting situation. Mr. Massee is a person of a certain charm, but he is very difficult to talk with, and hard to draw out. He's about forty and simply sweltering in money. We are living at a hotel while the boat is being provisioned and repairs made, and he is standing the whole thing — $15 or $20 a day for each person, with $100 tips to the orchestra and $10 tips to the waiters. I think he likes to feel that he is dispensing largesse and playing the grand host. His wife is about thirty-five, I should say, tall and with a splendid figure, but not particularly pretty. She has exquisite clothes, as she should have with the Palmolive millions to buy them, but she has absolutely no manners. She was formerly society editor of the *Chicago Tribune*. A shallow, superficial type, her new importance has gone to her head. She can't forget for a moment who she is, or let anyone else.

Then there are a Mr. and Mrs. Ward. He made his millions in Orange Crush. He is fat and middle aged, filthy with lucre, and as coarse and vulgar and stupid as anyone I ever met. If he can't twist some chance remark into a salacious double meaning, he isn't happy. His wife is in her thirties, beautifully groomed and with gorgeous clothes, and she treats all of us but LT as though we were carrion. Mr. Massee's two children and about a half dozen of their friends came, too.

One thing I can't complain about is lack of men. There are five women and fifteen men among the grown-ups. Two doctors are on board, Dr. William D. Jack, the cruise physician, big and fat and jolly, and his nephew, in his last year in Johns Hopkins Medical School.[1] Dr. Jack raised a row with the *Vaterland*, saying it needed fumigating and disinfecting and a dozen other things. Then we have Colonel Dan Edwards. He was in the First Division in France — the same company as my brother — and got the highest decoration, the Congressional Medal, and was one of the most decorated men. He has one stiff leg and one arm cut off at the elbow, and still he can throw the other men on board in a wrestling match. He is a big red-faced, raucous, blustering fellow, what is popularly known as a rough diamond — and under the influence of a few drinks he occasionally pulls a raw one, but Mr. Massee likes him because they both have such limitless capacities for hard likker.

Prosper Buranelli is on board. He is a feature writer on the *World*, and is often at Pawling. He was taken as official newspaperman, although he refused to write a line because it is too hot.

Another chap I met before is Rexford Barton, who used to be with the Century Publishing Company. He resigned this spring to go-west-young-man and pick up in health, but came along on this cruise instead. He is a Harvard man and by far the most first-rate person on the cruise, I think. I like him immensely — he's one of these utterly likable chaps. I'm sorry to say he is so diminutive. If he were not, I could fall desperately.

Count von Luckner's wife and brother Ferdinand are also on the trip. Then there is the explorer Carveth Wells,[2] the Englishman who has been doing that series on "Coldest Africa" in *World's Work*, and McClelland Barclay, the artist. Barclay is the chap who does those covers for *Pictorial Review* and *Country Gentleman* and the classy Fisher Body advertisements that you see in all the magazines — the ones with that corking looking girl. He's a good-looking scoundrel himself, about forty, I should say, not married and never will be, small black mustache type. He goes about all day in dirty sneakers and soccer pants, a blue jumper that exactly matches his eyes, and a blue beret. Half the time he is stripped to the waist; that shows off his powerful shoulders to wonderful advantage. He is doing sketches of everyone on board. He's a rare and racy laddie, from all accounts, and apparently not a bit slower personally than the speedboat *Dogfish* he has brought along, a neat job that does fifty miles an hour with no trouble at all. It is hoisted up on the deck, so that he can go jazzing off in it any time something interesting appears on the horizon. When I arrived, as my trunk was on the *Vaterland,* to even change for dinner I had to get out to the yacht and bring back some clothes. Barclay took me out in his speedboat, and we stayed for lunch on the boat.

One day thirteen of us piled into the *Dogfish* and went whizzing across the harbor to a lovely little uninhabited island — which I heard the Bermudians are trying to sell to some rich American for a million dollars cold. We climbed out on the coral rock and bathed for two hours on a beautiful beach. Except for a few slimy jellyfish, it was delightful — yes, even in spite of the violent sunburn I picked up on my shoulders.

Bermuda is the cleanest hot place I have ever seen. There is the same blinding sunlight that one finds in Italy, but in Italy the pink and blue houses mitigate things somewhat — here every house is glaring white, and so are the roofs, which are washed down with lime periodically and are used to catch rainwater, the only source for drinking water. Flowers give the only color — oleander and flaming hibiscus, with the green of palms and banana plants for contrast.

Every night we have dinner on the hotel roof garden, and each night our table grows longer. The hotel management should bless the Lord for us, for undoubtedly we are a drawing card, and the place has been crowded. We eat up there with the electric lights turned low to give the moonlight a chance to make us look interesting. It is so warm that our thinnest chiffons are sufficient without a wisp of wrap, and we eat and dance until midnight, and longer if we can persuade the orchestra to remain. One night Mr. Massee took the whole orchestra out on the ship, where they played until four a.m. There was no piano on board, so he just bought one from the hotel and sent it along. Frances heard two women talking about the hundred dollar tips Massee passes out and when Prosper and Sherm[3] picked up two barmaids down by the water front, the two girls could talk of nothing else but this marvelously rich American.

The Hamilton newspaper has been filled with our doings every day. Heaven knows what they will print when we leave, as we have taken up two thirds of the news section every morning. We've been meeting all kinds of interesting people. One afternoon we drove out to see Colonel Tom Dill, the Attorney General of the island, and the descendant of the early pirates who operated from here. He has one eye gone and hobbles about on a crutch, which makes him a pretty good Jolly Roger himself. He has a charming bungalow out on a cliff with a study built like a ship's cabin, and there he told me stories of early pirate activities. Another day I got a story from one Joe Heenan, formerly a commander in the British Navy, and now owner of a chicken ranch. He is a nice Englishman, and after we met him he came up to the roof every night to dance, which he did like a professional.

One afternoon the American consul and his wife had us all for tea at their place — and then actually served tea, much to the disappointment of the harder drinking members of the company. The Governor General of the Islands, Sir Louis Bols, honored us by attending, and we all rose and stood solemnly as they arrived and left. LT found that he had known General Bols in Palestine during the war. He and Lady Bols also came next day to the party that Mr. Massee gave on board the ship. He invited 250 people, and the checklist at the gangplank showed that over 600 actually appeared. It's nothing less than miraculous that the drinks and sandwiches went around. Mr. Massee imported a corps of waiters from the hotel, and had the entire orchestra come over to play all afternoon. I am appalled when I think of the money that man is spending.

Every night before dinner somebody in the bunch throws a cocktail party. The Thomases gave theirs out on the boat on the night that a water pageant and regatta was being held on shore. We ate so many sandwiches with the drinks that we didn't even want any dinner, and stayed out on the boat until ten o'clock. We set off a fireworks display for the benefit of people on shore. Then all the boats staged a sham attack on the yacht, and took the Count prisoner and carried him to shore to make him an honorary citizen and listen to him give a speech.

The fishing is marvelous. We caught sharks and barracudas and on one island we went out to do some deep sea diving with William Beebe, the scientist.[4] Everyone is as brown as an Indian from living in the sun.

On two different afternoons we took carriages and drove across the island to Coral Beach, where everyone bathed on those pinkish mauve sands, with the surf spray coming in like the top of a strawberry soda. Mauve and pink are the prevailing colors here. The beach is pink, the surf is mauve, and the water is a startling combination of brilliant green or deep purple. One afternoon the Wards gave a beach party, buying up all the bathing houses so nobody else could use the beach. Fancy umbrellas were stuck along the beach, drinks were served between swims, and afterwards the women all changed into beach pajamas, and we had drinks and hors d'oeuvres in a little craggy garden. The pièce de resistance was small ripe tomatoes stuffed solidly with caviar, and the accompanying masterpiece in the liquor line was something served in iced tea glasses, and with no dilution. I had two of them and they simply knocked me for a goal.

At sea, both mentally as well as geographically.

We have a man on board recovering from a scalp wound who says his head aches all the time because the new impressions come too fast. There's nothing wrong with my scalp but the impressions are coming too fast for me, too, and this cruise is a whirling maze of wild impossibilities — of cliques, scandals, gossip, too much drinking — as well as of tropic nights so lovely that one hurts, and falls in love with whomever has the nearest deck chair.

There is plenty of cabin space, and two salons beside the dining salon, but we all spend every minute on deck, even for sleeping. My own cabin is a double one and fairly cool with the fan on, but most of the party have taken to sleeping on deck in cots. It's simply a lazy life. Not only is work difficult, but ordinary letter writing is almost out of the question. Theoretically, I am being paid to work every morning from breakfast to lunch, but it is hard sledding. Today is an example. I got up at eight, was finished with breakfast at nine, and then started in to type some notes. An hour later I was drenched with perspiration, and a bit woozy from the motion in the dining room, where I had parked my typewriter. I went up on the top deck to read my notes and recuperate, and found everybody doing gymnastics. Of course I had to join, and the next thing I knew it was noon and the morning gone. After lunch we climb up in the bow and sit out on the jib boom, or loll in deck chairs and read or play bridge, or have a long nap, then afternoon tea on deck, then more reading or bridge, then the long evenings on deck.

We have cocktails and dinner up on the top deck every night, and then sit in the twilight watching those beautiful sunsets — poems in mauve and pearly translucence — until the stars come out, and the sailors begin to play their accordions and guitars up on the forecastle. It's the evenings, though, that are too unutterably lovely. If there is any wind at all, the auxiliary motors are stopped, and we float along under full sail, the sky overcrowded with stars, the lights and shadows of masts and rigging on the canvas creating something like those highly modernistic stage settings they do so well in Germany. There's always a rush after dinner up to the bow on top of the forecastle. All the sound of the mechanism of the boat is lost up there. I sit on the bowsprit amid lovely silence, with the path of the moon on the water in front of me, those enormous sails behind me, and those lofty masts swaying up above as we roll in the swell, and the phosphorescence sparkling and gleaming on the water, the air cool and fresh.

We five feminine passengers dress in pants, but the others are much more elegant than mine. I had only time to pick up something essential in Bermuda, and sailor pants were all I could get. I spent several hundred dollars buying more clothes for the tropics, only to find I haven't nearly enough, while what I have can in no whit compare with those purchased by the Palmolive, Colgate, and Orange Crush millions. The trouble with me is that I am trying to keep up with the millionaires on a working girl's salary, which is foolish in the extreme. This boat is swarming with millionaires and titles. Those of us who can't qualify for either class turn up our noses in the most approved intelligentsia way and get what consolation we can.

Fortunately, on the boat our money is simply no good. Laundry, pressing, cigarettes and drinks all come out of Massee's pocket, whether on land or shore. I heard yesterday that the cruise is costing him $125,000 [over $1.6 million in today's dollars], and I well believe it, especially after seeing the supplies that came from the most expensive grocery in New York. Every delicacy in and out of season is at our disposal. Caviar is dished about as though it were cowpeas.

I started on this cruise with the wild idea that I was going to do a lot of work, but lost that noble ambition long ago. It is utterly impossible to find a quiet place or the right mood. After a few hectic efforts, therefore, I have given up trying, and spend the day loafing like the rest, thinking of work only when I see the huge trunk of unfinished manuscripts the boss brought with him. We loll around with our feet propped up on the railing swapping stories most of the time, or playing bridge. I've won enough so far to buy a new hat. It is even difficult to drop into the mood for reading. For most of us, life at sea is plumb lazy.[5]

Prosper Buranelli and I, after two years of impersonal association and comradeship, have taken to holding hands under the moon. He said "My gosh, if this moonlight holds up I could hold even your hand." He's the chap with the nine children. Now and then we work up a game of handball or volleyball, but any kind of exertion proves too much. As long as we sit on deck in the breeze it is cool, but anything else makes me realize that tropics are tropic. At eleven o'clock the long cool drinks begin to make their way to the afterdeck, and the procession continues until we lunch at one. Thereupon everyone flops down for a nap, or merely passes out from the over-gorging on rich food, and for a couple of hours the only sounds are the flapping of sails, the snoring of Dan Edwards, and the half-hourly calls of the lookout.

We stir ourselves at half past three to bathe. At first we used to stop the ship and lower a big dip net overboard. It was the same principal as one of those wire buckets in which you cook French fried potatoes. We splashed about in that blissfully until one day we saw a shark at really close range and realized that the old boy could bite through it very nicely if he chose. The net was put in the hold and we now have our daily splash at the business end of the ship's fire hose on the lower deck. That lasts until coffee is served at four, when we gorge ourselves on German pastries. Everyone usually plays bridge or reads until seven when we gorge again. Dinner is always up on deck, where it seems nothing less than sacrilege to guzzle champagne and eat ham in the face of these flaming tropical sunsets.

One day we thought that we were in for a hurricane. It began to blow late in the afternoon. The sky turned a peculiar yellow, and a gust of wind snapped off one of the topmasts as though it had been a toothpick. The ship was heeling and the sailors were standing on one ear trying to reef in the sails, and the Count was bawling out orders like a foghorn. The hurricane was reported straight ahead of us, and so we turned around and went due east, expecting that if it didn't let up we should find ourselves in Africa instead of the United States. Three or four of us climbed up to the very front of the ship to watch the big waves and the lightning in the sky, but when a bolt came down the steel cables and gave us all an electric shock we got down out of there without any backward glances. We went down into the dining salon and played cards until about one o'clock, while the steward went around tying down all the trunks and warning us not to leave anything loose in our cabins. I turned in after awhile and was aware of pitching about in my berth during the night, but in the morning everything was peaceful and calm and we were back on our course.

At San Salvador, where Columbus first landed, we stopped and had a christening party. The Count changed the name of the boat from *Vaterland* to *Mopelia*, which is the name of the island in the South Pacific where his first raider was wrecked during the war.

Jamaica

Jamaica is the most beautiful island in the West Indies, I think. We came into the harbor of Kingston, which was completely destroyed by an earthquake about twenty years ago, but one would never guess it now. The most important building in the town is the hotel owned by the United Fruit Company, which owns all the banana plantations. I got a shampoo there, went into a little shop and bought another white linen dress, and then went out and sat on the veranda drinking absinthe frappes with Prosper until time for lunch. Lunch on shore wherever we stopped was always a feast of tropical fruits and vegetables.

Immediately after lunch several carloads of us started up into the mountains, where LT and Frances were giving a dinner party at a hotel. On the way we stopped in old Spanish Town to see the cathedral. I was in a car with Prosper and Rex. We rode for three hours, climbing steadily up the mountains all the time, through that wonderful tropical jungle, with waterfalls on every side, and those hibiscus trees blazing red as fire all over the mountainsides. Up at the hotel we picked up Countess von Luckner, and then went down the mountains to the opposite coast to see the Roaring River waterfalls. We fooled around there a while, and then drove through a marvelous forest of ferns higher than our heads and back to the hotel, where dinner was ready and waiting. Again it was mostly of tropical things — breadfruit, coconut milk, guavas, papayas, pineapples, plantains, alligator pears, and I can't remember what else. There were twenty-four of us there, and it was a gay party.

Santo Domingo

We got in here on a Tuesday and started the excitement by going hard aground just before noon. Every tug in Santo Domingo worked until nine o'clock that night trying to get us off. If they hadn't succeeded the old schooner would have been sitting there yet, just as two or three other boats were, including a U.S. naval cruiser that had gone on the rocks four years ago.

The British minister and his wife, whom the Massees had known in Chicago, started off by entertaining us at a cocktail party at their house. I got paired off with a very nice chap named Smith, from the Bank of Montreal. When we moved on from there to the country club where we were dining, I found my dinner partner was one Hinchcliffe, who was Smith's boss, the manager of the bank, likewise a most charming Canadian. There were twenty of us from the boat at the dinner, and about twenty others. We danced between courses out on the veranda, and afterwards guzzled Scotch highballs until after midnight, with intermittent dances. The club was formerly an old sugar plantation, about five miles from the city — a charming tropical setting in the moonlight. I had a great time (there were six men for every woman). In fact, the male preponderance was so strong that Dan, Carveth, and Barclay sneaked off after dessert and went down to the dives of the city.

The next morning Prosper, Rex, Sherm, and I strolled over to the town to see the old cathedral where Columbus is buried. It was hotter than what LT calls the hinges of Hades, and we were glad enough to drop wetly into a cafe and shout for long cold drinks. We spent the rest of the forenoon there watching the world of Santo Domingo go by.

Dinner was served on board, where we entertained the British minister. Afterwards, Carveth showed one of his moving pictures on the poop deck, and then we danced to the music of a native Dominican orchestra. Mr. Massee was so taken with the orchestra that he hired them to accompany the boat to the next island, and ordered his representative in the city to make the arrangements as to passports and the like. There were a dozen or more Dominicans at the dance, and I danced with one very swarthy gentleman who did the tango exquisitely but who spoke no word of English. It's a rather foolish feeling.

In the meantime the three deserters from the party the night before had been so enchanted with the haunts they found that they went off again, taking Prosper with them, and Prosper, with his engaging frankness, told us much about it. It seems that Dan had been looking forward with much anticipation to the beautiful Castilian girls he would find in Santo Domingo. Dan hasn't but a few words of Spanish, and his Castilians were all black, but he waded right into things, and they visited every questionable joint in the city. Before the night was over they had been in two fights, and Barclay had drawn sketches of all the dusky belles of the demi-monde. One dusky beau took exception to this and tore up the portrait and threw the shreds at his lady's feet, whereupon Mac drew it on the wall of the cafe where they were. The story was all over Santo Domingo the next day, and everybody in town repaired to the cafe to see the picture that caused so much commotion, and which was done by so famous an artist. Dan drew more notoriety than anybody else in the party. The day before, President Horatio Vasquez received a select few from the ship, but not Dan.

This morning Dan wanted to go boar hunting, so he boldly introduced himself as General Edwards to the Commandant of the army[6] and asked if he could get some advice on the best place to hunt. It was against the law both to hunt boars in August and to take firearms on shore from an alien vessel, but that small matter was soon disposed of, and Dan got his hunting. He also got a chance to tell what a great man he is, and the next thing we knew he was reviewing the Dominican army, being decorated by the President with the highest decoration they have, and getting presented with 20,000 acres of land situated God knows where. Every morning after that a limousine with a military escort presented itself at the dock and Dan swaggered off with all his medals strung across his buzzum. Everybody in Santo Domingo knew that Dan Edwards was the greatest soldier in the world and the champion ladies' man of the Western Hemisphere, which in no way decreased the curiosity or the crowds that centered on the entire cruising party.

The next morning at ten a couple of carloads of us went into the hills for luncheon as the guests of the German consul. He and the Luckners and the Thomases went in one car, and Rex, the young Doctor Ralph Jack, Mac and I in another. Santo Domingo is full of gorgeous mountains, and that drive was wonderful even to such a stuporous bunch as we were. Ralph slumped in one corner, I slept on his shoulder, and Rex slept on mine, with his feet hanging out of the side of the car, while Barclay sat in front and speculated on which hairpin curve would land us in Kingdom Come. We finally stopped at Bonao, about ninety miles up in the hills, and ate an enormous luncheon of everything native we could find in the dirtiest place I have ever seen, yet the food tasted wonderful.

Then we piled into the cars again and rode back down the mountains, this time at a more gosh awful pace than before, in order to get back on time for the inevitable cocktail party. Each day the cocktails seemed to get stronger, and these were like so much liquid dynamite. I didn't take any more than on the previous day, but it was quality and not quantity that played me tricks. By the time I reached the ship it was after eight o'clock and the others had gone on, thinking I wasn't coming. I sat down to talk to Sherm, and immediately became most horribly, desperately ill. Relations were immediately severed with all the nice cocktails, and Sherm took me up on the top deck and walked me up and down in the fresh air to make me feel better. He was so apprehensive that nobody know I was three sheets in the wind that he took me behind the chart house and brought me ice water and patted me on the shoulder. It happened that the top of the chart house, being inaccessible to stiff-kneed elders, was the favorite rendezvous of those fourteen- and fifteen-year-olds, who went up there for very intimate petting parties. Sherm had caught them up there one night, and now when they looked down and saw Sherm holding me up they retaliated and spread all over the boat that Sherm and I had been necking behind the chart house. Fortunately nobody took it seriously. I went down and went to bed and about midnight LT and Frances came staggering in. "Did Zhoshephine get home shafely," asks LT, as tight as an owl. "I'm mush afraid shesh had toomush drink."

This will give you an idea of the high intellectual tone of the party. I never in all my life saw so much drinking, and everyone was doing it. Everybody was rather meek the next day and stayed quiet. The regular Saturday night dance at the Country Club was that night, and Mrs. Massee, the British minister's wife, about fourteen men, and myself went out in a party. For the first time on the trip Mrs. Massee was really cordial to me, which made a difference.

We left Santo Domingo the next morning at daybreak, running aground two more times before we got clear and set sail. Two final incidents made a fitting climax to our stay. The day before, Mr. Massee had found that he would run into a lot of immigration red tape by taking the Dominicans with us, and so had notified the musicians that he couldn't carry out his plans. He found then, that through some hocus-pocus, the potential orchestra had wangled an advance of $200 out of his Dominican representative, and that they couldn't give it back because they had already spent it on new clothes suitable to going on a yachting party. "All right," says Mr. Massee, "then get the clothes."

General Trujillo, very indignant at his honored visitors being defrauded, had the orchestra thrown into jail. As we pulled out at daybreak the chain gang was starting out to dig ditches, among them four musicians in brand new tuxedos. The Dominican law said one could throw a man into jail for fraud, but one couldn't take his clothes away from him.

The other parting scene was of four very plump and very black maidens coming to the boat to demand of one Dan Edwards "payment for services rendered," to put a businesslike air upon it. They arrived there just in time to see Dan in all his panoply of decorations and medals chatting sociably to the General. Instead of demanding their stipends they gazed in amazement at this roughneck who was so friendly with the great General — evidently they knew that old boy, too — and slunk away. And that was Santo Domingo. It probably sounds on paper like a highly vulgar time. Well, I guess it was, but it was also a highly comic one.

The *Mopelia* made the 860-mile run through the Windward Passage to Nassau, where the Thomas contingent stayed in port for a few days, then sailed to New York, and on August 30th docked at Seventy-Ninth Street. My mother expected to return to Germany for more interviews to continue the work interrupted by the cruise, but LT changed his mind. In late September she wrote Commander Valentiner:

"I found your two letters waiting for me here in Pawling two days ago. It is good to be home after so much traveling. It was impossible to do any typing on board the ship and with so much work to do I cannot go back to Germany this month as I planned. I shall be very busy for several weeks typing your story, and the stories I got on the cruise. The second book about Count von Luckner will be printed next month, and the book about Captain Lauterbach comes next, and then I think the publishers would like something else before Mr. Thomas publishes a third German book. You have such a fine story that it will be more impressive if it comes after a book about an American or Englishman. I am glad to have the article from Admiral Spindler and shall translate it and then let one of my German friends read it also, to be sure I made no mistakes. Of course, we shall not use the same words in which it is written, so there will not be any trouble about the copyright.

"So now we have both reformed. I, too, have not smoked for three weeks. Everyone smoked and drank too much on the boat, so I stopped, although I couldn't refuse the excellent champagne that flowed so freely. I am very glad that everything is well again with the New York stock market. Mr. Massee in one day lost $400,000, but the next week he got it all back again. I am still refusing to speculate, and am pleased to see that the little piece of land I told you about has not yet been sold. I may buy it yet."

My mother considered moving from Pawling to New York City. In October she wrote Marian:

"I still haven't done anything about fall clothes. I can't decide whether I want to invest in a fur coat. In the days when I couldn't afford one I thought it was the height of luxury. Now I am not particularly interested. A fur coat is certainly too heavy to wear into New York for the average day of shopping, and a good cloth ensemble would be much more practical. I am half deciding to take an apartment in New York for a few months this winter. I could do very nicely with some opera and music and plays and city life for a while, and besides I can do my work for LT in New York just as well as here. I have all my notes from Europe still unfinished, another batch of stories and notes from the cruise to put into shape, and a book to finish that I was working on when I went abroad in April. I haven't made any decisions beyond that, principally because I still haven't got back to earth after that cruise."

The stock market crashed on October 29th. Massee lost $16 million ($208 million in today's dollars) and was wiped out. My mother did not buy the piece of land or the fur coat. In early November she wrote Marian:

"Pa needed a hundred dollars awfully bad, and for the first time I had to tell him I couldn't send it. All the money I had in my savings account I put into an investment so I would get more income, and now it's gone and I can't get it back."

NOTES

[1] *The nephew, Dr. Ralph Willis Jack, went on to become an OB/GYN and practiced in Miami ,Florida. In 2011, long after I finished the research for this book, I received an email from Janis Jack, the wife of W. D. Jack II, son of Dr. Jack, who found my name on the Count Felix von Luckner Society website. I shared the diary entry with the family and they sent me a copy of the film Sherm Shalley shot on the* Mopelia.

[2] *Carveth Wells was a cinematographer, writer and lecturer. Massee financed Wells' trip to the Mountains of the Moon in Africa, a mountain range once thought to be the source of the Nile River.*

[3] *Sherm Shalley was LT's staff cinematographer who also lived at Pawling and was a friend of my mother's.*

[4] *Naturalist Beebe developed a bathysphere to explore underwater reefs at Nonesuch Island. Massee was a fellow of the National Geographic Society and one of the backers of Beebe's research.*

[5] *Hard as it is to imagine, and in spite of the distractions, my mother did work. Thomas' second book about von Luckner,* The Sea Devil's Fo'c'sle, *was published at the end of the year, and he inscribed the flyleaf, "Dear Josephine: You did so much work on this that you really ought to autograph it to yourself."*

[6] *General Rafael Trujillo, who seized power in a military coup the following year and controlled the Dominican Republic until his assassination in 1961.*

12
1930 TO 1932
Jo Falls in Love

Jo the summer she met my father, 1930.

*"In 1932 I discovered I was going to have a baby and my husband's family
import business succumbed to the Depression."*

In June of 1930, my mother, now living in an apartment on 112th Street, on Manhattan's upper West Side, felt the initial pinch of what history would call the Great Depression. By the end of the month she moved to a farm in Washingtonville, northwest of West Point, New York. She complained to Marian:

"My work for Lowell is very sporadic; I just don't have enough money any more. I really have to be awfully economical until I get this book out. I came out from New York a week ago to this farm up the Hudson, where it will be cooler, but still near enough so that I can run into New York as necessary. It got very hot in the city, and very noisy with the windows open… I am so immersed in this book I think of nothing else."

Although Josephine might have tried to think of nothing else other than her book, at thirty-two, she fell in love with a man who distracted her from both work and financial worries. This was not one of the girlish crushes of the Washington years, but real love, and with a man whose Aunt Margaret had just left him a houseful of furniture and a portfolio worth $100,000 dollars. What surprises me, is that after so many entries in her Washington diary about a man not being tall enough, she chose a man an inch shorter than she was. Very handsome, but shorter.

Jo wrote a catch-up letter to her Michigan friend Elsie Scheurer:

"Lowell Thomas had put up his young English friend Don Gillingham at the Explorers Club in New York. He knew few people, and would rather lonesomely come around to talk shop with me. He and I were both doing research for LT at the public library on Forty-Second Street. One day he brought with him another man from the club; that man was Reynold Thomas (No, he is no relation to LT) — and that was my finish. Then I had an idea I wanted to write a book for myself, and took the summer off and went to a farm in New York State to do it. I did finish half — that was pretty good considering that Reynold was coming courting when I would be in the middle of my best paragraphs. I couldn't believe it at first, but he wanted the same things I did, not life in a big city, but somewhere with a yard, a place for flowers and vegetables and fruit trees."

I never found any remnants of the book my mother was writing nor did she ever mention it to me. I can only assume that either she was dissatisfied with the manuscript and destroyed it, or that it was lost in various moves. As she was rigorous in saving so much, I think she must have discarded it. I can picture her the summer she died, as she sat in a pink quilted housecoat by her desk, ripping papers and tossing them into the wastebasket. I was so involved with my own life that I never asked what she was throwing away.

After almost a decade of wandering, the Depression brought my father to New York City. When he met Jo he was taking business courses at Columbia University and working as a salesman for American Dyewood Co., where his Grandfather Percival Thomas had been CEO. After he returned from Germany in 1920 — where he had remained in the Army of Occupation after fighting in some of the deadliest battles of the World War — he moved from place to place and job to job. He homesteaded in Utah, worked in his uncle's eelgrass business in Harvey Cedars, New Jersey, ran a dairy in Chincoteague, Virginia and considered rejoining the Marines. Before the stock market crashed, my father moved to New York, where he lodged at the Explorers Club and signed up for business courses at Columbia.

Jo's letter to Elsie continues:

"When I came back from the farm in the autumn of 1930 I was torn away from my book by LT, who had just got his radio contract to broadcast for the *Literary Digest*, and for the rest of that year I helped write the news program every day. In odd times I did some work getting material for his Fox Film Movietone job, which was just beginning. I tried to polish up my own book and finish it, but it meant quicker money working for LT than for myself."

In an unpublished manuscript titled "Early Days in Radio, How It All Started," Thomas recalled his first months on the air: "In those days my staff included an unusual young woman who for years had been associated with Frank G. Carpenter, of high school Geographical Reader renown. After his death, his resourceful and experienced editor, who knew almost as much about the world and its inhabitants as her former employer, joined me. For several years I had been using her mainly for research... In her field I doubt whether Josephine Lehman had a peer."

In February 1931, my parents paid $2 for a license and married secretly at the New York City Hall. They lived in her apartment, very near the Cathedral of St. John and Columbia University, and near enough to Riverside Drive to overlook the Hudson River. They used to laugh and exchange an intimate look when they alluded to the blinking lights at the Palisades Amusement Park across the river in New Jersey. In November of that year, my mother received an enigmatic letter written from a friend that hints at a possible pregnancy: "I'm so sorry to hear you are sick but I imagine the complications at the present moment are better than if they were nine months later. I do hope you are all right now. For God's sake, be careful in the future!" She might have miscarried, or had an abortion because they had so little money and felt they could not afford a child.

In New York, my mother researched Lowell Thomas' biography about Sir Hubert Wilkins, *Sir Hubert Wilkins: His World of Adventure*. In the spring she left for Quantico, Virginia where for three months she lived at the Marine Corps base with General and Mrs. Smedley Butler until she "dug up enough material from him to do a story of his life." In LT's archives, I found a 1977 letter to Thomas written by one Hans Schmidt from the University of Zambia, with a reference to my mother's involvement in Butler's biography, *Old Gimlet Eye*. Schmidt was writing his biography of Butler, and asked Thomas, "Would you care to comment on an anecdote passed on to me by one of Butler's sons to the effect that *Old Gimlet Eye* was dictated by Butler to Josephine Lehman in Quantico, and that you never appeared there?"

That summer of 1931, while my mother worked in Quantico, my father bounced back and forth between Harvey Cedars, where he tried to find a house they could afford and where he was having a boat built, and attending to his mother in Ridgewood, New Jersey. Ridgewood is about fifteen miles west of the George Washington Bridge, (which would open that October) and convenient to New York, but isolated from the bustle and crowding of closer suburban towns. The bucolic village played a large part in my family's early years. My grandmother rented a comfortable Dutch-colonial home on Lincoln Avenue that she sometimes shared with my divorced Aunt Dorothy, my father's older sister, and Dorothy's son Bobby. (Aunt Dot was a free-lance writer and a publicity agent for various companies.)

My mother saved her husband's letters from that summer, written from Harvey Cedars. He had still not told his mother they were married. In early July he wrote:

"Mildred came down Saturday with George (his younger sister and her son). I had planned to tell Mother that we were married before they arrived but hadn't done it.

"I hate to mention how the boat's coming on — damn the soul of that Barnegat builder, the engine is scarcely in. If he just keeps poking along I'm going to take the job away from him. It's sure discouraging — and I'm getting so broke it's becoming serious. I hope to have her overboard in the early part of next week. I hear that bluefish are starting to run.

"There are quite a few cottages available but the damn pirates want $25 a week for one with electricity and bath but I could never pay that much. I'm still on the lookout. As soon as the boat gets overboard I'll get after it. Be sure and let me know as soon as you've an idea when you'll be coming so I can have things ready for you. I hope you'll be finishing this trip sooner than you expected, having so much material already in hand.

Good luck and speed to your work and Love Galore, Tommy."

A few weeks later my father wrote:

"I shan't ask you to pretend to your friends you're not married anymore, dear. I'll finish telling mother as soon as I see her." A fragment of a note in my mother's writing was inserted in the envelope with her husband's letter: "Dearest and best of husbands: I am at my desk editing the manuscript. But the General has gone out for a few minutes and perhaps there will be time for this letter to be finished…"

I don't know why my parents kept the marriage a secret — I didn't even know they had until I saw these letters. Daddy was very close to his mother, who was distraught with her own marital problems, and I think Daddy was timorous about exposing his own happiness.[1]

August 25

"Jodear — It was good hearing your voice last night, but how much more to have been able to see the lips it passed through. I said I was going to write as soon as I hung up, but forgot that we had no power in the house, just one candle. Today is the fifth day of storms and I've not been able to do a damn thing. My boat went back on the ways over a week ago. If the weather breaks it is coming off Tuesday or Wednesday so we can have one day of fishing. This is all costing us more money. Oh, I took out some insurance the other day — don't hit me lady — $2 a month — $580 when I die naturally, a thousand if by accident. I figured I could stand two bucks a month and that the $500 would pay my funeral expenses.

"Your idea of getting a cottage for the fall was a good one. I've got a wide eye on a peach, too. They never rent, but this year expenses are heavy and income low and the owners are disgusted with the weather. They suggested their house for me and my bride. I told 'em OK but no price was mentioned. I'll offer them $125 for six or eight weeks.

"When you get here I'll make a double effort to try and make you happy and comfortable. I certainly am unhappy at dragging you into this miserable family mess of mine. If I could make some money a lot of this would be eased. Let me know as soon as you are ready for me to come for you — and don't make it too far off. I'll be there if I have to hock the goddam boat. In the meantime, dear lovely wife — enjoy yourself all you can and remember me now and then, and write, and love this miserable wart. Kisses, Tommy"

My mother finished her work in Quantico and they spent the end of August and the fall in Harvey Cedars. By early November they were back on 112th Street My mother wrapped up *Old Gimlet Eye* and, as their investment income dried up — stocks dropped 90 percent from 1929 to 1932 — my father was trying to figure out a way to make some money. On December 28th he penciled a brief note from Ridgewood:

"Good morning dear — I hope you were comfortable and settled in and slept well last night. Personally, my bed was wide and empty. I hope you get quickly submerged in that book of yours and are happy with your work. I'll be in town some time Tuesday afternoon. I'll bring the typewriter. Love, Thomas — and I don't mean Lowell!"

My mother's catch-up letter to Elsie in Michigan concludes:

"In 1932 I discovered I was going to have a baby and my husband's family import business succumbed to the Depression. I was too ill for months to even look at a typewriter. (Excuse split infinitive.) We left New York and were living in Ridgewood with Reynold's mother. We finally decided we would come down to Harvey Cedars, as it would benefit us both in health. Reynold was very thin and jumpy from business and family worries, and for several months I could hardly hold my head up. He was gassed in the war and shell-shocked and was told by doctors he must live an outdoor life if he wanted to keep fit. We had just enough independent income to live on, but every time another dividend was passed we lived slimmer and slimmer. Reynold decided he could use his boat, his favorite plaything, for commercial fishing, and all that summer he went out with the deep-sea fishermen from Barnegat Inlet. By the end of the summer he was about $300 poorer than if he had just put the boat in dry-dock and twiddled his fingers. But, miraculously enough, he stopped having heart attacks for the first time in ten years."[2]

NOTES

[1] Before the war, Daddy's father, George Percival Thomas (a Catholic), had fallen in love with a vaudeville actress, Rose, and had two daughters (Rosemary in 1915 and Anne in 1918). He bounced back and forth between his wife and mistress and in 1928 asked for a divorce, but my grandmother (a Quaker) refused. In a letter to her lawyer she wrote, "I have lost the comfort of my husband, but I will not give up the comfort of his name." Her lawyer responded, "In considering the facts of your unfortunate position, your family has reason to be grateful to you for your restraint in the past, which has avoided scandal and front page notoriety." She sued for support because of "abandonment." A year later she was granted $125 a month from her husband's trust and one-third of any other income he received.

[2] What my mother called "heart attacks" were panic attacks, not diagnosed at the time. After World War I, soldiers who suffered what we know as post-traumatic stress disorder were called "shell-shocked." In January 1922, my father referred to these "spells" in a letter to Dorothy. He wrote: "I get funny spells every now and then — my legs give way from under me and I get hysterical. I'm ashamed but I can't seem to help it."

13
1933
Fisherman's Wife

My parents brought me to Harvey Cedars the summer of 1933

"If I can bring him into the world healthy and be a good mother to him, as I know you will be a good father, I'm willing to make the sacrifices."

In 1932, after my parents left Harvey Cedars, they returned to Ridgewood to await my birth — my mother was then three months pregnant. She wrote to her family in Michigan:

"We left the beach in November and came up to New York and Ridgewood for two or three weeks, then went back to the shore and closed up the cottage for the winter. We hadn't had the Franklin[1] for three months, as we couldn't afford to pay the bill to get it out of the garage (about $60 for new parts and repairs). Then Reynold made a connection with a travel bureau in New York, and now is in Florida for two weeks. That sounds rich, but he went down on business to make some arrangements with travel agents down there. He got the car and drove down, taking along four passengers, who paid all the expenses of the trip, so it cost him nothing, as he will bring other passengers back. The travel bureau gets passengers for people who want to drive someplace and want somebody to go along to help pay expenses, and Reynold made this trip for the experience. He will be back before Christmas and then we'll look for a new apartment in New York and stay there until summer."

My father's pencil-scrawled letters on hotel stationery, written along the Eastern Seaboard from New Jersey to St. Augustine, Florida, were a litany of love, loneliness and complaint. On one trip he wrote his wife:

"Jodear, I hope everything is going smoothly at mother's and in your precious stomach …This is a goddam rotten stinking world — in spots — when the margins shrink and I can barely make expenses — But then it's very sweet in other spots, you!"

Jo wrote back to him:

"Tommy Dearest. It's been so long since I wrote a letter that I started to say Dear Sir. Jean telephoned me today and wanted me to come in to New York to dinner and spend the night. I wanted to desperately, but I was working well, with genius crackling and sending sparks up the chimney, and my new dress was not finished, and my figure grows more and more like John Bull's. I put in a good day — from nine until three steady, except for an hour out to eat lunch, and I have something like 4,000 words of that fish story finished… I went out for a walk, but the sidewalks were not propitious for carefree strolling. Treacherous films of ice threatened the welfare of Reynold Thomas junior and I came home to take a nap.

"Oh, Tommy darling, I hope everything goes well and that the trip is worthwhile, in giving you a change of scenery even if not financially. You've been pretty close to the apron strings these last few months, but you've been such a comfort to me in the rough spots. When I've been physically miserable and nervous and unreasonable you've been grand. I really think the worst is over now and I'm looking forward to the little wretch.[2]

"If I can bring him into the world healthy and be a good mother to him, as I know you will be a good father, I'm willing to make the sacrifices. He's been doing somersaults and gymnastics more than usual today, probably as a protest against my sitting in one position so many hours. All this activity and squirming indicates the same yen for being on the move and going places that his old man has.

"I am going to bed now, and shall say good night to you after I get there. The bed grows larger during the night, and when I wake in the morning it seems very vast and uninhabited."

On February 10th, Jo brought her sister Marian up to date:

"Tommy's travel business cost more than he got out of it so now we are living on the income from his stocks and bonds, which isn't enough to pay for any luxuries, and we are still here with his mother in Ridgewood, but I want to find a place of our own before the baby comes. I haven't written for a long time because I didn't feel so well, but now I am fine again except awfully big and awfully lazy. I weigh 170 pounds and the doctor doesn't want me to get any heavier, so for every pound the baby puts on I am supposed to lose one... My doctor says I am getting along fine. My feet and legs don't swell any more. He says I am going to have a young elephant. I seem to have a tumor, so he is trying to keep little 'it' as small as possible. Tommy and I have a lot of fun out of life, limited as our pleasures are. I am so heavy I weigh my side of the bed down and Tommy is always rolling down the slope. He insists that I have trained 'little Tommy' to kick him every time he lands on me.

"This hospital where I am going seems very modern and satisfactory.[3] I like their ideas about babies. They say to feed them every four hours and they are less likely to colic, as it gives their stomachs a chance to empty before another feeding. They don't use long-sleeved wool shirts except for a trip out in the cold but they put on a little cotton mesh sleeveless shirt, a diaper and one other garment — a slip, kimono or a dress. Then you regulate the rest of its clothes (according to temperature) by sweaters. They say its best to have the wool on the outside instead of next to a baby's tender skin. It sounds sensible to me. My sister-in-law just brought me a big package of those new paper diapers, like Kleenex.[4]

"I am sending you a carbon of a story I did about life down at the shore. Being very personal, I changed a few details, but in the main it is true... The original is going the rounds of the editors. Don't be so conscientious you can't slip in a letter to me once in a while when you're at the office. All my love, Josie."

My mother sold her article, "Fisherman's Wife," to *Scribner's* magazine for $500 and, in July 1933, three months after I was born, she published it anonymously. My mother didn't use her name because she didn't want her friends in New York to know how difficult life was for them. She changed "Jo" to "Ann." I have restored her name.

Fisherman's Wife

The wind off the Atlantic is raw at four o'clock in the morning, even in summer, and I pull my sweater closer about my throat as Tom and I walk down the sandy road between the tarpaper shacks where the fishermen live. The long, low fish shed on the dock and the high round shaft of Barnegat Lighthouse are beginning to take form out of the darkness. The slightly sour smell of Barnegat Bay salt marshes is strong in the air.

The waves lap softly against the fishing skiffs tied in orderly rows along the breakwater. The fishermen, awkward in rubber hip boots and stiff yellow oilskins, shuffle clumsily past the piles of wooden boxes and wire baskets to stow their gear and tin lunch cans in their boats. They make their preparations swiftly and with little to say beyond an occasional speculative comment about the weather.

"What you think about it, Axel?" The names one hears are like that — Axel and Olaf, Sven and Hans. Except for Tom and two or three native Barnegaters, these men of the fishing fleet are Scandinavians with the blood of seafaring Norsemen in their veins.

Axel scans the sky, the stars overhead, the faint pinkish glow on the eastern horizon. "Looks all right to me."

The other is getting the feel of the wind. "I don't think she shift before night."

Tom climbs down into his skiff and does something with a monkey wrench. There is a staccato sputter, and the motor starts with a roar. As it warms up, he pulls on oilskins and boots, and listens to the speculation about the weather. Axel, the acknowledged weather prophet, takes another long look at the sky.

"I think she is a good day. I shove off," he announces.

When one man starts the others follow. Tom kisses me good-bye, and Olaf Svenson in the next boat looks embarrassed and nudges his partner. These Scandinavians would rather lose a day's catch of fish than be seen in a public gesture of affection toward their wives.

Lines are cast off, motors throttled down, and one by one the huge gray sea-skiffs slip out of the dock basin. Tom's boat leaves a scimitar of foam in its wake as it rounds a bend in the channel and disappears behind the low sand dunes, and I have my last glimpse of him as he stands at the tiller, fastening his oilskins more securely. It will be wet going through the narrow inlet where the tide is running swiftly out of Barnegat Bay and meeting the big rollers of the Atlantic.

The last boat is lost in the early morning grayness, and inside me is the dull emptiness I feel every time Tom puts to sea. I walk back down the road to where the Model T is parked, beside the little lunchroom where two fish-truck drivers are going in for early morning coffee and fried potatoes. They glance at me curiously as I hurry along, and one asks the other a question. The answer comes to me clearly in the still morning air:

"Her? Oh, just one of the fishermen's wives."

When Tom and I married, two years ago, my excellent journalistic salary, Tom's business, and the interest from his inherited securities gave us an income of almost a thousand dollars a month. Now we have not that much in a year. The business failed after being nursed through a year of steady losses. My salary ceased because of sickness and an ill-timed venture into freelancing. The income from our securities has shrunk two-thirds, chiefly because the aunt who bequeathed most of them to Tom had such unquestionable faith in South American bonds.

After months of forced idleness and fruitless search for a paying job, Tom had become sallow and thin, harassed by nervous indigestion and insomnia. To add to his worries, I discovered I was going to have a baby. The beginning of summer found us with few tangible assets, not counting the kind known as frozen, except a quantity of furniture (and no place to put it), an expensive automobile we could not afford to use, and a motor boat acquired in the last year of our prosperity and still unfinished.

Tom had spent his summers since childhood on Barnegat Bay, and his boat was the same type of huge oceangoing skiff the Barnegat fishermen use. That boat was more than a hobby to him — it was practically a mistress, the recipient of secret extravagances, the occasion for numerous trips, ostensibly to "see a man in Philadelphia," which invariably were made by the roundabout and wholly illogical way of Barnegat. We couldn't afford to keep the car, but I knew Tom would rather pawn his clothes than sell the boat. He decided to convert it from an expensive plaything into a commercial investment, and join the fishing fleet.

The fishing village clusters around Barnegat Lighthouse on the long sliver of island that lies six miles off the New Jersey shore between Barnegat Bay and the Atlantic. A mile or so down the road we found a scantily furnished cottage for twenty-five dollars a month, where one cooked and ate and lived and entertained in the same room. I did things to its glaring whitewashed walls with blue and red chintz, while Tom worked from dawn to dark fitting the skiff with what his optimistic nature considered the minimum of necessary equipment.

When the boat was being built, we pored over plans for trim-lined cabins and gay awninged cockpits where one served tall cold drinks in nautically monogrammed sea-going china and crystal. We made long lists of bronze and chromium fittings, chronome-ters, shining binnacles — all the enticing gadgets the more expensive yachting magazines advertise. Before we could buy them the money was gone, and instead of a smart cabin cruiser, we owned an open twenty-six-footer with no equipment except the powerful motor. Tom added fishing gear, three soggy life preservers, a homemade anchor, and a second-hand compass always at least four points off. He hired a native Barnegater as fishing partner, paid thirty dollars for a ten-year-old Model T to provide transportation between house and dock, and in a week was ready to go to sea.

A deep-sea fisherman's day begins at a quarter past three. There is no sign of dawn when we are wrenched awake by the strident alarm clock. Half asleep, I fumble for slip-pers and warm bathrobe. (The peach satin negligee that cost more than the Model T is packed away in New York.) I awake by degrees as I go through the routine of breakfast. Coffee on one burner of the smoky oil stove; water for the eggs on the other. The pound-ing of the surf sounds ominously loud to me. As I dash cold water on my face at the kitch-en sink, I am thinking about the treacherous bar at the inlet. I squeeze the oranges, fetch cream and bread and marmalade from the little icebox, and dress in snatches — woolen slacks, jumper and sneakers, a comb through my hair. Thank God I had that permanent. There is no time to put on powder or lipstick. My face looks pinched and old to me, and I hope Tom is too sleepy to notice.

The stove will not burn, and the first waves of early morning nausea make me short-tempered. "Damn it, darling, will you *please* not take my stove matches away." Tom says he is sorry, and I am ashamed. He is never irritable before breakfast or any other time.

He eats while I pack his lunch in a tin biscuit can. The four sandwiches. Two apples. The slab of chocolate cake. A bottle of lemonade. While he goes out to crank the Model

T, I manage a few swallows of orange juice, but my stomach revolts at coffee. I put on an extra sweater and ride with him to the dock to bring back the car.

If I am too ill, or do not want the car during the day, Tom goes alone. I stand at the window and watch the red rear light of the Model T until it is lost around a curve. A fish truck returning from a night trip to Philadelphia rumbles past and disappears, its clatter drowned by the boom of the surf. Then there is nothing but the dark empty road and the thundering Atlantic. "Please God, don't let the bar be too rough," I pray, as I prayed for things when I was a child. I put the butter and cream into the icebox and try to go back to sleep. The bed seems wide and empty. In the east are the first flaming streaks of dawn.

Slowly and laboriously, I grew accustomed to the new routine. For two months I was wretched and ill most of each day, and given to morbid brooding over our poverty. In my heart I knew that Tom's smile and the way he writes "JoDear" as one word meant more to me than all the money in the world — but as I dragged miserably through the morning housework, every domestic task seemed laden with reminders of another life. Washing the blue and red breakfast dishes brought back memories of Prague and the day my Vienna-bound plane was halted there by fog. Ironing my best embroidered napkins and table runners, I saw the crooked sun-drenched street in Rome where I paid three times too much for them. And emptying the ash trays with the crossed-sabre trademark invoked a gay picture of the January day I bought them in Dresden — afternoon coffee and *belegtes brotchen* at a table overlooking the ice cakes floating down the Elbe, the orchestra playing the latest seductive tango. All that was another existence, and that young woman was someone else, someone whose confident plans for the future had nothing to do with being a fisherman's wife on a barren island off the Jersey coast.

Lunch and a cup of hot tea usually induced a more cheerful mood. In the afternoons I walked far up the beach to lie in the sun on the hard white sand, alone except for a steamer crawling along the horizon, the gulls wheeling overhead, and the flocks of solemn little sandpipers, wholly absorbed in their own pursuits, running stiff-legged over the sand. I spent long drowsy hours there by the dunes, content to listen to the sound of the surf, captivated by the changing moods of the sea, until I grew to understand the lure it has for Tom, to comprehend how one can both love and hate it as one loves and hates a mistress who holds him in her spell.

One day is much like another. By four o'clock I begin to look for Tom. I go back to the cottage, prepare vegetables, try to read. By six o'clock I know he will be there any moment, and I put the potatoes and dessert into the oven. Forty minutes later I turn down the fire to retard the cooking, and sit at the window watching the automobiles coming around the bend in the road. By eight o'clock my imagination has encompassed every possible calamity that could beset him.

I remember the two Norwegians, veteran fishermen for twenty years, who were lost when their skiff capsized on the bar last year. I think about the bad heart Tom has had ever since Belleau Wood. It begins to rain, and I go down to the beach to see if the surf is heavier.

By nine o'clock I am numb and choked from worrying, and when at last Tom strides in, ruddy and glowing from the rain and preceded by a strong odor of fish, I cry weakly down his neck and search futilely for my handkerchief. He offers me his own, one of his best monogrammed ones, which has evidently been used to clean out the fish bin.

"Never mind, honey, let 'em drip. You can't make me any wetter. I'm sorry I'm so late, Jo. We had a swell catch and I didn't want to leave."

I light the stove again and bring his dressing gown and slippers while he peels off his wet clothes and drops them out of the window to air.

"My God, I'm hungry. Is that Brown Betty I smell? Come back here; you get another kiss. Look, JoDear, do I have to wash all over first?"

The fishy odor he exudes makes me deathly sick, but I compromise. "All right, just your hands and face then, and finish afterward." I hurry to put the food on the table. "You shouldn't go so long without eating. It must be ten hours."

"Thirteen."

"Thirteen what?"

"Thirteen hours since food." His voice is indistinct from baked potato and omelet. "I got hungry as a bear at nine o'clock this morning and polished off my lunch."

"Oh, Tom, all of it?"

"Well, no, but I gave the rest to Bill. He didn't have any breakfast."

Bill is another fisherman — a tall young Finlander, hair unbelievably yellow, shoulders unbelievably broad, and the coat of arms of Finland tattooed in violent blue on his powerful forearms. Tom brought him home to lunch one day. He speaks English slowly and carefully and pleasantly, but was ill at ease and inarticulate at first, and had to be urged to eat. He was puzzled by the cold jellied-beef consommé, and embarrassed by the extra spoon and the napkin. Both Tom and I liked him immensely.

Bill came often after his first shyness had gone. On rainy days he and Tom burrowed into our collection of yachting magazines and marine catalogs, and spent hours discussing trawling and squidding, self-bailing hulls, clinker construction, and other subjects unintelligible to me. Bill could not understand anyone's being afraid of the sea, as I was, and despite warning glances and surreptitious kicks from Tom he innocently divulged in his conversation all the nautical mishaps my well-meaning husband tried to conceal from me: Tom's rudder unshipped by a heavy following sea on the bar, the dead engine twenty miles at sea and the four-hour wait until a Coast Guard cutter saw his distress signal (his pale blue B.V.D.'s flying aloft), the number of times he went out without a compass or life preservers. Tom will never learn to take life preservers seriously.

Tom was anxious for me to go on a fishing trip to convince me it was merely a prosaic day's work. After waiting weeks, a day finally came when the weather report and my internal state were simultaneously favorable. We were off in the Model T together, through the daybreak scenes that had grown so familiar — the stunted cedars and silver-green bayberry bushes ghostly and shadowy on the white dunes, Barnegat Bay flat and calm to the west of the island, the pounding surf and rosy sky to the east, and the red and white buildings of the Coast Guard station with the charming name of Loveladies.

We shoved off as soon as we reached the dock, rounded the end of the island under the long beams Barnegat Light threw far out to sea, and approached the bar. There was just enough daylight to see the buoys. Tom was at the tiller, and Jim, his fishing partner, stood at the motor controls to adjust the speed at Tom's orders to meet the incoming seas. The big skiff breasted them beautifully, and ten minutes later we were riding the long even swells of the Atlantic. The throttle was opened wider, and a compass course set for the "ridge" — the shallow banks twenty miles offshore where the schools of bluefish run. It takes more than an hour to reach there, and the fish bite best at daybreak.

We passed the lightship nine miles out at sea. Turning to say something to Tom, I discovered the shoreline had disappeared behind the horizon. We were out of sight of land, and the skiff seemed very small in the wide expanse of water. I was glad of the half dozen other fishing boats nearby.

"Are you all right, Jo?" Tom was shouting above the roar of the unmuffled engine.

"Fine," I lied, sucking surreptitiously at the lemon I had put in my sweater pocket. Tom smoked at the tiller, and Jim, lazily chewing tobacco, began cutting up mossbunker, the oily fish used as bait. They were mossbunker that had been dead a long time, and I moved to windward of them.

We sighted the high masts of the big sailing smacks that come down here from New York, and altered course toward them. After cruising around to see which of the other skiffs were "pulling," we selected a spot not far from Axel, who has an uncanny instinct for finding fish if fish are to be found. The engine was stopped, the anchor lowered, and Jim began "grinding," putting the moss bunker bait through what looked like an over-sized kitchen meat chopper attached to the starboard gunwale of the skiff. The nauseous mess that emerged was thrown overboard a handful at a time. The oil in it smoothed the water and made a slick on the surface. Then larger pieces of the bait were put on the two lines let over the stern into the slick. Tom attended to the lines and Jim to the grinder. We waited five minutes, ten. I was eager and impatient, and anxious to help. Another five minutes. There was a flash of brilliant blue just under the surface, then another and another. The water became radiant with streaks of bright color. We had found a big school of bluefish. They were attracted by the slick, and darted greedily at the largest particles of bait in the water — the ones with the hooks inside.

The fish bit as fast as they could be pulled in and unhooked. Tom put on a pair of old leather gloves to protect his fingers from the wet lines and also from possible bites from vindictive victims. All about us, other boats were pulling in fully as many. The fish were biting so fast Tom could not attend to both lines, and I helped him bait the hooks, in my excitement and enthusiasm forgetting my distaste for the mossbunkers. Even the stoical Scandinavians grow excited over a catch like this.

"Look at the size of this baby, Jo." I admired it and Tom tossed the big blue into the bin.

A six-pounder lunged off Jim's hook, and the lanky Barnegater spat a resentful stream of tobacco juice after it. "God damn, there goes fifty cents."

The fish bit steadily until the bin was more than half full. Then the flashes of blue in the water grew scarcer, and it was several minutes between bites. The three of us amused ourselves throwing bits of bait to the flocks of Mother Carey's chickens twittering over the water. Watching the little birds catch the tidbits in midair, I realized I was very hungry, although it was still long before noon. We opened the lunch tin and ate sandwiches ravenously out of unspeakably dirty hands.

The midday sun was warm, and after the last sandwich had disappeared I took off my heavy hip boots and yellow oilskins and stretched out forward for a nap. When I awoke, a half dozen more fish had been caught but none of the skiffs had repeated the luck of early morning. Toward five o'clock, one boat started for shore, and the others raised anchor and followed.

A stiff westerly breeze had come up. We began to ship water, and I put on my oilskins and boots again. The waves grew higher as we neared the bar. I was very tired by this time, and worried about going through the inlet. Tom showed no apprehension, but his remark that "it's always worse coming back than going out" did nothing to allay my fears. I started to go forward — because the life jackets were stowed in the bow.

"Stay back here," Tom called sharply from the tiller. He knew the bow must be light to help the skiff ride the seas and keep her from burying her nose as she slid down into the trough of the waves. I clutched the gunwale in unconcealed terror as sea after sea rose into high curling crests and crashed into churning foam around us. This was the place where the two Norwegians were drowned. In that pounding surf even a good swimmer would have little chance.

Then suddenly we were through, and rounding the lighthouse into the bay. Throttles were wide open as each boat tried to reach the dock first. There was the noise of the ice crushers as we nosed in and tied up. Heavy baskets of fish were swung lightly from boat to dock — not only bluefish, but flounder and weakfish and sea bass, and squirming gray lobsters making futile slaps at their captors with their claws. The news of the big catch had been brought in by the first arrivals, and already trucks were backed up to the dock shed to load the fish and start the night drive to Philadelphia and New York.

The smell of fish and gasoline sickened me, and I walked down the road while Tom made fast the skiff. Around me the lobster pots and buoys were stacked everywhere, nets were stretched to dry, and boats lay pulled out to have their bottoms copper painted. I sat on an overturned lobster pot and listened to the sounds from the waterfront — broken clam shells crunching under foot as the fishermen hurried away to hot food and coffee, the chopping of ice, the thump of heavy boxes, the snorting trucks. The sound of the surf on the other side of the island was faint and dull. It was good to be on land again.

We brought in eleven hundred pounds of fish in that catch, more than a half ton after they were gutted, but the wholesale price was only four cents a pound. After paying for ice and boxes, shipping and commissions, gasoline and oil and bait, and sharing the proceeds with his partner, there was less than ten dollars left for Tom for the day's work.

And that was a good catch, one of the best of the season.

Often Tom did not make expenses. There were days when the bluefish could not be found, other days when they refused to bite for some reason known only to themselves. Or the sea was too choppy for fishing, and the end of a sixteen-hour working day would find Tom coming home exhausted and white and seasick, with nothing to show for seven dollars' worth of bait and gasoline except three small bluefish and a worthless young shark.

"And I used to do this for fun," he marveled.

There were long stretches of squally weather, when no boats ventured outside the bay, and the fishermen overhauled their engines and mended their gear, talking of the old days, two or three years ago, when bluefish sold in Fulton Market for fifty cents a pound, and five-hundred-dollar catches were not unusual.

For three weeks Tom did not have a catch big enough to pay expenses, and there was one weekend when we had nothing to eat but boiled rice and apples. As a last resort, he offered himself and the skiff for hire, to take weekenders deep sea fishing. A party of Philadelphians engaged him every Sunday for six weeks, and were satisfied if they caught one bluefish apiece to uphold their piscatorial reputations. They paid Tom twenty dollars a trip, and once they brought him a gift of old clothes — a half dozen coats and trousers of the type known ten years ago as "cake eater." I was first amused, thinking of the excellently tailored suits hanging unused in Tom's wardrobe, then indignant.

"How could they? Can't they see you're different?"

"The only way I'm different is that I'm not half so good a fisherman as the Squareheads. I don't look any different, you know."

He was right. In disreputable dungarees or oilskins, face and hands smeared with grease and perspiration, all men look pretty much alike. Tom's hands were never wholly clean any more, and his nails defied the stoutest mechanic's soap. He grew careless about shaving, and had his hair cut only when the tendrils began to curl about his ears.

These things no longer seemed important to me. I was content that he was growing strong and brown again, that the whites of his eyes were white instead of yellow, that the box of bicarbonate of soda stood neglected on the kitchen shelf, and that he slept the sleep of healthy fatigue and grinned at me when I shook him awake.

My own attacks of illness began to abate, and keeping house grew less laborious. The same grim satisfaction I once felt over scooping a rival foreign correspondent was now aroused by achieving a perfectly cooked meal, or ironing Tom's shirts without leaving a wrinkle in the collar. Doing my own washing and hanging clothes out on a line seemed a balder admission of poverty than any we had yet made, and at first I hung the wet things over an inadequate five-foot length of twine above the stove, where they remained damp for three days. After a month of this I said "what the Hell?" and put everything out to flap in the sun and wind and dry in two hours. After the first time, I didn't mind.

When the Sunday fishing party came no more with its weekly twenty dollars, I learned to practice economies I would have considered flatly impossible two years ago. I understood that the United States Army ration allows twelve cents a meal for food, but the best I could do was thirteen. Searching for sales on rice, butter, flour, and sugar, I dreamed of a shopping list that would again include mushrooms, Camembert cheese, sweetbreads — luxuries that are outlawed when every nickel is counted for staples.

By September I was reduced to my last pair of stockings, even though I had gone barelegged all summer. Three-dollar face powder and thirty-dollar French perfume were merely memories, and my toilet articles came from the five-and-ten.

We learned to take pleasure in simple things — our nightly extravagance of ice cream cones (the small five-cent ones) from the general store, an occasional movie, Tom being at home for a leisurely Sunday morning breakfast of waffles and both of us trying to get the *Times* book review first, the yellow-haired Bill bringing us a basket of succulent baby lobsters. They were "bootleg" lobsters, below the minimum legal size, but we asked no questions.

It was a gala day when Tom came home with a bunch of golden calendulas bought at a wayside stand on the mainland, for few flowers grow on this sandy island. Their tawny brightness recalled the talisman roses that played a persuasive role in his courtship.

"They only cost ten cents a dozen," he admitted. "I remembered you liked yellow."

The ten cents was the amount he allowed himself daily for the cheap cigarettes he had substituted for his favorite brand.

The months passed. The scrub cedars that cling precariously to the white dunes turned a duller green, the bayberry bushes grew brown, the summer bathers were gone, and the long white beach was left to the gulls and sandpipers. The wild ducks and geese began to fly south, and the sound of firing was heard all day from the shooting blinds in the marshes across the bay. Heavy autumn fogs hung over the island, and at night the hoarse uneasy rumble of the fog horns of passing steamers punctuated the boom of the surf.

One day there was an ominous sky, a long ground swell, and an uncertain wind that veered and shifted. The barometer fell steadily, and the surf pounded more heavily. In the afternoon Tom brought his boat from the fishing dock and anchored it in a cove of the bay near the cottage to have it within sight.

That night the first northeaster came howling out of the Atlantic. The cottage shook and quivered in the sharp gusts, and the rain dashed against the panes like handfuls of gravel. The electric current was off, and Tom stumbled about barefoot in the dark, closing windows, swearing fluently when he stepped on the sharp heels of my overturned bedroom slippers. In ten minutes he was asleep again, but I lay awake listening to the wind, and plagued by the vague worries and forebodings a pregnant woman has in the night. I knew this was the beginning of winter, and we had to plan what to do when we left the island — to face again the disheartening search for a job.

Tom heard me stirring and turning and asked if I was all right. "I can't sleep either," he lied. "Let's play rummy."

He lighted a candle, wrapped my bathrobe around my shoulders, and dragged out a hatbox to put between us in bed for a card table. It was pleasant and intimate in the little circle of candlelight, with the cards clicking down on the gay pink and black stripes of the pasteboard hatbox. The box bore the name of a great establishment in the rue St.-Honoré, and the 900 francs I paid for the scrap of black felt it originally contained did not seem excessive then. I lunched in the Bois that day — but Paris is far away and long ago, and Tom beside me concealing his own weariness to help me through a wakeful night is very real.

The gale raged through the night and the next day, shaking the little cottage until I feared it would be torn from its foundations. By mid-afternoon the sea was breaking over the bulkheads and through the dunes, and sweeping broken timbers as far as the post office. The high wind sent icy blasts through loose window sashes and under the doors, and I shivered in three sweaters as I stoked the little stove with driftwood.

The second morning of the northeaster the tide was over the island and the cottage was surrounded by water. In hip-boots and oilskins we waded through it to the beach, shutting our eyes and lowering our heads against the sand that whirled off the tops of the dunes and cut into the skin like powdered glass. On the other side of the dunes everything was gray and white — pale gray sky, lines of white breakers foaming to the horizon on the mountainous waves of a dark gray sea, white suds of spume and spindrift whirling over the sand. The rain lashed at our faces and the wind tore at our breath. Walking against it was like pushing a solid weight, and I made little more progress than the gulls that hovered almost motionless overhead as they tried to fly out to sea. The beach was deserted except for Tom and me and an occasional plucky little sandpiper.

The northeaster blew itself out, calmer weather followed, and other storms came and went. The bluefish season ended, and the fishermen changed to cod-fishing gear, although by this time there were only a few days each month when it was safe for the fleet to venture far outside.

Shut in together for days at a time by long stretches of stormy weather, I found it tragically easy to slump, physically and mentally, especially in the inertia natural to my condition. I had to force myself to put on a bright dress, to polish my nails and wave my hair, to cook Tom's favorite dishes, to manufacture foolish little surprises to stimulate and vivify the continual contact of marriage. Preserving an illusion of loveliness and romance is difficult when there is utter lack of privacy, when the only plumbing is at the kitchen sink, and icy draughts from outside make Spartan fortitude necessary for even the minimum of bathing. The "jolly little coarsenesses of life" are not always jolly.

Nevertheless, we were happy. It was a satisfaction to Tom to know he was providing a living for us, even by manual labor, and some answering primitive instinct made me content to cook and tend the hearth and breed. We stayed on the island until two months before the child was born, and when we left, we left reluctantly. Besides health, this simple elemental life, in all its barrenness and frugality, had given us a deeper feeling of fulfillment in marriage, the common bond of each having worked hard for the other. Something much finer was welded between us than we found in the first prosperous days of our marriage, when our lives followed two distinct paths and we couldn't afford a baby.

****

Four days after giving birth to nine-pound me, my mother wrote from the hospital to Marian:

"Little Maggie is a fine baby, big and plump and nicely shaped. It was a disappointment at first having the stork lose my requisition for a blue-eyed boy and sending me a black-eyed girl instead, but we decided to keep her just the same… She has an appetite just like her mother's and when they bring her in to nurse, she goes at it with both feet in the trough. I've hardly had time to make her acquaintance, however, because I still have this awful cold, and they put a mask over my face before they bring her in. She probably thinks she was born into the Ku Klux Klan."

Jo told her sister that the $500 she received from *Scribner's* would keep them for a year and that they had decided to live in Harvey Cedars[5] and she could make some money by writing. Soon afterwards, my parents settled into the house they rented from my father's uncle.

NOTES

[1] *In 1931, when my great-grandfather Thomas died and left my grandfather money, he bought a Franklin touring car, and my father used it in his ultimately unsuccessful travel business. I found the sales slip among my parents' papers; Grandfather paid almost $3,000, including $125 extra for a trunk. The Franklin Sedan model 145 pumped out 100 horsepower from an eight-cylinder engine. The market for luxury cars collapsed during the Depression, and the company declared bankruptcy in 1934.*

[2] *Wretch! My mother liked this descriptive; she used "wretch" to describe me before I was born and even afterward, when I was a small child; as in "If I ever catch you doing that again, you little wretch…" or, "Come here, you little wretch." She also called my brother and me "heathens" and "wild Indians." In those guilt-free, pre-Freudian days, children were often reminded that they were imperfect goods, in urgent need of finishing.*

[3] *The Park East Hospital, on East 84th Street, New York City. My mother saved the bill — $23.85, including $2.90 phone charge.*

[4] *This reference to paper diapers is a mystery; 1942 is the official year that the diaper industry states as the first manufacture of disposable diapers.*

[5] *My family had more than deep and strong roots in Harvey Cedars; my father's Kinsey forebears had founded the town. The Kinsey roots in New Jersey go back to 1677, when the first John Kinsey emigrated from England with the Quakers who followed William Penn. After the Civil War, newly mustered out of the New Jersey Volunteers, my father's grandfather, John Warner Kinsey, bought the Ashley House, a seasonal hotel near Barnegat Inlet, on the north end of Long Beach Island. In 1884 his son, my father's uncle, Josiah B. Kinsey, always known as JB, bought a large parcel of land and developed the small town of High Point, later renamed Harvey Cedars. Throughout my father's childhood, he and his family summered here until he left home in 1917 to fight in World War I. During the 1920s, he returned to the town often and it became his refuge as he tried to find his way in life.*

PART 2
Harvey Cedars

Clockwise from top: The house on Bay Terrace, 1935; Playing in a rowboat 1936; Storm tide surrounds the house, 1935; My mother, my brother Michael and me, 1936.

14
1933
The Move to the Island

My mother introduces me to the 80th Street beach

"To the east, more bayberry, goldenrod, morning glory, prickly weeds, wild roses, heather, and the grey-stemmed beach plum; and then a double row of dunes dimpled by sandy hollows, in the fall filled with the red glow of sumac and poison ivy. The high dunes blocked the view of the ocean, but we knew the sea was there. We could smell it."

Early in the summer of 1933 my parents made their most significant return to the island, and it is this trip that became the family legend. The myth was often revisited: My parents, both thirty-five years old, packed the trunk of the Franklin and headed south from Ridgewood. I lay innocent of the momentous change in my life, in my sturdy bassinet in the back seat, long before the advent of the child car seat or infant carrier. I know this bassinet was sturdy because three years later it held my brother and then, throughout the rest of my childhood, the laundry.

In 1933, the drive took four to five hours on two-lane cement roads; today it is a two-hour run from exit 163 to 63 on the Garden State Parkway. We drove through the silk-manufacturing city of Paterson, through Elizabeth, across the river from New York City, and onward south on Route 9 to Englishtown, where we stopped at the Village Inn for lunch, theirs and mine; the inn provided a private space where my mother could nurse me. Here — so the story is told — Daddy spilled his coffee on the red and white checked tablecloth and my mother offered to take the cloth home to wash and then return it on the next trip; but when the manager heard they were starting a new life along the shore he said, "Keep it." When I was three, my mother transformed it into a dress for me.[1]

Daddy turned west toward Freehold, and drove through horse country to pick up Route 9, the major north-south coastal road. In the early 1930s, New Jersey was rural and the ride south on Route 9 went through farmland until we reached Lakewood, a resort town surrounded by chicken farms. Whenever my mother spotted a handwritten sign, "Fresh Eggs," she stopped to buy some. She said the eggs reminded her of her family farm in Michigan. At Toms River, we reached the eastern edge of the Pine Barrens, a vast area of scrub pine and oak, with white sandy soil too acidic for farming, and Daddy always kept a watchful eye out for deer, which could bound out of the woods and leap across the road in one jump.

A highlight of later trips — I was too young on this initial journey — was the full-sized dinosaur statue at the side of the road in Bayville, just south of Toms River, that advertised "Sinclair." On later trips from Ridgewood, when we reached the dinosaur, with its gaudy green paint and toothy grin, I knew we would be home in an hour. We continued south through the Pine Barrens, and passed through the hamlets of Forked River ("Forked" always pronounced in the old English way, with two syllables) and Barnegat.

My father loved to recite the story of how his grandmother Emily Kinsey, pregnant with his mother, had come across the bay in a twenty-eight-foot catboat in an attempt to get home to Crosswicks to give birth, but only got as far as Barnegat, where his mother Evelyn was born.

Daddy drove the last six miles south to Manahawkin, a sleepy crossroads town surrounded by pinewoods and a few farms. We turned east through town at the main intersection by the National Hotel, where in 1944 my mother, brother and I would shelter from the great hurricane. We left the village and its streets lined with 19th century homes, and drove through a patch of woodland to the edge of the meadows — the salt marsh that borders Barnegat Bay along all undeveloped land on its west side. These tidal wetlands are laced with pools and creeks and are rich in organic matter. As soon as we emerged from the woods we smelled the pungent, sulfurous aroma of mud and decayed organisms mixed with the tang of the ocean, five miles across the bay, which shimmered in the afternoon sun.

The two-mile long, wooden plank causeway we crossed was only six feet above the water and lined on both sides with a four-foot high pipe railing. When the heavy Franklin drove onto it, the reverberation of tires on the loose boards made a grumbling, growling sound. Much later, when we lived in our house five miles north in Harvey Cedars, we could hear that rumbling, amplified by the volume of traffic on a Friday or Sunday evening, that the southwest breeze carried across the water. It was a distant, subdued roar, and I missed it when the state demolished the roadway.

In 1914, this first causeway was laid out parallel to the railroad trestle fifty feet to the north. It was too low to the water to afford a good view of the whole island to the right and left of us, but in 1958, at the apex of a high-arched new causeway, the narrow, eighteen-mile barrier island could be seen spread out ahead in two wings with the ocean beyond. My mother always rolled down the car window to smell the air and she would say, "Oh, smell the salt in that air." It was her oxygen. From the low roadway, we could spot the 172-foot, red and white Barnegat Lighthouse at the north end of the island, very close to the swirling, turbulent Barnegat Inlet — which was, in 1933, much too close; erosion had washed out the land around the base and the lighthouse was about to topple into the inlet. After four miles, the causeway touched down on a tiny marsh island, set out again over water, then landed on another island, this one with a few ramshackle cottages. A drawbridge over the last narrow channel led traffic onto Long Beach Island.[2]

From the top of the bridge, we got the first glimpse of wheaten, grass-covered dunes as we drove into Ship Bottom, the town in the middle of the island, and turned left at the intersection, then north through Surf City, another of the string of six island communities with a huddle of houses settled around a railroad station and hotel.

After twenty blocks lined with cottages, the natural, wild section of the island remained as the hustling waves and hissing winds had formed it. This was my mother's favorite part of the island. To the left (the west) of the narrow road and train track that bisected the island, were stands of bayberry, holly thickets, clumps of dusty miller, cattails and pink mallow and red cedar, and then the verdant meadows to the bay's shoreline. To the east, more bayberry, goldenrod, morning glory, prickly weeds, wild roses, heather, and the grey-stemmed beach plum; and then a double row of dunes dimpled by sandy hollows, in the fall filled with the red glow of sumac and poison ivy. The high dunes blocked the view of the wind-rumpled ocean, but we knew the sea was there. We could smell it. We could hear it roil, as the surf slammed onto the sand.

The Franklin cruised down the main road, past the red-roofed Coast Guard station on Cape May Avenue surrounded by a few cedar shake shacks built among the dunes, and past the vast, rambling, three-story mid-19th-century wooden Harvey Cedars hotel. Standing on a peninsula across a cove on the bayside, this was a significant landmark — the great wooden "castle" haunted my childhood. The Philadelphia YWCA had bought the hotel a few years earlier, but as the Depression deepened, the organization was forced to close it and the structure stood, with peeled paint, a ghost hotel. In 1941, a Bible Presbyterian Conference took over the building as a summer hotel, and after the war, painted and expanded it.

Another mile and we were in the middle of the 12-block long town that I could fairly describe as "ours." JB Kinsey had at one time owned most of the commercial structures and many of the rental cottages. In 1910 he built a general store with a single gas tank and a post office; he hauled an 1840s gunning club from Loveladies and converted it into an ice cream parlor and grocery store; his wife, Anna, ran a real-estate office, and he converted his old hay barn into a tavern (Prohibition had just been repealed). JB built the Harvey Cedars Inn, and a yacht club that he had started in 1917 on 78th Street was now located on the bay at 76th Street. All the side streets that led to the ocean a block to the east, and to the bay a block to the west, were gravel, and had, until recently, been sand. Small summer cottages perched here and there on spindly cedar pilings a few feet above sandy lots; a few had outhouses, but most had modern inside toilets and a cesspool — the putrid stink of an overflowing cesspool was unavoidable after a heavy rain. There were no lawns, no shrubs, no gardens — just sand, gravel, more sand, and some scrubby patches of bayberry bushes.

My parents drove past the tavern on 80th Street, at the end of which they would shortly build our new house, and then the final two blocks to one of JB's rental cottages on Kinsey Lane. This cottage, a sun-faded, clapboard, four-room bungalow faced Kinsey Cove. We stayed in that cottage until our house was finished. JB had owned all the land at the north end of town; beginning in the early twenties he sold it off, small lot by small lot. Much of this property surrounded Kinsey Cove. The oval cove had a meandering creek named, yes, Kinsey Creek, that led out to the bay from the northwest corner. Gravel-paved 80th Street went straight down the south side of the cove, two blocks long, with undeveloped land between it and the water — one boathouse stood in the middle of the block and one house at the end; none of the land was filled or graded, and flood tide submerged it. When 80th Street reached the bay, it curved right and ended; only a sandy path encircled the cove like a fishhook and continued to the spot where the creek joined the bay. JB sold Daddy a big piece of land in the middle of the peninsula between the bay and cove for practically nothing, and he, in turn, sold off some lots when times were tough during World War II. In 1938, a street, Bay Terrace, replaced that path. Today, it is my address.

July 15, 1933: "How are you, dear Marian? Fortunately I don't get so tired any more and Margaret has been almost angelic for a week. She'll be all right until some more company comes along to spoil her. It took me a week after some company left before she would go to sleep without howling, and then, when she was calm again, I upset things myself. July third was a special date for Tommy and me, and Tommy wanted to take me out to dinner. The woman who comes in occasionally couldn't come, so we put the bassinet on the back seat of the car, and after her six o'clock feeding we drove down to Beach Haven, the big resort with a boardwalk at the south end of the island, and ate in a restaurant where we had a table in the window where we could watch the car. Margaret slept beautifully through it all, and we had a lovely evening, but the next night she evidently craved traveling again, because she howled until I was distracted, and it was ten days until she consented to go to sleep quietly.

"Now she is functioning just like clockwork. Awakes at six sharp, eats, and goes back to sleep in her crib. At eight when I get up, she is awake, and I take her downstairs and ensconce her on the davenport, where she listens to the radio and plays with her fingers while we breakfast. She takes a very short afternoon nap, and then we go outside. I either wheel her in her coach, or we sit in the sun together, or Tommy takes us riding in the car if he is going places, which she just loves.

"She sleeps right through the radio, loud conversation and even this clacking typewriter, and is a great comfort to me. I could play with her for hours, if I only had the time. I never realized little girls were so sweet. I am making her a sunbonnet so I can take her down to the beach. She holds up her head all the time now, and can pull herself to a sitting posture on my fingers. But listen to proud mother rave about her child. I don't do it to people who don't have babies themselves, but having a sweet little girl of your own, you can sympathize."

My mother was big on lists and schedules. I found scribbled on the back of a yellowed *Scribner's* envelope, perhaps the one the $500 check had come in, an hourly schedule of her day with the new baby — what time she'd nurse, have breakfast, do housework, rest outdoors, write letters, prep dinner, and "write! 10:30 to 1:30."

August 15, 1933: "Dear Sis, I sent off to the Children's Bureau in Washington today for a long list of booklets on how to raise children (don't laugh). I get a lot of help and reassurance out of their publications. I am trying to finish another piece for *Scribner's* and hope to Heaven I can sell something more, because living in a tent would be awfully hard for little Margaret this winter, but there is so little time! If we were absolutely isolated, I might succeed better, but people drop in on us so often.

"Last Saturday was a hectic day. Margaret cried with the heat and I was trying to clean the whole house. I tied my hair in a towel and put on an old pair of dirty overalls and scrubbed and swept and dusted and cleaned. At six o'clock I was just finishing. The house was immaculate, even the garbage pail scrubbed, but I was a mess. I nursed the baby and put her to bed and wanted to just flop down as I was and rest. It's lucky I didn't. I heated water and took a bath and manicured and shampooed and set a water wave in my hair and put on a white sweater and clean white linen trousers and really looked quite like a summer vacationer with nothing to do. It was just seven when I walked into the living room and said to myself, "I wish someone would come once when my house and I are clean," and immediately a long, grey, swanky Lincoln stopped in front and there was Frances Thomas, LT's sister Pherbia, his secretary, another girl, little Sonny Thomas and another boy. I hadn't seen them for over a year except for the time Frances called after Margaret was born. They had read my *Scribner's* story and evidently expected to find me half starving and bent over a washtub, and they were all very elegant in sports clothes of the type I can no longer

155

afford. Just then Tommy came in with the boat and took us all for a ride on Barnegat Bay and then all six stayed for supper. They insisted we eat with them over at the inn, but I fixed scrambled eggs and bacon and toast and coffee and we set two tables and had a fine time. It was like old times and a glimpse of another life. With much love, from Tommy and Margaret and me, Josie."

Daddy wrote his mother in Ridgewood:

"Mr. Snyder has certainly made a dandy job of my boat. It looks absolutely ship-shape and as added much to its seaworthiness and comfort. She is now much more desirable for parties. He has sure worked hard — I can't slow him up. He says he's having a good time. The weather has been fitful and most of the time been damp and unpleasant. We have been quite comfortable in the house, though, with the oil stove. It is fine today except for a high wind. We expect to finish the boat Tuesday."

The fishing skiff that Mr. Snyder built was a new boat. The "pleasure boat" that my mother described in "Fisherman's Wife" did not actually exist — Daddy fished in another man's boat; as she wrote Marian, she "changed a few details" in the story. The Independent Dock in Barnegat Light — in 1948 the name was changed from Barnegat City (not to be confused with Barnegat on the mainland) — looks much the same as it did when my father fished there. It is still owned by one of the original Norwegian families.[3]

NOTES

[1] *The checked tablecloth dress reappears again, as if through familial alchemy, on a baby quilt my grandmother in Michigan sewed for my doll cradle. I found in the attic a cardboard carton that contained four of her quilted tops and one silk crazy quilt. I recognized some of the fabrics that had been my mother's dresses and then, to my delight, I saw the red and white checks, the final recycled use for the fateful tablecloth.*

[2] *To allow water traffic to continue on the narrow ribbon of deep water that was the Intracoastal Waterway, which extended from New Jersey to Florida, a boat captain blasted his horn to rouse the bridge keeper to raise the drawbridge. When I was a teenager, a friend and I sailed south down the bay just to see if the bridge tender would open it for us — the mast of our sailboat was too high to pass under. This action stopped traffic in both directions. He did raise the bridge, and a long line of cars waited while we, with satisfied smiles on our faces, sailed through; after fifteen minutes we tacked and sailed back north. This time, on to our prank, the bridge tender made us sit and stew at anchor until he was good and ready, and later he phoned my father. It was an early lesson on what I could not get away with on a small island, where everyone knew everyone, especially my father.*

[3] *Barnegat Light is headquarters for a major fishing industry, shipping scallops and fish to wholesalers between New York and Washington. Forty-three ocean-going fishing boats dock at the harbor under the shadow of Barnegat Lighthouse. The dock and fishing sheds have been restored and modernized to keep up with the industry, and the remaining bait and storage sheds are in their original line, perpendicular to the dock, although they have been tarted up and converted to shops. The complex is called Viking Village.*

15
1934 TO 1937
Struggling to Survive

My father and his sister, Milly Johnstone, on his first dredge.

"Reynold and his partner with the dredge are on the trail of a big contract for building streets down the island, and if they get it, it may mean a little extra money for us. The trouble is that they work and work, and the money they get hardly pays their expenses."

The winter of 1933-34 was exceptionally frigid; the bay froze to the mainland and when the cold became unbearable, my parents retreated. For several months we lived in Elizabeth with their friend, George Mauthe, a bachelor with live-in help. My father looked for work in New York and also kept an eye on his mother in nearby Ridgewood. By early March 1934, my parents were back in Harvey Cedars, but my grandmother was hospitalized and Daddy drove back and forth to Ridgewood. He said that his mother was seriously ill and he'd stay until she was back from the hospital. He wrote:

"Jodear: Tell the Pooch to keep her toes turned out and take good care of you and

157

don't let the fire go out. Much Love, Much Kiss, Tommy. PS: the nurses are like the weather — rotten."

Just after my first birthday my mother wrote home to Michigan:

"Dear Father, Dear Mother, Dear anyone else at home in Ionia: I'll try to slip in a note while the little squealer is asleep. Thanks very much for the lovely handkerchief for my birthday. I didn't think I was going to have a birthday this year, because Reynold was called to Ridgewood by his mother's being sick again, but about eight o'clock of the night of my birthday along came Reynold and our friend George (the banker who gave us the Chevy) in George's big car, bringing birthday cake, birthday pie, candy, wine, pair of gloves for me, funny presents from the five and ten and all the necessities for a party, which we had. They stayed all night and went back the next morning. Reynold stayed up there another week until his mother was out of danger.

"Sunday afternoon we got a neighbor girl to stay with Margaret, and Reynold and I drove to Atlantic City, which is only thirty miles away. There was a huge crowd on the boardwalk, but we didn't have any money to spend, and went for supper with some friends who live there. It was a nice holiday and practically the first time I have been off the island in three months.

"My hungry husband, at a quarter before noon, keeps coming in and asking if it isn't time to eat, so I'll go and humor him. Affectionately, Josie."

In December 1934, my mother wrote her younger sister:

"Dear Lillian: You can send me a big spank by long distance and I will deserve it. For three weeks I've had laid out something that should have gone for your birthday, but I was running around looking for jobs, dashing back and forth trying to keep one eye on Maggie and one eye on the big outside world:

"I've got a job reading letters for Floyd Gibbons.[1] He prints a prize adventure letter in the *New York Journal* every day and my job is to go to New York and take as many as I can carry, bring them down here and wade through them, picking out the good ones for the prizes. I've only had one check from him so far and just as soon as I got a chance at the job I had an infected finger and sat around for a week with my hand in hot Epsom salts. Finally the doctor had to cut it to the bone, and it healed.

"It has been bitterly cold here and of course that northwest wind blowing across ten miles of frozen bay doesn't get any warmer before it hits us. Fortunately, the house is tightly built, and no wind can get in. Our house is still not finished. Every time we can spare a few dollars we buy a few more pieces of lumber or cans of paint. Most of the inside is still to be painted, and all the outside, but it is quite comfortable."

I wondered if my mother was in her right mind when she wrote this, or just tried to reassure her family that she didn't live in a ramshackle hut — 70 years later the northwest wind still finds its way through the west wall. But the winter of 1934 recorded the lowest temperatures in 64 years. The water mains in town froze; and, the story goes, a bottle of ink froze on the table just four feet away from a neighbor's glowing potbelly stove.

"Maggie is blooming in this weather, and talking a blue streak. Her hair is about the color of yours, and very shiny, but absolutely straight. I wanted to get some really good pictures of her for Christmas, but we simply couldn't afford it. The price of living has gone up terrifically here. Eggs are forty-eight cents, and meat so high we can hardly afford to buy it. Every time we go through the countryside on our way from New York, we buy things from the farmers, at roadside stands, which helps cut down the H.C.L.

"Are you doing any more stories? I just got a rejection slip for one. Affectionately, Josie."

My mother told her sister how difficult it was to find hired help to care for me while she worked for Floyd Gibbons. She said that I forgot my "housebreaking," got fresh, and wanted my own way for months before I got back into a routine. Nonetheless, she took the train to Manhattan off and on that winter. My diligent mother left a typed schedule for the baby-sitter, whom we would later call Auntie Nan.

Between 7 a.m. and 10 p.m., my mother told Mrs. Weiseisen exactly what to do and how to do it. For example: "8:15: Two teaspoons cod liver oil. Juice half orange diluted with little warm water. If she seems hungry before this, give her dry crust." Bathing instructions included "put diaper under her to prevent skidding" and "wash carefully in creases." After I had my cereal and milk I would go "on the potty chair... If no bowel movement in ten or 15 minutes, use soap stick... Put on potty-chair every 40 minutes." In addition to all the practical instructions, I was "handled and played with after four o'clock."

My mother loved to walk on the desolate beach. She said walking is good for the soul and walking on the beach is good for the mind, body, and soul. I found this 1935 report of one of her expeditions. The four mile strip of open land between Harvey Cedars and Barnegat Light is called Loveladies, after Thomas Lovelady, a sea captain who built a gunning club there 100 years earlier.

"A schooner somewhere out in the Atlantic had her deck load of lumber washed off in a northeast storm. The next morning the beach from Barnegat City to Harvey Cedars was strewn with lumber, with more coming in continuously. By noon the sand was thronged with beachcombers salvaging lumber and piling it up — 2 x 4s, 1 x 6s, 2 x 6s, etc. By afternoon trucks from the mainland were on the scene to share in the haul, especially to snatch any pile left unwatched for ten minutes.

"As the day wore on and the timbers kept floating in, the teenagers took to swimming out and riding lumber in through the breakers like surfboards. Draper Lewis, who is now an important, and we presume dignified, official in the National Broadcasting Co. in New York, was one of the boys who had the time of his life swimming out and bringing in timbers. The timber snatching grew to such a pitch that nobody dared to go home for lunch and leave a pile unguarded. One woman even gave her children their naps under an improvised tent made of a rain slicker — it was raining hard — and while the children slept marked all her husband's lumber with red and blue crayon from the children's box.

"By darkness the truck drivers from the mainland grew discouraged by the rain and the refusal of the islanders to go home and leave what lumber was still there unguarded. The two men whose adjoining stacks had been marked with crayons went to the beach at nine o'clock and found everything undisturbed. When they made another trip around midnight, they discovered a big truck driven down a sandy road once used by the old fishery, just about at the north end of town on the Loveladies border. Two men had carried the two big piles of lumber over the dunes and were now ready to load it into their truck. It was their lumber, they said; they had pulled it out of the surf. But the red and blue marks made by the children's crayons turned the trick. The truckers finally gave up the argument and the twice-rescued lumber was eventually built into a garage. It disappeared in a hurricane a few years later, back to the foam whence it came, but that's another story."

In June 1935, Mommy wrote her mother:

"Dear Ma: Margaret plays every day with the little doll quilt you sent her. She is growing an inch a day it seems. Reynold says she'll be another big horse like me. She plays outdoors all day and is healthy and brown. Right this minute she is bothering me until I can hardly think. She wants to write to gamma, she says.

"Reynold and his partner with the deep-sea dredge are on the trail of a big contract for building streets down the island, and if they get it, it may mean a little extra money for us.[2] The trouble is that they work and work, and the money they get hardly pays their expenses. It is time to get dinner, and my child is hungry. We just about live on soup these days. I bought fifty cents worth of strawberries on the mainland; then I came home and made preserves. Affectionately, Josie."

Daddy and Luther Carver, who owned the dredge, were now partners, but within a year Daddy swapped his fishing boat for the dredge and continued alone, and founded the Barnegat Bay Dredging Company, which, over the years, pumped sand from the bottom of the bay to create building lots on the island and mainland. Luther went back to fishing. A very early memory is my father taking me to "Uncle Lute's" shack near the Independent Dock in Barnegat City — the same dock my mother described in "Fisherman's Wife." We often took food; Daddy said Lute was a "rummy," and needed our help. In the 1950s, when Lute died, Daddy flew to Florida to be certain he was properly buried.

In August, my mother complained to Marian how difficult it was to get any writing done at the shore when friends dropped in and spoiled her concentration. I found this fragment on half a sheet of typed paper:

"It was one of those days when you sit at your typewriter hour after hour, tearing half written sheets of yellow copy paper out of the typewriter — sheets with only one paragraph, sheets with only one line, sheets with line after line Xed out. At the end of the day, instead of a book 3000 words nearer completion than it was the day before, or 2000 words, or 1000 words, you have produced only a drift of crumpled sheets of paper, some in the waste basket, some scattered over the floor — only that drift of waste paper and the glum conviction that you were fool ever to think you could spend a winter on the island and finish a novel. A fool to think you could write in this summer cottage. A fool to think you could write."

She told her sister:

"Marie Smith Dunne (Smittie) drove up from Cape May to see me this month. She is the girl I lived with in Washington who was in Berlin when I was. She is in Washington again for a few months. And Ethel Ford Boyce [my mother's pal from the Frank Carpenter days] drove up from Atlantic City with her two boys last week. She is big and fat and I hardly recognized her. I had a card from Grace Leonard this week. She has taken an ocean trip to Quebec and Bermuda and sent Meg a beautiful convent-made dress. For some reason I've had loads of presents this month, including your hanky. A cousin of Reynold's sent us a coffee table as a belated wedding present and my sister-in-law Mildred came down and probably was appalled at my chipped dishes. She presented me with an entire set. Write soon Sis, and to heck with the state's time!"[3]

The November 1935 northeaster, which washed out the railroad to the island and caused record high tides, is one of my earliest memories. My mother was three months pregnant with my brother, Michael, and my father was in New York. The tide was rising fast in the bay and water surrounded the house, high enough to cover the steps to the front door. My mother, who had never learned to swim, was terrified. I was too heavy for her to carry. Foaming white caps splashed close to my eye level, which was somewhere between my mother's knees and hips, as she clutched my hand and dragged me through the water to the house at the end of 80th Street, where a Coast Guard truck picked us up. They took the few residents in town to the oceanfront home of Frederick P. Small, the president of American Express, considered indestructible behind its fortress-like bulkhead. (It was destroyed in The Great March Storm of 1962.) The winter of 1935-1936 was even colder than the one two years earlier. For two months, Barnegat Bay was frozen solid, and in some places the ice measured thirty-seven inches deep. Anglers who fished the waters fifteen miles offshore, on the Barnegat Ridge, predicted the cold weather when, in June, they spotted icebergs. When the bay freezes solid to the mainland, the house is especially cold. The northwest wind whips over the ice and chills it, much as the southerly breeze over the water cools the house in the summer. During this frigid winter, the government fed the starving wildfowl corn, dropped by blimps out of the Lakehurst Naval Air Station.

April 1936: "Dear Sis: I have been lucky about my child catching things. That's the advantage of living at the seashore. She hasn't had anything yet but some intestinal grippe when it went the rounds. I hope the mumps are not too awful and I'm sorry you've all had such a siege. Today Meggie got her first bad burn — not deep but about three inches wide, right on her fanny. She backed up against the kerosene heater while being dressed.

"The 'event' won't be until the latter part of May. The doctor says I figured wrong when I thought April. I may have to go to the hospital in Lakewood, about 45 miles north, as the little hospital[4] on this island, 15 miles south at the other end, is only for emergencies. And this house is too small. Our wing is started but I don't see enough money in sight to finish it.

"I wish I still had the sewing machine I borrowed during the winter, and I could sew for you. If I get one again this fall I'll try to run up some clothes for your children. I made Meg four dresses, two pajamas, bathing suit and sun suit, a little jersey sweater and slacks. I am all ready for the new one except that I can't finish the bassinet until the girl I lent it to brings it back.

"I am feeling very well, but terribly clumsy and ponderous. It's an effort to get up from a chair. Tommy is painting the kitchen yellow, the curtains are red checked and the canisters and things bright blue and it looks very gay. I recovered six pillows today for the divan and window seat — navy blue with red and white cord edging. We shall be so darn nautical we shan't know what to do! Love, Joey."

In April 1937, my mother wrote her sister Marian, who, with her daughter Dorothy, had visited us the summer after Michael was born on May 31st:

"There is no excuse for my not having written you before, except being worn out all the time. This has been a siege of everybody sick for weeks — everything at once — bad colds — teething — swollen glands — grippe — neuritis — accidents and what have you. Things seem to be better now. It hasn't been a cold winter, but we haven't been as healthy as we are in bitter weather. Poochy[5] has been running a fever all day and is muttering in her sleep now, and coughing.

"I haven't had time to do any thinking about spring clothes. Bobby Bloomer, Tommy's nephew, is here this week so I have a little easier time as he helps with the housework. Tommy is very busy in the dredge, building a street here in Harvey Cedars. He has two men working for him, and if everything works out all right he should make some money.

"Michael is now walking around and around his playpen. He sat out in the sun this afternoon and watched Bobby build a walk. You wouldn't recognize our yard, all the wood is picked up; it is filled in high and level with sand and Bay Terrace is now a real road. Two more houses are being built along the shore to the north of us. Tell Dorothy that Poochy learned to read this winter and is ready for the first grade reader. It's eleven p.m. and Mike thinks it amusing to awake at five. I don't. Please write when you can fool the boss."

NOTES

[1] *Floyd Gibbons was a well-known journalist and the first daily network radio newscaster.*

[2] *Government money offered relief during the Depression through the Works Progress Administration (WPA).*

[3] *Marian worked for the State of Michigan in Lansing, the capital.*

[4] *Michael was born in that little hospital in Beach Haven; it was barely a hospital, just the size of a comfortable home. Dr. Dodd and his wife, who was his nurse, lived on the third floor; his office was on the first, and a small surgery unit with one patient room with two beds on the second. My mother saved the doctor's bill. Michael's birth cost $118 — plus five dollars for his circumcision; they stayed for twelve days. My parents paid off the bill a year later. In the waiting room, there was a bulletin board display of fishhooks that the doctor had removed from the body parts of anglers with bad aim.*

[5] *This is the first reference in a letter where my mother called me "Poochy." Unfortunately, my father won the battle of what nickname to call me, as I would have much rather been Meg or Maggie than Poochy. If I hadn't seen these letters I never would have known my mother's choice. An early reference to my unforgettable nickname appears in a letter from Aunt Dot to my mother: "Did I tell you that a hostess in Child's Restaurant on Columbus Circle came up and said to me, 'How is Poochy?' I couldn't imagine how she could have known Poochy and I asked if she came from Harvey Cedars, but no, she had been the hostess in that Spanish Childs restaurant where Poochy made such a hit that night she went dancing there with Brother and me. Small world!"*

16
1938
A Terrifying Northeaster

Cousin Bobby, Mommy, Aunt Milly, Grandperce, Daddy, his mother, Aunt Dot, Cousin George and Michael and me in front, Christmas in Ridgewood, 1938

"The whole west end of the house was cracking and shivering. I figured that if the west end of the house stove in, the best place for us to get out was through the east window in Poochy's room."

In July 1938, Mommy wrote to Marian about how much she wanted to visit her parents in Michigan but that she never seemed to have any time: "I have been so busy I hardly ever powder my nose anymore. I have been trying to paint, make slipcovers and curtains, plant flowers and a hundred other things. We have a fence all the way around our house now and I thought that would give me relief from watching Michael all the time, but he has learned to place one wobbly toy on top of another and make something high enough for him to almost climb over, so I still must watch him. Again, I am sorry for the delayed birthday present — half the time I don't even know what date it is."

There was also the continuing matter of not enough money as Daddy scuffled to make a living. An accident my father had on the job compounded the problem. The letter continues: "When you came to visit, Tommy had a smashed foot. Now he has a smashed head. An iron railing on the dredge struck him on the head and laid it wide open, right across the top of his head. He is thankful it was not a fractured skull."

The "shack" had been enlarged, and blossomed into a real house. A wooden bulk-head protected our home from the bay. Daddy graded the land and covered it with gravel, and for a total cost of $340 my parents built a bedroom wing on the east side, with a small sun porch at the southeast corner. Mommy created a flowerbed that was sheltered by the house and lined it with pieces of gray driftwood, sculpted by the sea in an infinite variety of shapes. The garden is still there.

Aunt Dot visited in August. She reported to her friend Carmen:

"Brother saved my life by having me down there each weekend of August through Labor Day. I did nothing but sit in the sun, dunk in the bay, romp with the children, go to the movies and dance at night. You know how much I love to dance. I wish you could see these young jitterbugs dance. It really is an amazing festival of youth — you feel like Methuselah if you're a day over eighteen. It's not like the dancing one sees at the Waldorf and St. Regis. These youngsters have evolved their own release for their buoyant sprits and an escape from the frustration that assails the average young person who is searching for a job in these desperate times.

Brother's children are perfectly enchanting and act as entertainers to their father and mother as well as guests. I went over to Jo's around ten every morning and fixed my breakfast, which the children called a 'tea party' and at which they joined me. Brother's terrace overlooking the bay is very pleasant and now that it is fenced in, makes a safe place for the children to play. Jo is smarter and better looking than she has been since her marriage. She has been so clever about making sophisticated sports outfits to wear down there. Her table is always charming and her food delicious. Brother does not look so well - but then he has had to do heavy labor that I sometimes fear is beyond his strength and I wonder how late in life he can continue to do it.[1] But he is no brighter than I at making money. However, they enjoy their children and their friends and live a civilized life. They were grand to have me there each weekend."

On September 19th Mommy wrote to Marian:

"I still have hopes of coming home before cold weather, but I doubt if I could bring the children. Perhaps I could dash home for a week, anyway, and I might borrow a few dollars of you if you had it, but we shall have some money later and I could pay you back in a month or two. Tommy has not had a piece of work since July but he now has two contracts to start next month and prospects for three more which should keep him busy until the end of the year. However, we go so deeply in debt in such times, that we never catch up. But please don't say anything to the folks except that I hope to come. I worry about them being so old and not well, and I don't want to disappoint them if I cannot. Do you think it would be a disappointment to Ma if I came without the children? I know she would like to see them, but Margaret is in school and Michael is so temperamental I am afraid to travel with him. I am terribly tired after having so many people about all summer, and I should like a vacation myself."

Two days after my mother wrote her sister that she longed to come to Michigan, a rapidly moving hurricane spiraled up the coast, swirling 100 mile-per-hour winds 80 miles offshore. It was the perfect opportunity for one of my mother's long narrative letters — this time to her mother-in-law in Ridgewood, with a carbon copy for her friend Martha Taylor. Martha's letter, marked "please return," has a sketch at the top that illustrates the relationship of the house between Kinsey Cove, the bay and the ocean.

Hurricane

"We had been hearing news of a hurricane in the West Indies for two or three days, until we paid no attention. Our radio still was not working and the last news we had yesterday morning was that the storm had sheered off into the Atlantic and probably would not hit here. There was no particular wind all forenoon — no more than an ordinary high wind — although it rained steadily and profusely and I spent the morning making piccadilly (seven jars). Everything began to happen just about noon. Within one hour the tide in the bay had risen from its ordinary mark to the edge of the road, while the meadows between here and the cove across the street were completely covered. Tommy sent Rodney over to the mainland to fetch the big anchor, then began tightening lines on the dredge and the skiff, both of which were at the little dock in the cove. The pontoon line was still in the bay beyond the Lane house. (Later he found half of it out in the middle of the bay and the other half on the Loveladies' meadows). I blithely announced that I would go over and get the mail, that "I liked to walk in the rain and wanted to see a newspaper." Tommy wouldn't let me take his oilskins as he said he wanted to be ready to dash out at any minute if any of the anchors on his two craft started to go. So off I went in raincoat and sneakers, intending to just get good and wet, and change when I came home, rather than try to keep dry.

"Well, when I got from the lee of the house and that wind, now northwest instead of northeast, struck me I was somewhat staggered but it didn't seem any worse than plenty of blizzards I have walked in during the winter. It was only when I got past Gordon's and started east down the exposed length of 80th Street that I realized how bad it was. I got about opposite Charlton's and decided I had best turn back — only I couldn't. The rain hit me in the face with the force of a fire hose, and instead of making any headway I just lifted one foot after another from the ground and stayed in the same place. So I headed for the post office again and ran all the way, afraid that if I slowed down to a walk the wind would turn me end over end. At the post office I got my paper and a letter from Dorothy, tucked them inside my raincoat, got my breath, heard the reassuring news that the barometer was lower than it had been in six years, and went outside to see if the wind had abated any.

"As I stepped on Lear's porch, Andy went by with the truck but although I hollered my loudest he neither heard nor saw me. The wind had not let up any and I knew I could never get down that unprotected length of 80th Street alone, so I stopped across the road at Hartman's to telephone home to have Andy come back in the truck and get me. Tommy greeted me over the phone with the first bawling out he has ever given me — evidently he had no idea I would keep on going and he had just let me go outdoors to see what I thought of it.

"So I waited some more, dripping all over the Hartman's kitchen, which didn't make any difference as the water from the bay was coming under the back door so fast Mary couldn't keep it mopped up. I tried to reassure her by saying I had seen the tide much higher in other storms, but I saw no reason to tell her I had never seen the wind as bad.

"Andy came along in a half hour and I got home to find Tommy drenched to the skin in spite of his oilskins and unable to get any hot coffee because the electricity was off. The house was draped with wet clothes and Tommy was looking about for still another change. About this time the big front window started buckling, bending inward as though it were made of rubber, and while Tommy yelled at me to take Michael and stay in the other end of the house, he and Andy got boards from the attic and nailed them across the window. I moved the breakable things into the bedroom, stacked all pillows and cushions away, moved the couch to the other side of the room and started moving books away, as water was pouring down from that little gable window, which has never leaked before. Andy went to see how his own family was faring and Tommy went back to the dredge to change some lines as the wind kept shifting more and more southwest.

"The whole west end of the house was cracking and shivering. I figured that if the west end of the house stove in, the best place for us to get out was through the east window in Poochy's room. I got a hammer and knocked out the screen, carried my raincoat and hood in there and a heavy coat and boots for Michael, and sat on Poochy's bed with him, partly to keep him quiet and partly to see what was happening to Tommy. Between gusts of spray I could see him, now in the skiff, now in the dredge, and then making his way, half crawling, over that rickety little bridge of Boone Stewart's.[2] Then the spray blotted him out again, and to keep from collapsing from anxiety I began to read Mother Goose to Michael, who didn't want to stay in his sister's room.

"Then I saw that Tommy was rescuing Stewart's birdbath and some other things they had left outside. 'Blankety blank,' I raged, 'isn't that just like Reynold Thomas to get himself drowned trying to save a damned old birdbath' — 'Yes, Michael, yes, Michael, storm go boom' — where, oh where is Tommy — oh, why did he go across that little bridge — 'Michael, please be quiet just a minute' — now he's coming across the bridge — 'MICHAEL BE QUIET — don't cry, honey, mommy didn't mean it — here, mommy will read all about Little Bo Peep — see, Little Bo Peep lost her sheep' — oh, there he comes across that bridge again — and so on and on and on. I was as close as I have ever been to having a good dose of hysterics.

"The wind was too hard now for Tommy to get across the bridge except on his hands and knees. He got over all right and ploughed through the water in the meadow that was almost to his hips, literally fighting every foot of the way. Back in the house he had once more to strip to the skin. By this time he was using my sweaters for undershirts and just forgetting about his wet pants. The water was sweeping over our bulkhead in a torrent, the spray pounding on that west window and the surf roaring even above the howl of the wind.

"Suddenly I thought of Poochy. It was almost time for school to be out and I had so many other things on my mind I had practically forgotten her. Tommy telephoned to the wife of the bus driver who said he had gone down the road to make sure his bus could get through, and that he would take every child all the way home. He was still not here fully an hour after that and we could get no response from the Barnegat City police. Finally a telephone call came from the manager at Small's place. The bus driver had tried to come down our street but he couldn't see a thing driving into that rain and he would keep Poochy in the bus if Tommy would come and get her. But Andy had the truck and the car wouldn't start, it was so wet. While Tommy was trying to have Poochy left somewhere else, the yellow bus finally loomed out of the rain and Tommy carried her in.

"She was shivering with fright because she heard somebody say the ocean was breaking through. She thought our house was going to be washed away, and especially after I explained why she and Michael must keep away from the big window. Tommy said later he thought the house might go and that he had the skiff in readiness all afternoon, as our best bet would have been to head straight across the bay to Manahawkin. About four o'clock the tide and wind began to slacken as quickly as they had come up, and in another hour the bay had dropped back to its usual level.

"The Atlantic Ocean three blocks east, however, had not. From our kitchen window as far as we could see up to Loveladies, the surf was dashing high into the air above the dunes. It was a magnificent sight, but I fear I didn't appreciate the magnificence — then. I would have preferred a nice, flat millpond to look at. Tommy got the car started and we drove over to see the ocean. It was right to the top of the dunes and breaking through in dozens of places, washing down every street south of Lear's where it cut a gash through the dune as even and perpendicular as a slice cut out of a cake. All the houses there were surrounded by from one to two feet of water. At Small's, about half of those glass panes from his greenhouses were smashed and flying across the road, his flowers beaten to shreds. On the ocean side, the wind lifted his boardwalk until the boards stood straight up in the air like a picket fence. Beyond the Coast Guard station one of those new little houses on the bay was lying on its side. Everywhere along the bay, boats were high and dry, smashed to pieces or floating upside down in the water. The house next to Hartman's had three boats on the flowerbeds.

"We tried to drive to Loveladies, but the water was over the road in several places. As we reached home we met the entire Hartman family in their car. The water was still pouring into their yard from the gash in the dunes and they wanted to stay here until after high tide at seven. Their maid fed all the children while I rustled cans of beans and Herb went to the store for hot dogs and whatever he could find and we had a very hectic meal, with little Anne Hartman and Michael and Pooch all too nervous and excited to calm down, and we four parents much too exhausted to have any patience with them. (The electricity had come on about six o'clock.)

"The Hartman's went home at eight and Tommy simply collapsed on the bunk. I tried to make him go to bed but he said he would have to go out and pump the dredge about midnight or she would sink from all the rain. I went to sleep myself and awoke about one-thirty. Tommy was still asleep on the bunk, and I put an extra blanket on him, hoping he wouldn't awake until morning. I didn't care if that dredge sunk to China — I didn't want him to go out there again. In the morning, however, I found out he got up at two-thirty, put on boots and oilskins, and made another trip to pump 'er out.

"And that was the famous hurricane of 1938. It did very little damage to us, although the yard looks very bedraggled; all the flowers are flat. I spent the whole day getting wet things on the line and thanking heaven for sunshine. Tell Dorothy her letter almost was among the casualties. As I came out of the post office, the wind took my newspaper and her letter out from under my raincoat and had them out in the meadows before I knew what happened. I crossed off the paper to profit and loss, but did go after the letter and finally tracked it down in a puddle, very soggy and ink-stained but still legible."

The milder, western edge of this hurricane passed New Jersey; but two hours later the storm's full force surged across Long Island and submerged Providence, Rhode Island, under thirteen feet of water. This unnamed hurricane killed almost 700 people throughout New York and New England. My only memory is of the big, wooden X formed by boards across the bay window. In my subconscious, however, the experience in both this and the 1935 storm, and the 1944 hurricane still to come, are very alive. I have a repetitive anxiety dream where I run from a tidal wave — sometimes the wave comes across the bay and sometimes it rolls in from the Atlantic Ocean — think of one of those tidal wave movies and you have the picture.

In November 1938, Jo wrote her mother and apologized for not being able to come home, and said she had "a slight operation," but did not elaborate. Over the years she complained of neuritis, which can be caused from sitting in one position too long. She told her mother:

"Margaret has been home from school with sore throats quite a lot but she likes to study and has her nose in a book all the time. (Whom does this remind you of?) Michael has been getting bigger and bigger and talks all day long. Margaret is very, very smart, and oh, so stubborn. I think I will train her to be a woman lawyer. She asks me a million questions a day and then trips me up when I don't answer right. Michael probably won't be so smart, but he is a loving little fellow, and hugs everybody."

That September, I had entered first grade at the one-room schoolhouse in Barnegat City. I trudged down Bay Terrace to 80th Street, where I turned east, and bent into the gritty wind. In the winter it was a tough trek for a little girl — 1,150 steps; I counted them. The school bus picked us up at the corner bar, which opened on cold mornings to shelter the four children who waited there.

The school nurtured its students. One large sunny room with tall, paned windows filled the east wall. Five rows of desks, graduated in size from kindergarten-tiny to barely-adequate-for-a-fast-growing-11-year-old-boy, stretched from one end to the other, one grade in each row. A round, pressed iron, black coal stove nestled in a corner; blackboards lined the west wall. Our teacher taught grades one through three as one group, and four and five as another; she was also the custodian and principal, a service for which she received an additional $10 a month over her $1,200 annual salary. She had to stoke the fire on Friday night and start it up on Monday morning, and be sure the toilets didn't freeze. Mothers brought in pots of soup for our lunch on the coldest days and a milkman delivered pint bottles of milk with cream on top. My schoolmates were mostly of Scandinavian descent, children of the fisherman who had settled there in the 1920s, and of the fishermen my father had worked with that summer before I was born. Their names told their lineage: Larson, Olsen, Swenson, Svelling, Bjornberg, Benestad, Englesen, Eliason, Carlson, Jensen, Hansen.

Just before Christmas, my mother wrote to Marian:

"We have been having bitterly cold weather and high winds here all the time, but our house is nice and warm with a big potbelly coal stove. We got rid of the kerosene burner because it never kept us warm. I suppose we are going to have Christmas right here. Reynold's mother wants us to come up to Ridgewood, but it is hard to take two noisy children to an apartment, and I'd hate to get caught in our old car in a blizzard.

My teenage cousin Bobby wanted us all together in Ridgewood so badly he said he would "save up his allowance to buy the plum pudding and the brandy and pour it over himself." We did so and Aunt Milly and George came and we had Christmas in my Grandmother's large, rambling apartment in the middle of town. It was our last Christmas with three generations gathered together.

NOTES

[1] *Aunt Dot worried unnecessarily about my father. He worked hard, was healthy, and after World War II built a successful business.*

[2] *Boone Stewart and his wife summered in a houseboat no bigger than a good-sized bedroom. They beached it on a marsh island in Kinsey Cove, just behind our empty land on the east side of Bay Terrace. A wooden plank bridge about fifteen feet long connected the land to the miniature island, about thirty-five feet wide by fifty feet long.*

17
1939
The Great Depression Ends

Portrait of Jo and me, painted by Sue May Gill.

"Here I live, piling up the most marvelous material for writing, but it's almost impossible to find the time or strength to do it. I still write all the time in spirit, and in another two years, when Michael is in school, I don't see why I can't put in at least five mornings a week at steady work."

In January 1939, my mother responded to a letter from her Washington friend Mabel Simpson, whom she hadn't seen since 1928. Mabel asked how to market her writing, and asked for an introduction to Lowell Thomas. Jo said he was harder to see than the Pope; and continued her long letter with many apologies for not answering sooner, and explained that she'd been ill most of the year and had an operation a few weeks before Christmas.

"Dear Mabel: For the first time in months I am without a backache. All these things notwithstanding, I still apologize, because I wanted so much to write you, and just didn't. I was terribly interested to hear all about you, as I had wondered if you were still in Washington. I once worked at a small town daily paper in Michigan, you know, and reported everything from society to drunks, and I have always been keen to try it again. What a shame that yours went bankrupt. I take it you have no family, and I know if I didn't have the two young hoodlums I have, I would bank everything on a book. In fact, I was half through a book of my own when romance came barging along and I got married. Since the stork put the Indian sign on me I tried once to finish it. I vowed to myself that I would finish it — that no matter how busy I was I could surely find one hour a day. Well, I nearly went crazy. I try no more books until both my children are in school.

"Re-reading your letter just now brought up so many memories of Washington that I fetched my diary from those days — it's right here on the bookshelf beside me — and delved back to May 1918. Great guns Mabel, that was twenty-one years ago. There you were, arriving in Washington, your attic room, dancing at Neighborhood House. You were too much of a lady to go as often as the rest of us.

"I haven't been in Washington since 1931. I have lost touch entirely with Dell. Grace Leonard is still in the Department of Agriculture. She married in 1927. I see her occasionally in New York when she comes up to visit her sister. Martha Taylor, the girl from my hometown, is also still there. She made fifty thousand dollars in the stock market and lost it all in 1929, and in 1933 the whole Department of Commerce was wiped out and she lost her job. Smittie was in Berlin that winter of 1927-28 that I was in Europe, and I saw her and her husband constantly, and frequently in New York afterward. Three years ago she popped in here to see me. Her second husband died just a few months ago and she is coming back to New York to live. Margaret Black married Robert Lynch and stayed in Washington.

"As to how much writing I have done, you can judge by the way I answered your letter. These last five years have gone in house building, painting, slip covers, curtains, bedspreads, gardening, stenographing for Reynold's business and having babies. Margaret and Michael are little monkeys. Michael is a funny little fellow who catches every germ that comes within range and has been so hard to raise that I wonder I am not a wreck. Margaret has always been a big healthy horse, so blooming and radiant, that she has already earned a fair amount posing. This is an artist's colony in summer and she has been painted several times. One of her portraits has been shown at the National Academy in New York.[1] However, she is beginning to be long-legged and freckled and I suppose her teeth will drop out soon.

"Our house was the first one on a little peninsula jutting out into Barnegat Bay, and for a couple of years we lived a primitive life in winter, often cut off for days at a time by high tides surrounding the house. Once a hard storm destroyed six houses on the ocean side near us and we thought ours was going. In 1935, in the dead of winter,

173

when I was three months pregnant, we had to be evacuated by the Coast Guard.

"Those days are now history. The land about us has been filled in and a road built to the end of our point. I rather regret the passing of our isolation, although I realize it is a material and physical advantage not to have to take off my shoes and stockings in the middle of November, as I have done when Reynold's hip boots were not home, and wade a couple of hundred feet through high tide to the butcher's truck.

"But it really is a grand healthy life on this island. In summer it is very gay, in fact, too gay for us working people. Reynold and I try to keep away from the cocktail parties and beach picnics during the week and confine our frivolity to dancing Saturday nights and spending most of Sunday in the boat out on the bay. In winter, we might as well live in Alaska. There are about a dozen families in this village then, the nearest movie is fifteen miles away, the nearest railroad the same distance, and we even have to go five miles for ice cream. The beach is deserted, and it's grand walking there alone. It is then I get something accomplished. Just at present Reynold is on a three-month's job forty miles up the bay and comes home only on weekends, so I have an early supper with the children and try to take advantage of a long undisturbed evening. This is why you are getting a letter, I suppose. That, and the fact that I can once more sit at a typewriter for more than ten minutes without my back almost killing me.

"Well, my dear, that seems to bring me up to date. Here I live, piling up the most marvelous material for writing, but it's almost impossible to find the time or strength to do it. One winter when Margaret was a year old and the weather here was hellish, we stayed with Reynold's mother and I read fan mail for Floyd Gibbons, which I could do at home, but there are not many jobs one can do with one eye while the other is on the baby. I have a fairly reliable woman who looks after the children when I need her, but in the few times I have tried to turn the responsibility over to her and do a regular half day of writing it hasn't paid. Margaret was afraid to go to sleep because she thought she would die ('if I should die before I wake,' etc.); both children got upset stomachs from irregular eating, and she used deplorable grammar (Auntie Nan says 'ain't got,' Mommy). They generally developed so many fiendish traits that I said, 'To heck with a career.'

"I still write all the time in spirit, and in another two years, when Michael is in school, I don't see why I can't put in at least five mornings a week at steady work. [At some later date, my mother penciled in "Ha!" next to this line.] I can stand somebody else's housework, but I feel it's my job to raise my children at this age."

In June 1939, my mother visited her family in Michigan, but left us behind. When she returned to Harvey Cedars, she wrote to her mother:

"The children were fine while I was gone, at least Michael was. Dorothy said he was simply angelic. Reynold's mother said he hardly mentioned my name while I was away, but every day since I have been back he comes to give me a big hug and say, 'I'm glad my Mommy back from Milligan.' Margaret is still in Bethlehem. Mildred writes

174

she had a fine time, has been playing with a lot of children at the country club."

I found the following snippet about Ionia that my mother typed on the back of an election board flyer. She typed on the backs of lots of papers — old school programs, municipal affidavits, other people's letters:

"Spring and Summer in Michigan: I still remember wash day, my bright gingham dresses blowing on the clothesline — red, yellow, green, blue — above the orange and magenta and scarlet of the zinnias and petunias in the flower beds below them. It was the only time I lived in a household where Monday was wash day, Tuesday ironing day, Wednesday sewing, Thursday upstairs bedrooms, Friday downstairs, Saturday baking, Sunday church and homemade strawberry ice cream and chocolate layer cake. It had been the happiest time of my life — the creek where the cowslips grew, going barefoot in April on a dare, the trilliums and violets in the woods, the baby calves, rides on hay wagons, apple blossoms."

Whenever my mother said that she wanted to take a trip "home" to Michigan, Michael and I wailed, "Mommy, this is your home!" In the summer my parents had a small circle of friends, the kind of people with whom my mother could talk books, she said. My mother was a big reader, but couldn't afford to buy books. In the summer, there was a small library in the general store, but during the winter the Bookmobile came to each house once a month. My mother always had a pile of books ready to exchange. She was a big supporter of a branch library on the island, and in 1959 the county built a branch library in Ship Bottom and dedicated it to her.

A Philco executive from Philadelphia bought an ocean-to-bay tract and my father filled in the bayside land. Several colleagues followed his lead and built oceanfront summer homes. Daddy got a big job at the other end of the island, when WPA funds financed a new municipal building in Brant Beach; and as the stock market began its slow rise, small dividend checks reappeared in box twenty three at the post office. We had a telephone now, a four-party line. The newer homes had refrigerators, but an iceman, with a melting block of ice wrapped in canvas slung over his back, twice a week delivered ice to our house; it was not cold enough to keep ice cream frozen.

Mr. Small completed his multi-dwelling estate during the Depression — two homes on the beach, one bayfront home for his manager, a farmer's cottage for the gardener, a clubhouse and a boathouse surrounding an expanse of greenhouses and gardens. He was a man of generous community spirit. In the 1930s and during the war, town families received a turkey at Christmas and Thanksgiving. (We shared our Thanksgiving dinners with an old Lithuanian fisherman who lived nearby; it was Michael's and my ritual to carry the dinner plate to Mr. Janutis.) Every Sunday throughout my childhood, Mr. Small delivered flowers to Milburn Hall, the one-room Sunday school on 73rd Street, built in 1906 by a group of women. (That women built it was recorded in August of that year by the *Philadelphia North American*, which published a photograph of a dozen women in long skirts on ladders, clambering on the roof, and wielding saws and hammers.)

On a mild early September night in 1939, my parents, and the Hartmans and a group of friends planned to go to Hans Bar in Barnegat City to dance. Before they left, my mother received a phone call from Mary, who told her to turn on the radio — Germany had invaded Poland. Herb was a colonel in the Army Air Corps. Eating my mother's special chocolate cake and drinking coffee, they spent the evening huddled around our tabletop Philco. A yellow light glowed behind the dial of its arched, Gothic façade. The ensuing war would change the island and all our lives.

NOTE

[1] *In 1963, I lived in Philadelphia, and on impulse I phoned Sue May Gill, the artist who painted this portrait. It was still in her studio. In 1935 "Child of the Sand" was exhibited at the Pennsylvania Academy of Fine Arts, and in 1936 was published in the catalog of the National Association of Women Painters and Sculptors' annual exhibition. My parents couldn't afford to buy the portrait, but thirty years later I paid the artist $600 in three monthly installments and it hangs on my living room wall.*

18
1940 TO 1942
German U-Boats Offshore

899024 CZ

UNITED STATES OF AMERICA
OFFICE OF PRICE ADMINISTRATION

WAR RATION BOOK FOUR

Issued to *Josephine Thomas*

(Print first, middle, and last names)

Complete address _____

READ BEFORE SIGNING

In accepting this book, I recognize that it remains the property of the United States Government. I will use it only in the manner and for the purposes authorized by the Office of Price Administration.

Void if Altered _____

(Signature)

It is a criminal offense to violate rationing regulations.

OPA Form R-145

16— 35570-1

We tore out little coupons from these ration books for butter, sugar, coffee and meat and gave them to the storekeeper, along with money.

"The German subs had a field day, and by the end of March, U-boats sank over two hundred ships off New Jersey. Navy blimps patrolled the coast with a primitive radar system, on the alert for the Nazi raiders. Most torpedoed ships were tankers, and black oil oozed from the sunken hulls, and like chocolate on vanilla ice cream, streaked over the white sandy beach."

Of my mother's letters from the 1940s, half are long and typewritten and half are short, handwritten notes, most to Marian and a few to my grandmother in Michigan. They were notable for what they did not say — very little about my polio, the war, or the 1944 hurricane, although she did write about the war and hurricane in future newspaper articles. And so little about her breast cancer in 1940. In April of that year Mommy told Marian about her new job as tax collector and worried about her mother's illness:

"Dear Sis: Don't fail to let me know if Ma's condition gets dangerous. I can manage somehow to get the money to get out there. I have a new job as tax collector and have been half crazy since April first. I counted on Mrs. Weiseisen to be here. There is not a soul to look after my children when I have to keep office hours. We had another one of those winters, with the dredge frozen up for three months, and no work and no income, so now we are living on borrowed money until we can crawl out of the depths.[1]

"I don't get any wages until May and it's only thirty dollars a month. The only office time I have to put in is four hours at the borough hall every other Saturday for tax collecting, and then keep the books in my 'spare time.' Ha. That's a joke. Just now, while I am learning the ropes, of course I must put in a lot of time. I think the former collector is going to be facing a charge of shortage — the tax books are a mess, and I have to check for months back with the bank, the state auditor, and lots of other people. When the books are in order I ought to be able to do all the bookkeeping in one evening a week."[2]

The first echoes of the European war reached our shore; the National Guard transferred some state contingents into coastal artillery units and local boat owners registered with a national defense program under the State Board of Commerce and Navigation. The Norwegian Consul came from Washington to Barnegat Light to form an Aid to Norway Committee to gather money that would buy food to send to German occupied Norway. The little fishing village raised $500 by the end of the summer.

On Labor Day weekend, the four Hartmans and our family drove to Atlantic City to walk on the Boardwalk. This was an unusual outing, as we rarely left the Island except to visit relatives. A boardwalk artist sketched my brother and me in pastels — me with my pigtails sticking out from under the Tam o' Shanter perched on my head. On that fun excursion, did my mother know that just two weeks later she would be in the hospital?

I found only two specific references to my mother's mastectomy. A brief item in the *Beach Haven Times* informed readers, "Mrs. Josephine Thomas underwent an operation on September 16 at the Paul Kimball Hospital and is improving fast." I was in school, but Michael spent six weeks in Ridgewood with Grandma and Aunt Dot. The hospital bill was $87 at $4 a day for the thirteen-day stay, and included $15 for the operating room.[3] That, plus this hand-written note to Marian dated October 11th was the only direct reference to the cancer.

"Dear Marian: Thanks for your nice letter. I don't know what Reynold's sister wrote you, but probably not the whole truth. They had to remove my entire right breast, but the doctor assures me there is no more sign of cancer, of which I was so afraid. I haven't told anyone here the truth — I just said it was to remove a tumor — I hate to have people scrutinizing me and trying to figure out which side is me and which is ART. So skillfully do they make these 'spare parts' now that you can't tell a thing when I'm dressed. I've been considerably depressed at being so butchered, but it's not as bad as I thought it would be. My arm is still in a sling. It affected the muscles and

I can't type yet or write much. Don't tell Ma this — she would just worry. The doctor assures me that in a few weeks I shall be quite all right, but I'm afraid my trip home has gone glimmering. More later when I can write more easily. With much love, Josie."

When I read this letter I burst into tears so suddenly I surprised myself. Children have no concept of what a parent suffers, nor would they know what to do if they did. If only I could hug her now and say, "I understand. I have been there too." I do remember that for years my mother complained about her aching arm. The tissues swell when lymph nodes are removed and exercising the arm is very important — but in 1940 it was not a recommended part of breast cancer patients' therapy. When I, and several of my friends, had breast cancer, after surgery we were told to immediately start to "walk up the wall with your fingers" to exercise the arm muscles. Many serious events have a comic side and with my mother it was the "spare parts." The prophylaxis she wore never really matched her other breast, and I remember her as she sat in her sewing room and either pragmatically or absent-mindedly used her falsie as a pincushion. When I asked my father why Mommy was lopsided, he said, "Michael bit her when he was nursing." The "C" word was not mentioned.

In December 1940 Mommy wrote home:

"Dear Ma: My arm has been bothering me again, and it's been hard to typewrite or use a pencil. Mrs. Weiseisen has left for Florida so I have been tired out all the time... I may send a little Christmas box to you, but goodness knows it won't be much. We are always broke at this time of the year, and now everything we have is going for hospital and doctor bills and notes at the bank. Ever since Labor Day, Reynold has been dredging out a yacht basin up near Barnegat Lighthouse. Today I see him out in the bay towing the dredge to a place about twenty miles south. If the bay doesn't freeze he has a good job ahead. I think things will be better after the first of the year. Still, I don't suppose we should complain. Our house is paid for and clear of mortgage. As soon as Michael goes to school next year I should be able to earn some money again. Excuse me for always talking so broke, but I so wish I could send you big Christmas boxes as in the old days."

The summer of 1941 was calm. My mother was feeling better, and now that I was eight, she let me help in the kitchen and dig with her in the garden. She showed me how to hold the knife to scrape the carrots I pulled from the garden, how to snap the beans and peel the apples in one peel. If her arm ached, I got to use the trowel to dig the holes into which she dropped seeds or seedlings. This was the first summer I could wander around town on my own and she let me take a list and go to the general store alone. Sometimes we went together; she'd rather walk on the beach than the street. In one photo someone snapped, she is nicely dressed in "beach pyjamas" and I'm in a stretched out bathing suit.

Sand played a large part in my childhood; it stuck on my feet or between my toes, blew into my hair, nose, and eyes. I rolled in it, built castles with it. I tracked it into the house. It leeched into the bed sheets, got stuck in my underpants. After I swam Mommy would say, "Be sure to get all the sand out of your crack." When my younger brother Michael and I fought we threw it at each other. My mother announced in a loud voice: "Sand is the bane of my existence!"

On Sunday, December 7, 1941, the Hartmans were at our house for lunch. I went with Colonel Hartman in his big black Buick, which had a radio — rare in a car then — when he had to run an errand. We were still on 80th Street when a news bulletin interrupted the music to announce that the Japanese had bombed Pearl Harbor. No adult I knew swore, so when the Colonel said, "Son of a bitch!" I knew it was serious. He made a U-turn and we drove back to my house.

The surprise attack galvanized the country, and by the end of December island boat captains joined the Naval Reserve and the government formed the Civil Defense Administration. It was nationwide in scope, but here on the island, residents feared a landing from German U-Boats, or an attack by Luftwaffe bombers. During the previous summer, from the beach, we'd seen ships on the way to Great Britain, transporting goods as part of the Lend-Lease program. Citizens swung into action. By January 2nd, my Grandfather was standing watch for German aircraft. Aunt Dot recorded in her diary: "Dad came in about 10 pm from his vigil of watching for enemy planes… I made hot chocolate for him and mother, lemonade with whiskey for myself."

In an April letter, my mother told her sister Marian: "Since January, Reynold and I have been airplane spotting and listening to torpedoes explode offshore. For a peaceful Easter, we stayed in Mildred's new log cabin." War was good for the steel business and Uncle Bill was a vice-president at Bethlehem Steel, the country's second largest steel manufacturer. He built a guest cottage in the grove of trees by a small stream at the far end of their property.

In the spring of 1942, on the way to Ridgewood, our parents took Michael and me to see the French liner, *S.S. Normandie,* which in February caught fire and burned at its West 49th Street pier in Manhattan. When the fire started, the War Department was in the process of transforming the 83,000-ton luxury liner into a troop ship. The *Normandie* was top heavy with the firefighters' water pumped into it and, after the fire was extinguished and the tide came in, it keeled over and rested on the bottom of the river. Although I had been in and out of New York since I was born — my earliest memory is when I tossed my Teddy bear out of the top of a Fifth Avenue bus and cried when it wouldn't stop — this is my first memory of the skyline, heightened by the sight of the massive hull in the foreground, lying on its side like a giant beached whale. We crossed the Hudson River on the George Washington Bridge and drove on to Ridgewood, where we left Michael for a visit.

Aunt Dot came to Harvey Cedars for Decoration Day weekend. She wrote in her diary:

"A dither of shopping to go to the seashore. Bought the only red rubber bathing cap left in town, but no rubber bathing shoes to be had… Took five o'clock train for Barnegat. Dad joined me. It was so nostalgic passing through New Jersey towns I've lived in — Middletown, Red Bank, Eatontown, Lakewood, Toms River — then the pines and scrub oak and ferns, little narrow winding creeks, marshland, farmland, daisies, laurel, all bathed in good sun. The nice fat conductor greeted us as though we were royalty. Generations of family have come to Barnegat and apparently old Mr. Perrine knew them all.

"I hear the sound of the bay swishing outside my window. Pleasant supper on terrace then on to Scandinavian fisherman's bar where the summer colony congregates to dance the folk dances which Brother and I do better than anyone on the island. Dancing transports me as nothing else and I can dance down any five men, except my brother.

"Brother is charming, graceful, gentle — a really good and lovely spirit. He thinks no evil, sees no evil, hears no evil. Josephine has tamed him — jealous wife doesn't let him out of her sight. She's a handsome, competent brunette, gets herself up cleverly, can even cook and sew. But she certainly has the ball and chain on Brother. Marriage is a wonderful racket for those who know how to work it."

In June 1942 my mother typed the following letter on Borough of Harvey Cedars stationery, with "Josephine Thomas, Collector and Treasurer" on the letterhead. She penned "Lehman" between her names.

"Dear Mother: I hoped all the time I could jump on a bus or train and get out to Michigan for your birthday and strawberry time, but I just couldn't. Reynold has to be away from home, the children's school wasn't out yet, and I am tied up with this tax collector job, plus being secretary of the rationing board. I issue all the ration cards for sugar, tires, inner tubes, cars, gas, typewriters and bicycles. I was offered a job to take charge of the county rationing board in Toms River, the county seat, but it didn't pay enough money so I could afford a housekeeper and the gas for driving sixty miles back and forth.

"The children got your things. Meg was tickled by them. Michael likes the sweater a lot. Maggie[4] would have written you a letter but she has been so busy learning parts for the school play that I can hardly make her eat and go to bed. It has been hot here and I have the house shut up with all the curtains closed to try to keep it cool. Of course, I could always go in the bay; it's shallow right in front."

Mommy wasn't a strong swimmer. The summer I turned three, I escaped from the fenced yard and she watched me fall over a bulkhead about 200 feet south of the house. As she sprinted to rescue me, a clam-digger working close to shore hauled me out. That summer, two gym teachers who rented the cottage next door taught me how to swim and from then on my mother had trouble keeping me out of the water. When she was in the bay she never felt comfortable unless her feet could touch bottom.

"We can't go in the ocean however, for the entire beach is covered with a thick coat of black gummy oil from the torpedoed tankers off shore. We now have one of them sticking up out of the water in front of us, and the other night two airships crashed a few miles to the north. They are flying over our house all the time. Four of them went over at one time yesterday. The island is full of barracks for soldiers as well as Coast Guards, and they are now putting up kennels for the dogs to be used on beach patrol.

"Reynold keeps surprising himself by being busy. As soon as the work plays out he is going to put his dredge in dry dock and get a defense job, or maybe go back in the Marine Corps. He was in the Second Division during the last war. He keeps thinking his work is all finished, and then something else turns up. With the beach so covered with oil the rich people with oceanfront homes, who also own bay front land, had him build them bathing beaches on the bay — that is, pump up enough sand to make a nice sandy slope into the water. With much love, your affectionate daughter, Josie."

Sinking ships were the constant, and not always distant, background to our life in the early war years. After Pearl Harbor, for the first half of 1942, German submarines lurked off the New Jersey coast, where they torpedoed U.S. shipping with impunity. German U-boat captains spoke of the "American shooting gallery," and the German man whom I would later marry, told me that as a boy he saw a newsreel of Atlantic City filmed from a submarine, the city's oceanfront hotels ablaze with lights; the War Department did not order a blackout until May. Winston Churchill called this one-sided fight The Battle of the Atlantic. The German subs were voracious, and by the end of March, U-boats sank over 200 ships off New Jersey, and in June alone, forty U-boats prowled the Eastern Seaboard and sank an average of three ships a day. Navy blimps patrolled the coast with a primitive radar system, on the alert for the Nazi raiders. Most torpedoed ships were tankers, and black oil oozed from the sunken hulls, and like chocolate on vanilla ice cream, streaked over the white sandy beach.

The Germans sank two tankers near Barnegat Inlet — the *R.P. Resor* in February and the *Persephone* in May. In her letter, my mother referred to the *Persephone,* which was so close to shore we could see it from the beach. Daddy took me with him to the Barnegat City Coast Guard station, where I watched local women painstakingly scrape and clean black crude oil from rescued seamen. Michael and I later used the same kerosene-and-soap technique on a stranded, oil-matted, wild duck.

That June, the government organized convoys of merchant ships along the coast to transport troops and war materiel to Europe. Destroyers and cruisers, like sheepdogs herding flocks, hovered around the edges of the slower ships, alert for submarines. Beach access after dusk was forbidden, and Army personnel who were billeted in Coast Guard stations patrolled the beach on horseback with Doberman pinschers and German shepherds, which wore booties to protect their feet from the thick oil. Michael had trouble understanding why we were using German dogs to capture German soldiers. That beach was my playground, and the threat of those ferocious, snarling animals left me with a fear of dogs I've never completely overcome.

In an article twelve years later, my mother recalled this first wartime spring.

"German submarines were having a field day off this coast, and patrol dirigibles and destroyers dropped bombs like ripe plums into the ocean. Hardly a day passed that spring when the windows did not rattle from an explosion or the dishes dance on their shelves.

"In the primitive radar devices of that time, a submerged enemy submarine and a whale gave back the same kind of signal, and more depth charges were dropped on whales than on U-boats. It was not uncommon to see a depth-charged whale washed up on the beach, and one of the acute problems of that spring, in addition to ration cards and no gas, was what to do with the whales. As the weather got warmer, the problem got more acute. One lay on the beach near the boundary between Loveladies and Harvey Cedars for several days while the town fathers debated as to whose whale it was. I never heard who won — or lost. I do remember that when I took an incredulous guest up to see it sometime later, it had disappeared. We wondered how it had been disposed of, but not for long. As we strolled along the beach we became aware of a peculiar condition underfoot. We had the same sensation we might have had walking over a large expanse of Jello. The whale had been buried, but 'not deeply and not well.' "

A rumor of Nazi spies coming ashore traveled up and down the island and my mother took off with this idea and began a story about two children discovering a cache of arms and a radio hidden in their dugout hut on the beach. It never went anywhere, but she left a folder of typed pages of dialog, an outline, lots of "cut and pasted" pages and notes in shorthand. One fragment describes the blimps on patrol as they passed overhead: "There was a deep hoarse sound of motors, louder than the roar of the surf, and I tiptoed to the window to look. It was directly overhead, one of the airships from Lakehurst speeding homeward through the night. 'Late for supper again,' I thought. Directly overhead it seemed gigantic, incredibly big. It slid off to the northwest, the running lights flicking on and off, and faded into the darkness above Barnegat Bay until only the small pinpoint of the stern light was visible."

In early July, Aunt Dot was anticipating a month in Harvey Cedars. She would stay next door in a small studio. She wrote in her diary:

"Hope all goes well for my month at the shore. It seems now to be shaping up naturally and easily. I have not wanted to go there in years — recent visits have been depressing due to deflated family fortunes and the likewise deflating effect my sister-in-law has on me. But this time I'll have friends who are stimulating. And I love riding Poochy's bike, and the beautiful free feeling of being under the open sky. I can only hope the July mosquitoes and heat won't spoil my visit."

The scourge of mosquitoes was a constant problem on the island, but had been somewhat controlled by a WPA project five years earlier. The Civilian Conservation Corps dug drainage ditches on the marshes across the bay from one tip of the island to the other, eliminating much of the standing water in which the mosquitoes breed. The voracious little beasts finally disappeared — almost — in the 1950s, when the county sprayed DDT.

Michael was Aunt Dot's favorite — he ran to her whenever he could. Again, from her diary:

July 15: In came a very vexed Pooch in pigtails to say she'd been looking all over the island for Michael and was he here? He'd been hiding under the cushions because he knew his mother wanted him to do his morning chores. Later I took a long walk, fighting the wind and the fine sand it stirred up. The sea and sky were a vast expanse of blue and the sunshine clean and strong. I saw a blimp and tankers quite close to shore. Stopped to chat with a Coast Guard from Iowa on patrol — very young, very lonely. 'This beach don't look like Coney Island,' he complained."

A week later she wrote:

"A pearl gray day with soft moisture. The heat has made me too indolent for real walking. But today was right for it. The bayberry has just shown its grey berries and the goldenrod will be out any day. Huge, blowsy marsh mallows show pink in the meadows. There is tiny meadow pink and the lavender morning glories, and cattails, long and strong and brown, and the soft old rose of milkweed. I saw sand moss, too — that strange gray-green which is the color of many growing plants here between the bay and the ocean. But alas, the beach is black with long gummy strings of oil, and you see it floating on the waves in dark, ugly masses — oil from tankers sunk by German raiders."

On October 27, 1942, Mommy wrote her mother:

"Dear Ma: I have tried every day to write you since the package came, but I have been so busy being tax collector. I had to arrange a tax sale to sell the properties of the owners who can't pay taxes, and I have been away from home at the borough hall every day.

"I get back at four when the children come from school, do all the housework between then and suppertime, and after supper try to write a letter, maybe, but somebody always comes, to see either me or Reynold on business, and that is the way the days go. The quilt is very pretty and I had fun picking out the pieces I recognized. It is gay and bright and I have it in my bedroom, although Margaret says she may take it any time. When housekeeping her room, I threw away an old doll quilt you made her several years ago. It was in shreds, and now that she has the new one you sent last spring I decided this one could go to the rag bag, although I wanted to keep it for sentiment, it had so many pieces of old dresses of mine — my King Tut dress from 1923, a piece of yellow satin ribbon that was a belt on a very elegant dress in 1918, and things like that.

"Does Clem [her brother] expect to be drafted? If he goes to war and if Reynold goes too, ask Clem if he will rent me his farm. I think I would like to get away from this seacoast for a while. Reynold may re-enlist in the Marine Corps. I hope you and Pa keep well. I had my misery all summer but have been feeling better since the children started to school. Maybe I've just been too busy. Your affectionate daughter, Josie."

Daddy tried to enlist in the Marine Corps but they rejected him because he was colorblind; he grumbled they didn't care about that in 1917. In early December he started war work at the New York Shipbuilding Co. in Camden, sixty miles west, on the Delaware River across from Philadelphia. He wrote to his wife:

"Jodear — Well, I'm a shipyard worker now! Can you hear my ears ringing? They tell me I'll get used to the terrific noise in a few days, or a couple of weeks, or months. Each man has a different guess. I have been lucky to get a nice clean place to room in a private family, one other boarder, within walking distance of the yards. I use the bus, though, for five cents, and make it in that many minutes. I leave the house at seven and stop at an all-night lunch wagon for breakfast. Two eggs and coffee — 40 cents. It is still dark when I finish and pick up a box lunch for 25 cents and a pint of milk for a dime. Then I punch in at number seven gate and go to the office. It is nice and warm there. I greet the boys and change clothes. (Remind me to bring back a wooden coat hanger.) Then to work. I carry a paint pot along in back of the 'counter' who is breaking me in.

"But listen to this: Monday morning I stood around in the dark waiting to get my badge. When it got light I found I was standing next to Ben McClellan. I went to their house for dinner last night. Monday afternoon I bumped into Warren Reno. I went there for dinner tonight and just got home. Tuesday morning, on the job, Jack Gordon yelled at me. I haven't been there for dinner yet.[5] My first paycheck will be December 17th, at which time I'll get one week's pay. The rest is held back until I leave.[6] Tell Poochy I saw Jimmy McClellan. Tell Mike to take care of the tools. I'll be home for dinner Saturday around six-thirty. My love to all of you, Tommy!"

I wrote a letter to my father in February 1943 when, one after the other, Michael and I had measles, a highly contagious disease that knocked children out for weeks, sometimes in isolation (a vaccine wasn't developed until the early 1960s). After telling Daddy that he left a fish on the back seat of the car and that the cat had dragged it in by the tail, I asked, "Will you please bring me home a good book and some valentines. And if you can get them please bring me some lead soldiers. Mommy could not write because she had to take care of His Royal Highness the Duke of Spots — that's Michael." What Daddy did bring me was a blue and red metal dump truck that was my favorite toy for years.

Just before Christmas, Mommy wrote her sister.
"Dear Marian: I put a package for you in the mail today and it was the measliest

one I have ever sent you, I think. And this Christmas we even <u>have</u> a little money. I had planned to do some shopping when I went down the island over the weekend, when Reynold was home, but I don't know if he will be able to buy enough gas to come home today (it is Saturday) and he may have to come by bus. Michael is sick with tonsillitis and has been home all week. I hope the box reaches you by Christmas and finds you having a happy day. We will just stay home, the second time since we have been married that we haven't driven up to Ridgewood or Bethlehem. Last Christmas we were in Bethlehem and had a marvelous time. Mildred's boy George is in North Africa now, driving an ambulance, and Dorothy's son Bob just enlisted in the Navy.

"I am glad to say that Margaret is good in school, but Michael, who is just as smart, spends his time fooling around. He has a marvelous memory, and went through the first grade learning all the stories by heart and not able to recognize a single word by himself."

When my mother read the comment on Michael's report card that he was "deficient in reading skills," she didn't believe it. She told her sister: "With an absent husband away on war work, a ten-year-old daughter, and a municipal job, I probably have not paid as much attention to Mike's schoolwork as I would have otherwise. Still, his earlier report cards didn't prepare me for this blow. He passed from first to second grade with no derogatory comment."

My mother spent the next two summers teaching Michael to read — it became her summer project. Of course she turned the experience into an article — several pages are left in her files—and she was bitterly disappointed when *The Ladies Home Journal* (as I recall) came out with an article "Why Can't Johnny Read?" before she completed hers. My mother's technique can be seen in this paragraph from the unfinished manuscript:

"I continued to use an offbeat approach. My next trick was to write sentences with misspelled words for him to find. Every one he discovered meant a penny for him, and if this be bribery make the most of it. Nearly every evening now, after catching up on my other job, found me writing little stories about 'a boy sevven years old, who lived on an isleand, and plaid with a boy elleven. I wrote what they eight, what they sed, what they didd, what they bawt at the store, and what they woor'." (Michael read very well when he entered third grade.)

The December letter to her sister continues:

"My plans for the winter are very unsettled. Nearly everybody has left here, and even the one store that is left may close and the post office keeps open only a few hours a day. There is no transportation out of here anymore. We have to go six miles to get a bus and fifteen to the nearest railroad. Still, to go up to Camden where Reynold is working, would mean paying terrific rent and living in some little apartment if we could find it, with the children penned up when they have been used to plenty of room to run. Also, it wouldn't be any cheaper because what Reynold pays for room and board is balanced by my pay here as tax collector. I don't get lonesome, but I do miss him, and don't like being a widow, so, I don't know. I'll probably just let events take their course.

"I have been terribly busy with that tax job taking about twice as much time as it did, and I am doing Reynold's job on the rationing board. He is a member, but is not here to take care of things. I can type better than this [There were lots of typos in this paragraph] — it's my cold fingers. It has been bitterly cold here, nothing but sleet and wind, and I have been the fireman, and every night I stay awake most of the night worrying for fear the stove will go out. We are lucky we have our iron potbelly (the stove, not me) that burns wood or coal. All the people who burn oil are much colder than we are. Much Love, Josie"

On the coldest nights, before we installed central heating, I fought with my brother over who would get the thick, rough Hudson Bay blanket, striped in red, green and black. The loser got Daddy's Coast Guard Auxiliary pea coat; I can still feel the weight of it. Sometimes, when the temperature dropped below zero, Michael slept with our parents and I had all the extra blankets, and I was allowed to wear my underwear and socks under my flannel nightgown. I lay on my back, solemn and still as a mummy while Mommy piled on the layers: cotton sheet, flannelette blanket, wool blanket, and Grandmother's patchwork quilt. After my goodnight kiss, my cat Greypuss crawled through a minute opening next to my neck, slithered along my body and curled around my ankles, securely tented for the night.

A winter blizzard left the beach so white any exposed sand became gray by contrast. A veil of white obliterated the few beachfront homes. Michael and I sledded down sand dunes on flattened cardboard boxes, or a Flexible Flyer when we had one. Right after a snowstorm the snow hugged the dunes, but snow on the beach melts quickly. Although Mommy didn't approve, when we were older, after a thick snowstorm Daddy tied ropes to the back of his 1939 Dodge pickup and towed us around town; when we slid fast enough we let go of the rope and coasted to a stop. And then we did it all over again.

I remember those frigid winters as a study in white and red. The frozen, crystal white bay, snowy white yard, frosty white windows and vaporous white breath. Red was the stove in the morning, a bulbous iron potbelly in the middle of the room. One of my parents had to get up early, shake down the ashes, put on more coal and open the draft. In less than ten minutes the bottom half was glowing as hot and red as my mother's lipstick or the holly berries in the garden.

NOTES

[1] *In a seasonal economy, many businesses borrow from the bank to carry them until the next year; I did the same fifteen years later. During the Depression, if the owner of a business knew that eventually you'd be good for it, he carried you. I found a running tab from Paxson's Drug Store in Beach Haven for the years 1936 to 1941 — the yellowing sheets are fastened with a rusted straight pin. In July 1941 the balance due was $70; in September, my*

mother paid ten dollars on account. A 1940 itemized bill from Mrs. Weiseisen, our sitter, scribbled in pencil, indicated my mother paid her 25 cents for an evening and 50 cents for an afternoon. The total for that May was $14.

[2] The town discovered the previous tax collector had embezzled $400; she was sentenced to three years in jail.

[3] The bills my mother saved showed that they paid her doctors a little at a time from 1938, finally catching up in 1945.

[4] Yes, two nicknames in one paragraph.

[5] All three men and their families had summer homes in Harvey Cedars. The McClellans moved to town permanently during the war.

[6] Daddy's salary for 1943 was almost $600.

19
1943
The War on the Homefront

I now have enough hair for pigtails; with Michael.

"One day there is a blizzard from the northwest and the next day a wet storm from the ocean and then vice-versa. I stay indoors and dream of working in the flower garden. Raising flowers on the edge of this salt water is harder than raising children, but I always manage to get some results."

While Daddy worked at his defense industry job, Mommy went back to the type-writer. Night after night my brother and I were lulled to sleep by pounding surf punctuated by the staccato of clacking keys. The sound of the typewriter in the evening assured me she was there, and became almost a lullaby. Uncle Bill gave my mother an Underwood upright when the Bethlehem Steel offices upgraded, and the little Royal portable from the 1920s moved into the attic, where it still rests. She worked on the war story, the article about teaching Michael to read, and probably other articles that were long ago fed to the potbelly stove. Inspired by that stove and the coal shortage during the war — a repeat of the one in 1919 when she boarded at Mrs. Dudley's — my mother transformed the incident into what she again termed "barely disguised fiction."

No Coal on the Island

Jo realized the coal pile was low and thought, "I must order some today," as she carried in the bucket. But she turned out four thousand words that day after Meg, proud and delighted to be riding in Ollie's noisy truck, left with him to go to the mainland for lumber. She remembered only after she covered the typewriter and went out to bring in the coal for the night.

"Not even a lump," was the cheerful reply when she rang up to order a ton from Flack, ten miles down the island. "We been outta coal week or more. Been promising it all week, too. Sure, I'll have you some up there just soon's it comes."

Two days later there was still no coal on the island. She telephoned another dealer, who said, "Who?" three times when she gave her name and address, and then informed her that he, too, was out of coal. She doubted it and hung up. Back in the coal bin, she stooped over laboriously and picked up a few last pieces out of the cracks around the edge and looked about the shed to see what she could burn. There was an orange crate, two vegetable baskets she had promised to return to the huckster, and boards too big and heavy for her to chop with an ax. She made a fine roaring blaze for ten minutes, and the crate and baskets were ashes in less than a half hour.

Calling Meg, they walked along the bayshore toward the point and came back with a skirt-front full of driftwood, old barrel staves and a pile of blocks the carpenters on the Basset house had given Meg the summer before.

"I'll get you some more," Jo promised at her protests at having them burned up, even as she remembered that nobody was building houses any more. "We'll come back in the morning and find a lot more."

Jo used only enough to make a small fire while she and Meg ate plates of hot soup, and went to bed as soon as Meg did. Sometime in the night she was awakened by rain lashing the east windows and thought, "There goes my wood." She went in to cover Meg, who had squirmed out of her covers and lay in a small huddled knot. In the morning she started a fire with the driftwood, putting in only two pieces at a time, and telephoned Flack again.

"Same old story, Mrs. Thomas," he told her. "Them people just keep promising and promising and don't do nothin' about it. The only way I'm keeping my own furnace going is borrowing."

Very few people were burning coal. Most people had changed to oil furnaces. She remembered the Hatfield's coal bin in their laundry. There was probably coal there, but the laundry was locked and they were in Florida, which had been their solution to the problem of keeping warm in their eighteen-room home on the Main Line.

Extracting Meg's promise that she would not get out of bed, Jo put on her raincoat and walked over to Ollie's house. There was no answer to her shouts, and the truck was gone. If Ollie was working somewhere, he wouldn't be back until five o'clock, and you couldn't ask a man tired and hungry from a hard day's work to come over and split wood for you.

Jo went out to the shed again and looked about, making a mental list. She noted the stepladder, three surfboards, three or four toy sailboats. At Meg's handsomest toy, an airplane model of polished wood, she hesitated, then put it back on the shelf. Inside were two wooden trays, the salad bowl, the cheese tray, the rolling pin, the kitchen stool, books — she wondered why she had not thought of the books before, the rows of books on the top shelves that nobody read, and which she had thought of getting rid of to use the shelves for her Quimper plates. She did not have the nerve to give them to the USO. She admitted she didn't buy war stamps the way she should, but she still was not the kind of person who expected soldiers to read *How to Raise Rabbits*, *Europe's Answer in 1914*, *Manual of Composition and Rhetoric* or the best sellers of 1932.

She piled them inside the stove, went over the shelves again and brought down four Old World Almanacs, a set of Emerson which she always meant to read and never had, a heavy volume of gossip from Paris in the second Empire, and fourteen paper-covered Tauchnitz editions. One of them she turned over reminiscently and then put back on the shelf. It reminded her of the blonde young Austrian on the train trip from Salzburg to Kitzbuhel, where she had bought it. He had written to her for three months afterward. When you are a woman with one child sick in bed and another one what is known as six months along, with your figure and your looks gone, and your body so uncomfortable you swear under your breath all day and would do it louder if it were not for Meg hearing, it is good to be reminded that once you had been a glamour girl.

She was laying out a pile of choice things to burn when a car drove into the yard, and something landed on the back porch with a thump. It was two bags of coal.

"Rest of the ton will be up tomorrow," Flack told her as he dumped them in the empty bin. "Truck just come in, and I thought I'd take care of you as soon's I could. I sure hope you got along all right."

"I sure did," she said. Jo thought she had never seen anything so beautiful.

All letters between my mother and her sister Marian have lengthy discussions about clothes, formerly their own, and now their children's. My older cousin Dorothy sent me all her hand-me-downs and Dorothy's younger brother, also named Michael after our Grandfather Lehman, got my brother's. Before my mother got so busy, she offered to sew clothes for Marian. Aside from sitting at her typewriter, most of the visual memories I have of my mother are either in the kitchen or her sewing room — I hated to stand still for fittings and even with all my squirming, my mother turned out some beautiful clothes.

March 18, 1943:

"Dear Marian: Margaret is delighted with the little suit. The shoulders and waist-line are exactly right for her, and I shall only have to shorten the sleeves and hem. The sweater and blouse are very pretty and fit her exactly. She can't wait until it's warm enough to wear them. I keep her in woolens all winter because these Arctic winds make the house drafty.

"I am fed up with birthdays and wouldn't have celebrated mine but the children would have been very sad. [This was her 45th.] They worked like little Indians wrapping up 'surprises' for me, and spent an hour decorating the table so I had to get busy and make a cake for myself that I didn't really want, and put ten candles on it. The joke pops up every year — is that your mental age? Ice cream is a big event as the nearest is five miles away. We had so much left I sent a plateful to the Lithuanian fisherman who lives down the bay, and when he brought the plate back the next day, he brought me six big duck eggs. I couldn't think of what to do with them at first, but finally put them all into a sponge cake. It was the best I ever made.

"Congratulations on the raise. I know you deserve it. As for the gray hair, I just use my little mascara brush and touch up the temples a bit, or what shows under my hat, and to heck with the rest of it … The children are back in school this week and I'm glad to have the time during the day to get organized. Your comment about a secretary's desk drawers appealed to me. I am still a better office worker than housekeeper. My desk over at the Borough Hall where I keep my tax books is neat and in perfect order, but my own desk here in the house is pretty awful. But I have given up hope, with two children to use the paper, pull out the erasers, lose the ruler and ruin the pens.

"Tommy is working the night shift at the shipyard now, which he hates, and it will complicate his getting home unless he takes the car up there. With much love and thanks. Josie"

March 23, 1943:

"Dear Ma and Pa: Still having very bad weather here after the mild winter. One day there is a blizzard from the northwest and the next day a wet storm from the ocean and then vice-versa. I stay indoors and dream of working in the flower garden. Raising flowers on the edge of this salt water is harder than raising children, but I always manage to get some results. Tulips, daffodils and hyacinths are up. More later. Josie"

My mother was depressed by the war news and attacked her garden with renewed energy. She produced amazing flowers, vegetables and tomatoes; her farm upbringing gave her a powerful green thumb. We composted our garbage and worked the mixture of coffee grounds, tea leaves, egg shells, and the carcasses of lobsters and hard-shell crabs into the soil around the base of tomato plants. My mother battled the segmented, medieval looking tomato worms. She picked them off with her bare fingers while I hopped from one foot to another, making all sorts of groans and squeals, horrified that she would actually touch the iridescent green monster. In addition to parsley, Mommy planted rosemary, thyme, and oregano, not usual ingredients for a 1940s cook. She liked to "pick something green and fresh" for her soups, stews and sauces. She longed for the rich mainland soil that had to be trucked over to the island. It was difficult to grow flowers in sand, she said. My mother dug aggressively; she moved a plant here, then there, then back again. When I asked why she didn't just leave it in one place, she said, "Because I can't afford a psychiatrist."

During the war, it was a homeowner's patriotic duty to provide her own fruits and produce so our garden became a Victory Garden filled with carrots, spinach, tomatoes, broccoli, radishes, green onions, and probably more that I can't remember. Green beans clung to tall poles against the house; the carrot plot doubled and green peas, with stuffed

Jo's Meatloaf

Her meatloaf was light and flavorful, with slices of bacon draped across the top. This recipe was one of the few that my mother listed the ingredients. She said: "A meatloaf can be as rubbery and tasteless as a mixture of old inner tube shavings or as crisply crusted and flavorful as a roast. This recipe is the best I have ever tasted."

2 slices dense white bread
1/2 cup milk
   Let these two soak in large bowl until the bread can be crumbled finely, then add
   2 cloves garlic minced very fine
   1/3 cup Heinz ketchup
   1 T. horseradish
   1/2 t. dried mustard
   1/4 t. each ginger, nutmeg and oregano
   1/2 t. coarse ground pepper
   3 lbs. Ground beef, preferable lean chuck, with one or two pork chops ground with beef
   2 raw eggs
   1 large chopped onion
   2 stalks celery chopped fine
   1 T Worcestershire sauce
   1T A-1 Sauce
   Mix all this with both hands as though you were mixing bread. (Does anyone how to mix bread anymore?) However you do it, mix it well, shape into a long loaf and put in a buttered Pyrex or ovenproof casserole, put two or three strips of bacon across the top and bake 1 1/2 hours in a 350 oven. Serve in the same dish, with or without thickening the drippings into gravy. Even better, for those who have tossed the calorie list into Barnegat Bay, is a horseradish sauce made of whipped heavy cream and horseradish. Nobody ever refuses this, but your plump friends will hate you.

pods begging to be popped, scrambled across the sandy soil. We planted an apple tree, still growing, although not producing any apples. I planted a peach pit and a small tree was growing three or four years later; it bore a handful of peaches each summer and stayed in the garden long after my mother died.

My mother was a very good cook and ahead of her time in her use of herbs, imported cheese, and olive oil. When butter was rationed she tried oleomargarine, a lard-like glob of white fat that came packaged with yellow dye, which the housewife would mix and hope it looked like butter. It didn't look like it or taste like it and we rarely used it. Mommy rolled out her pie crusts with lard and laced the apple pies with cinnamon and a shot of brandy, if she had it. We ate simple food, but always well flavored. "You're not a real cook unless there's a fresh lemon in the icebox," was one of her dictates.

For Sunday night supper, we often had hash patties of leftover meat and potatoes and carrots served with a poached egg on top and a spicy red sauce on the side. Mommy knew how to sear a steak in a hot iron frying pan so it was red and juicy inside; and she cringed when Michael insisted on slopping ketchup on it. My mother didn't overcook our fresh vegetables and always squeezed a little lemon juice on them. Green beans, asparagus and broccoli in season were the best, and at the table, we were allowed to pick up the asparagus with our fingers. The way it was done in France, mommy told us. We didn't eat as much fish as we might have, even though it was plentiful and cheap — Daddy said he never wanted to see another fish.

Scribbled on the back of a cancelled check I found my mother's marinade for leg of lamb, which she cooked only until pink in the center, not well done, as most cooks in the '40s and '50s did. She rubbed it with garlic, juice of lemon, salt, pepper, paprika, and a "sprinkle of thyme or rosemary." In another recipe she cut it in cubes and marinated it overnight in "1/3 cup sherry, 2 T. olive oil, chunks of onions and a little oregano, salt, pepper and vinegar. Broil or fry in butter."

Mommy expressed her love with food and their flavors carried meaning; sometimes she called me Sweetie or Sweet Pea and other times Sourpuss or Picklepuss. She made junket when we were sick and I can still remember the cooling softness as it slithered down my sore throat.

April 7, 1943:

"Dear Marian: That handkerchief is lovely, and I am a louse not to write before. I claim forgiveness for having been sick. I celebrated my birthday flat in bed. I passed out in a faint for almost the first time in my life, from what the doctor says is nervous exhaustion. It was a terrible winter, first Michael's ear infection for three weeks. Then I broke a bone in my foot.[1] Then a month of measles, then Reynold had a bad accident to his knee so that after five weeks he is still on crutches. For two weeks he was not allowed out of bed, and with nobody to help me — all the trays and work wore me out. I am slowly getting better, but every day about eleven a pain starts to pound in the back of my head and then I am finished for the day. It is very annoying.

"Thank you sis, for the nice birthday remembrance, especially the dollar. I'll really spend it on myself. With Love. Josie"

This was my last year at the one-room school and in my final report card — comments only, no numerical grade — Mrs. Moffett wrote: "I have been more than pleased with the progress that Margaret has made this year and feel that she will continue to do so. The only trouble with her arithmetic (which is not up to her other marks) is that she does not always think logically, but I'm sure she will overcome this. She is still very young." In June 1943, as soon as school was out, I visited Aunt Milly in Bethlehem. My mother saved a postcard I wrote: "There will be a circus July 5th. I want to go but I'd rather come home. I have been going to bed at eight, would you change it to nine? Grandperce is here. Could I go to Ridgewood with him then go home on the Barnegat train? Love to all. With love, Margaret."

I was ten this summer and earned 15 cents a week allowance helping my mother with the housework; then I was free to roam. The bay crawled with crabs then and, from the time I was eight, I was obsessed with clamming and crabbing. Crabs hid behind the pilings — one piling, one crab. I could almost count on it. I didn't use a crab trap, but waded in the water with a net and pushed the crab into the net with my foot, protected by an old sneaker.

My younger brother Michael and I had two methods of catching clams — the very easy and the easy. Daddy was a dredging contractor, and if the dredge was filling a lot in town, we would stand on the edge of the crater made by the force of the sand and water that gushed out of the end of the dredge pipe; the turbulence looked like boiling oatmeal. The force of the pump sucked the clams from the bottom of the bay along with the sand and shot them out of the pipe into the roiling cauldron. I had but to bend down and pick up a clam as it rolled down the watery slope. We skittered from one to the next and soon had a basketful. That was the very easy method. The easy method was treading. It was impossible to dig your toes into the soft sand at the bottom of the bay and not hit a clam. I walked through chest high water and squiggled my toes into the sand, one foot after the other, half floating, and moved with a swivel-hipped motion, arms extended for balance, until I felt the hard ridge of the bivalve. With my toes, I worked the clam up the opposite leg until I could dunk down and reach it with my hand and drop it into a basket floating in an inner tube. Clams and crabs provided a steady source of income in the summer. Houghton's Clam Bar paid 25 cents for a good-sized soft-shell crab or a dozen clams. My mother suggested peddling them directly to summer renters who had trouble turning down fresh seafood offered by two smiling children. It was a good lesson in productivity and reward, plus it augmented my 15 cents a week allowance.

That winter, on December 15th, my mother wrote a catch-up letter to Marian:
"Dear Sis: You can call me anything you like for not writing for so long but don't be too harsh on this typing as the typewriter is frozen up and won't slide along and

half the keys won't hit.

"This was the first summer that I had absolutely nobody but Margaret to help me with the housework, as Mrs. Weiseisen, whom I have had for ten years, had a fulltime job and everybody has left the island for war jobs. I had more work than ever for my tax collector job, and more work taking care of the money as I could get no gas for making the fifteen mile trip to the nearest bank to deposit the cash, and day after day had to stand in long lines at the post office to buy money orders.[2]

"All of us have had flu for the last month. I have gone down twice with it; probably because I am the one that can't stay in bed to get any rest. I hope this flu epidemic has missed your family. Margaret's school on the mainland is closed, but Michael is still going.[3]

"Tommy has finally been discharged by the Insurance Company with a 10 percent permanent disability in one leg. It doesn't hamper him to any extent, but he must be careful of it the rest of his life. He doesn't limp, fortunately. He is doing some odd contracting jobs for the county, although his own business is now folded up for the rest of the war.

"I can't struggle with this typewriter any longer. It needs to have the oil changed to winter grade, I guess. Remember the French opera glasses you gave me so long ago? I use them to look across the bay at boats stuck in the ice. With all our love. Josie"

Daddy left New York Shipbuilding and took a job with Eastern Engineering Co., a firm building a rock jetty to help control the current at Barnegat Inlet, where in March he broke his knee. He received a $350 disability settlement for the sixteen weeks he was unable to work. Daddy also joined the U.S. Coast Guard Auxiliary about this time. These men stood watch in the towers at the five Coast Guard stations up and down the island, which relieved the Coast Guards for sea duty.

During these war years, dinner ended at quarter of seven, when we listened to Lowell Thomas's news broadcast on CBS. This time was sacrosanct; when LT went on the air we were not allowed to interrupt. We followed the war's progress on a large world map tacked to the wall. My mother wept when she tried to explain the difference between a German and a Nazi, but the distinction was lost on me. Sometimes, when she read the Sunday *New York Times,* she would slam down the paper and head into the garden. My father taught my brother and me to present arms using a stick for a rifle, and we sang the Marines hymn and the Air Corps song, "Off we go into the wild blue yonder..." At first I thought a "yonder" was a type of plane. I carved models of Spitfires, Zeroes, Messerschmitts, B-17 bombers, Mustangs and my favorite, the twin-fuselage P-38.

Harvey Cedars had its own war hero, Colonel Russell Ives, who was captured by the Japanese during the battle of Corregidor. His wife spent the war years at their summer home on our street, and forlornly walked the beach, not knowing her husband's fate; it wasn't until after Japan's surrender that she learned he survived the 1942 Bataan Death March.

As for all Americans, our food was rationed. My mother tore butter, sugar, coffee, and meat coupons from our ration books, and often Uncle Bill and Aunt Milly augmented our coffee and sugar.[4]

My mother sent her chocolate cake recipe to Marian:

"The best and most delicate chocolate cake in flavor and texture is one made with real sour milk, not sweet milk with vinegar added. But thick, naturally soured milk is impossible to find anymore, and even the superiority of the cake hardly justifies keeping a cow. The next best recipe I know uses sweet milk. For weeks I hesitated to try it, as I suspected it was a misprint. When I mixed it the first time, I was still dubious. An cake batter than uses almost as much milk as flour, and that goes into the oven looking like thick brown soup — well, what cook wouldn't be skeptical?

"I needn't have been. This cake is fine-grained, moist, fudge-like and tastes richly of chocolate. Here it is: An hour or more before starting to make it, take out of the refrigerator a half cup butter, three eggs, one and one-half cups milk, to lose that sepulchral chill. Grease two large layer cake tins. When the butter has softened, set your oven to preheat at 350 degrees, and put four squares of Baker's bitter chocolate (none other) in it to melt. Use a thick pottery dish so the chocolate won't burn, and don't forget it.

"Mix quarter cup butter (use the other quarter cup) for frosting, one and one-half cups granulated sugar and two egg yolks until the mixture is very smooth and creamy. Take the chocolate from the oven as soon as it's softened, don't let it bubble, and let it cool while you are sifting one and three-quarter cups flour. You don't need cake flour, just ordinary Gold Medal, three and a half level teaspoons of Royal baking powder (a poor baking powder can ruin this cake) and a half-teaspoon of salt.

"Now beat the three egg whites (what you do with the third egg yolk is your problem) until stiff, then add a half cup granulated sugar in about four installments, beating each time. The mixture should look like a nice thick fluffy shaving lather.

"From now on work fast. Stir the warm chocolate into the butter, egg and sugar mixture and beat thoroughly, then add two teaspoons real vanilla, the cup and a half of milk and the sifted flour mixture and beat all together until perfectly smooth, but no more. Too much beating makes a tough cake. You can use an electric mixer, but hand mixing produces the best results.

"Now empty the egg white mixture on the chocolate batter and with the lightest possible strokes, fold it in. Don't beat. Don't stir. Move your mixing spoon up and over, softly and stealthily, until the mixtures are combined and you can see no streaks, but for no longer. Pour the batter in the cake tins and bake 30 minutes on the top shelf of the oven. If the cake hasn't pulled away at the edges, give it another five or ten minutes. Be sure it isn't soggy in the center. It must spring back when you press a finger on it gently. If you are doubtful, turn off the oven and leave it in another five minutes.

"Let the layers cook, and not on the windowsill, as a sudden blast of cold air can make the cake fall flat. Don't frost until it is cool, or the butter frosting will melt and float away.

"For the icing, mix the remaining quarter cup butter with three-quarters of a package of XXXX confectioners sugar, two melted squares bitter chocolate, one teaspoon or less of instant coffee powder, one teaspoon vanilla and then dribble in mild or cream, stirring constantly until it will hold its shape when spread. If you get it too thin, add more XXXX sugar. Spread the icing and put cake in the refrigerator a half hour or so to set it. This cake will keep moist and delicious for a week in cool weather if kept airtight and the teenagers don't know about it."

In fifth grade my poster of fat being poured from a frying pan into a coffee can won the school competition. Mommy saved a letter from school that I wrote on lined paper: "Dear Mother, Will you please put out any scrap that you don't need. Our school has started a salvage collection to help win the war. We want iron, steel, rubber, copper, brass, lead, old rags and rope. Thank you. Lieutenant Thomas."

Propaganda posters lined the entrance hall wall at school: in one, a red, white and blue Uncle Sam emerged from a cloud backed by a billowing American flag; a squadron of bombers flew overhead while troops with bayonets ready marched on the ground. The text read, "Buy War Bonds." Another poster invited children to join the American Junior Red Cross.

Black oilcloth blinds covered all windows on the east side of our house, and car headlights were painted with black eyelids for those times when the gas ration was sufficient for night driving. Barnegat Lighthouse was blacked out on its seaward side. Civil Defense gave every homeowner and renter — the few that were here during wartime summers — a card with instructions on what to do in case of air-raid or poison gas attack, and our parents turned this serious concern into a game. When the air-raid siren let out its terrifying screech, we were to turn the radio dial to 650, close the curtains, and turn out all lights. Michael and I pulled cushions under the sturdy drop-leaf table and kept a picture book, flashlight, and Milky Way bar there. Michael liked making a game of all this, but I wanted to know what to do if a bomb hit the house, or if paratroopers landed, or if a U-boat came up and shot at us. Would we really be safe under the table? Would the German soldiers kill us if my mother spoke to them in German?

V-mail[5] from Cousin George let us know of his progress across North Africa and confirmed his part in the invasion of Italy. Michael and I created our own Anzio beachhead on the little beach next to our house. We took turns being either George-and-the-liberators landing in the rowboat, or the soon-to-be-defeated Italians and Germans entrenched on the beach behind the bayberry bushes. I discovered my father's World War I gas mask and helmet in the attic, but my mother didn't allow me to wear it; she said it would upset Daddy. After futile attempts to stop them, she bore our war games, but she allowed no gunplay in the house.

We were allowed on the beach during the day, and Michael and I became first-rate scavengers. Beachcombing yielded an abundance of artifacts: waterlogged tar-stained life jackets stamped "USN," a deflated rubber raft, tins of pure water, C-rations (tasteless biscuits), K-rations (biscuits and pithy, tasteless chocolate), and the rare but more desirable A-rations. We opened one square tin of A-rations that had hard candy, coffee, sugar, Spam, and a little tin of fruit cups. Sometimes we found yellow-bombs, the name we gave to the four-inch, tubular, sealed-glass vials containing a yellow, zeolitic exchange resin that purified salt water. The vials made a small but satisfying explosion when thrown vigorously onto the street, leaving a white smear on the black tar.

One evening, while trying to concentrate on my homework, I overheard my father tell my mother that a Coast Guard had pulled a body out of the surf; when he grabbed one of the hands to haul it to shore, the skin peeled off like a formal evening glove. Suddenly I understood the significance of the sailor caps and uniform fragments Michael and I found at the high tide line.

NOTES

[1] *After we had gone to sleep on Christmas Eve, Mommy stubbed and broke her toe when she didn't turn on the light as she put presents under the Christmas tree.*

[2] *In the attic, I found all my parents' tax bills and income tax forms. Real estate tax on our property in 1943 was $56 on an assessment of $1,000, which included our house and six separate lots — so it is conceivable that a taxpayer could come into the office clutching a $10 bill to pay the tax. My parents' declared income, called "Individual Income and Victory Tax" on Form 1040, was a bit over $1,500. The tax collector's job netted $950. They paid $18 income tax.*

[3] *Twenty-one thousand persons died during this epidemic. My school was 16 miles by bus across the bay in Barnegat; Michael went to the one-room school in Barnegat Light that I had attended for the first five years.*

[4] *Joseph Wood, a wealthy summer resident, brought my mother extra butter and sugar when he could, knowing she would bake a chocolate cake and give him half. On the sly, Michael and I called him Jesus Christ Wood, because of his double goatee. We thought he looked like the romanticized paintings of Jesus we saw in Sunday school. Mr. Wood sat in the living room, his animated chin wagging, as he discussed the war in Europe with Mommy, and reminisced about their travels there. In a later article, my mother described him as a, "distinguished artist, World War I aviator, mountain climber, English sports car owner and Loveladies summer resident."*

[5] *Victory Mail. Letters to and from servicemen overseas were microfilmed to reduce bulk and weight of letters transported by ship.*

20
1944 TO 1945
Hurrricane Devastates
Harvey Cedars

The Hartmans and my parents at our house overlooking Barnegat Bay. I am standing, left.

*"Daddy watched the tidal wave overwhelm the town. He told us that the
wave lifted itself twenty-five feet above the dunes and advanced toward
the boulevard in a solid wall of green water, no foam. Lloyd Good's huge,
oceanfront home split in two, and the north and south wings rose
up in the air like a 'V'. Water covered the island as
far as he could see, from ocean to bay."*

During the summer of 1944, life at the shore flowed in a subdued rhythm, marked by events of the war. In June, the Allied Forces invaded Europe, and young men who in another summer might have guarded our beaches, fought their way across France. The Battle of the Atlantic was declared officially over; U-Boats no longer stalked shipping off the coast. Although the last attack was in December 1943, Daddy, with the Coast Guard Auxiliary, still stood six-hour watches. By Labor Day, in Europe, battle toughened veterans of the First Army penetrated the Siegfried Line. The end of the war was in sight that hot dry summer, and an optimism that sons and husbands would soon return was in the air. Even though gas rationing was still in effect, summer residents trickled back to Long Beach Island. Daddy anticipated getting back to work and Mommy thought that finally she could visit her parents in Michigan.

Harvey Cedars had more on its mind than the war. On August 1st, a hurricane passed offshore and seriously eroded the Harvey Cedars beach. The volunteer fire company retrieved the contents of two homes, which were so undermined they were about to topple into the ocean. My father had been elected a town Commissioner the year before and, together with Mayor Joe Yearly, was lobbying the state for aid to erect some sort of barrier along the beach. They worried that the ocean was trying to force an inlet through the town. The state promised emergency aid when the borough submitted a plan.

On September 13th, the *Philadelphia Inquirer* warned, "A great hurricane fraught with peril for life and property is bearing down on the North Carolina coast; only a last minute change of direction could save the coastline from a raking by winds of a force comparable to the New England hurricane of 1938." Searching for excitement was second nature to me as a child, so that Tuesday morning, September 14th when I heard my parents speak in hushed voices about a hurricane, I thought it would be a neat adventure. Mommy was packing my lunch as Daddy tapped the barometer on the wall by the kitchen door; it was below 28.9 inches and dropping. I begged not to be sent to school; I tried to convince Daddy that he needed me, a skinny eleven-year-old, to help him move the boats.

My mother's words came down from on high: "Poochy has to go to school." So off I went, grudgingly, and scuffed down 80th Street to wait for the school bus that would take me the sixteen miles to the mainland, where I was in sixth grade. It was a warm day, too warm for mid-September, still and sunny early in the morning, with an oppressive humidity. As I waited for the bus, I saw the red-and-black hurricane-watch flag flying over the general store two blocks away. In 1944, hurricane advisories as we know them now did not exist; and because of the war, radio silence at sea precluded any warships from sending — or receiving — advance warnings.

The early morning news from radio station WFPG in Atlantic City reported that the hurricane had hit Cape Hatteras and veered out to sea, so some families turned off their radio and went about their business. Others phoned the Coast Guard stations to ask whether or not to evacuate, but their responses were not consistent. The Ship Bottom station advised one of my mother's friends with two babies to leave. The Barnegat Light station told another, "If you have a well built house, stay put." My father took no chances. He prepared to tow his dredge into the relative safety of Harvest Cove at the south end of town, just east of the Bible Conference.

At the old stone school, I tried to pay attention to our teacher. But as the wind increased, it swiped the trees against the multi-paned windows; all I wanted was to get back on the island. By eleven o'clock it was raining and blowing about thirty-five knots. The school board, in an inexplicable distortion of safety, sent all the "beach kids" back to the island.

We boarded our buses and lumbered back east across the low causeway — it seemed even lower than usual as the storm pushed more ocean water through the two inlets into the bay, which was solid white and frothing. The powerful northeast wind buffeted our snaking yellow convoy; spray splashed against the windows and the buses rocked back and forth. Ned Galbraith, a boy four years older, who lived in Harvey Cedars, sat behind me and we decided to ride our bikes and meet at Mr. Small's oceanfront house after we had lunch. As I got off the bus I noticed that the dried salt spray had coated one side white.

Mommy was in the kitchen distractedly baking a cake — my mother cooked when she got nervous. I grabbed a peanut butter and pickle sandwich, told her I was meeting Ned at Small's, and ran out. I tried to eat my sandwich while I pedaled but I needed both hands to hold the heavy Schwinn as the wind strengthened and pushed me south. Ned and I dropped our bikes in the lee of the house and crouched and crawled to get near the high bulkhead that was built to protect the home facing the ocean.

We cupped our hands around our eyes in a futile attempt to protect them from stinging sand, borne on the northeast wind. Neither of us had ever experienced an ocean like this — no longer our friendly swimming hole, but a sea of white churning foam all the way to the horizon. The beach had disappeared. Huge waves slammed against the bulkhead and sprayed geysers of sticky warm water over our flattened bodies. We lay on our bellies and looked at each other, awestruck. We couldn't talk because our voices blew away with the wind. The sky had an oppressive yellow tinge. Ned stood up and broke into a run. I followed, shoved by the wind back into the lee of the house. Ned shouted in my ear that he'd better get home in case his mother needed help. I leaned into the wind and pushed the bike the five blocks along the two-lane main road — no way could I ride against that blast. As the tide rose, I saw the first water splash through the break in the dunes at the end of the block-long streets that lead from the main road to the ocean.

Mommy was frantic when I got home. The tide in the bay was about to come over the bulkhead into the yard. Daddy nailed wide boards over the bay window and cracked the kitchen window an inch so the house wouldn't explode under the low pressure. "Go out and find the cats," she said. I knew it was serious when Mommy let all the cats in the house when we were out. She packed food, made thermoses of coffee for Daddy who would stay to change the lines on the dredge as the wind shifted. We were evacuating to the mainland; my mother would drive us in the pickup. Daddy wouldn't need it because the next high tide would cover the road.

It was two in the afternoon and the wind was blowing a gale; by four it would reach hurricane force. I remember the fear in my mother's face during the drive back to the mainland, as she struggled through water almost up to the hubcaps; but my memory doesn't resurface again until it is dark and my brother and I are huddled with my mother in a bed at the National Hotel in Manahawkin, pretending to concentrate on a game of gin rummy. The wind shrieked — wind really does shriek — and the 19th-century building swayed, flying shingles ricocheted against the hotel and a tree crashed onto the roof. We were all scared now.

From the dredge, riding high but secure in the cove, Daddy watched the storm surge overwhelm the town. He told us that the wave lifted itself twenty-five feet above the dunes and

Jo's Meatballs

Two pounds beef ground with one thick pork chop with fat removed, one medium onion cut very fine, one egg, quarter cup of catsup (Heinz is best); one large clove garlic, grated or cut to one-fifteen thousandth of an inch; about a rounded tablespoon of bread crumbs or one slice bread or leftover toast. Dip toast in water to soften and crumble up. Add two teaspoons salt and a dash of pepper.

Put all this in a good-sized bowl and mix with your hands (of course you washed them) until blended and smooth, with no lumps of bread, but work gently and fashion into balls about the size of a plum or small egg. In a heavy iron skillet or kettle put enough olive oil just to cover the bottom. When hot, put in as many meatballs as you can without them touching each other. Adjust heat so meat gets a good dark brown without burning. Brown on other side and lift out, then fry another batch until all done. I turn up the heat before each batch, and then turn it down again. I use high and medium on an electric stove. The pan must be hot enough or the meatballs will lose their juice and cook up a sorry gray color.

Sauce: When all meat balls are dark brown and crusty on outside, turn heat to low and slice into fat in pan three large onions, one green pepper shredded thin, three or four stalks of celery cut fine, two cloves garlic and let this cook about five minutes or more, so that the onions turn golden but not brown. (The garlic must not get too hot.) If I have a nice sweet carrot from the garden I shred it in now — I learned this trick from that chef in Rome. While this is cooking, open two large cans of tomatoes and one of tomato paste. Combine everything, using about two cans of water to rinse out the tomato paste can. Stir well and simmer at very low heat with seasonings in thick pot for two or three hours, stirring occasionally to make sure it does not stick to bottom. Simmer soup bone with it for added flavor.

Seasonings: Two teaspoons of salt, one scant teaspoon Worcestershire sauce, one tablespoon A-1 sauce, one tablespoon catsup, one bay leaf, one generous pinch of thyme, oregano and marjoram. I add some chopped parsley when I have it. Optional: slice in some mushrooms. If sauce becomes too thick, add water.

split Lloyd Good's huge oceanfront house in two, and the north and south wings rose up in the air like a "V." Water covered the island as far as he could see, from ocean to bay. Whole houses and pieces of houses floated by the dredge.

The Great Atlantic Hurricane, named by the Miami Weather Bureau, passed Long Beach Island at high tide about 30 miles offshore; its maximum winds registered 96 miles an hour. Witnesses described the storm surge — that massive mound of moving water topped by a cresting wave — as anywhere from 30 to 100 feet high. The eye passed about six in the evening and the wind shifted to westerly and pushed all the debris-filled water that had washed into the bay from the ocean back out again.

We returned to the island at dawn the next morning; because we were residents, the State Police let us back on. When I saw what was left of my town my awe changed to shock. Sand covered everything; it looked like a two-mile stretch of beach sprinkled with whole buildings, homes belly-up and fragments of homes — a wall and a floor here, half a house there, roofs at rakish angles — all scattered like my brother's toys on our sandlot across the street. The soldiers' barracks next to the Coast Guard station had washed over near the bay. Mr. Gurney's real estate office was plop in the middle of the road. Our friend Jimmy McClellan's house on 76th Street had disappeared; every home on his street was gone. He was crying, and Jimmy never cried. The tide had peaked at a record nine and a half feet and the storm surge destroyed almost all the oceanside homes I'd passed on my bike the day before. Front yards on the bay were a mess of smashed timbers, porches, stairways, refrigerators, cupboards, deck chairs, benches, rowboats, sailboats, wicker furniture, cushions, dead seagulls, and chicken coops. (It was wartime and people kept chickens.) People stood around in small groups, not sure of what to do. Soldiers billeted at the Coast Guard station wore bold, black, and white Military Police armbands, and took charge of the town, alert for looters who tried to come by boat from the mainland.

All the windows on the east side of our house were blown out and a scummy line on the wall about four inches above the floor marked how high the water had been. Sand and grit was over everything below that level, but our two cats and four kittens purred placidly on the rolled-up rugs and waited for food. The garage and everything in it was gone; the front of the car looked like an accordion.

In a newspaper article eleven years later, my mother wrote about the experience from a cook's point of view:

"All the water mains were broken and water was obtainable only at the pump house. I brought my own bucket and walked it home. Walked, because hardly a street was passable with a car, even if the car didn't have a hundred pounds of sand under the hood. People with gas stoves could still cook, but with no electricity on the island, food in shops was spoiling by the ton.

"At noon the day after the hurricane, the Red Cross sent down food trucks and handed out sandwiches, coffee and soup. The next day, they set up shop in the firehouse. A few days later, a local woman took over the responsibility for the cooking. In one way that was a mistake. Her food — I still remember her bread pudding, and ordinarily I hate bread pudding — was so good that more and more people crowded in three times a day for meals. A Red Cross official, who knew that the crowds being fed were supposed to taper off as electricity was restored to the various streets, found they were increasing instead. One man, who was told that the food was only for the homeless, replied, 'Look lady, give me that piece of pie and I'll give you what's left of my home.'"

For Michael and me, the following week was a blur of no school, drying pillows, clothing and books and shots in the arm doled out by a doctor at the Coast Guard station. People came together and exchanged stories. Dozens of buildings disappeared without a trace. Nobody knew whether they washed out to sea or were carried across the island and broke into kindling in the bay or mainland.

I didn't pay much attention to my parents' problems, nor did I listen to them when they told me what not to do, like climb into damaged houses. Michael and I had a week of unexpected exploration. We burrowed under roofs and into sections of homes with a screwdriver and a crow bar, and unscrewed pulleys and jimmied dangling boards. Why the fascination with pulleys I can't remember, but they seemed very important and I accumulated a bucket full. We roped and nailed together a fine hut in the bayberry grove between our houses — a hut, I realized much later, built from the sad losses of my neighbors.

The hurricane destroyed 20 percent of Harvey Cedars' homes and businesses, smashed both beach pavilions into kindling, and obliterated all boundaries under two feet of sand. The mayor traveled to Washington to appeal for reconstruction funds. As tax collector, my mother and the mayor worked together for the next several months, while the town was surveyed so streets could be rebuilt. Mommy said how disorienting it was to have the landmarks gone. (Daddy said he couldn't imagine a worse storm — but he wouldn't have to: in March 1962, when he was mayor, a job he held from 1955 until he died — a three-day northeaster inundated Harvey Cedars, transforming two streets into channels where the ocean met the bay, and washed away a third of the town's buildings and all its infrastructure.)

In early December 1944 my mother wrote her sister Marian: "Our Chevy didn't survive the hurricane, it finally played out completely, and we were lucky to sell it for $200, after putting out that much in repairs in the last year, so now there is only the truck, which Tommy drives, and I am entirely carless, which is not convenient on this island with no transportation. It is easier to get to Philadelphia than to the drug store in Beach Haven, as a bus leaves our corner every morning for the city, but nothing public goes down the island... I am finally sending you that spaghetti recipe you asked for. Between the destruction of the borough hall in the hurricane and the tax collecting, the book goes slowly."

My mother was working on a cookbook she titled *Home on the Range*, and a large manila file bulged with recipes. Again, someone else beat her to the draw, but the recipes remained in her files. Spaghetti (never pasta, we didn't know the word) and meatballs was a family favorite — she sent her sister a copy and I have the original, on disintegrating, brown-lined school paper. We always ate the spaghetti on special Italian pottery deep-dish plates with a hand-painted boat on the bottom, a souvenir from my mother's trip to

Italy years earlier. When she fried it with a squeeze of lemon, my mother could make even leftover spaghetti taste good.

In May 1945, my mother wrote another sorry-I-haven't-written-sooner letter to Marian:

"Dear Sis: This winter has been something of a strain, trying to take care of my tax work and Reynold's business from this end, while he is mostly marooned out in the middle of Barnegat Bay. He has been forty miles from home all winter dredging in a landing field for a company that has menhaden fish factories all along the Atlantic coast. They have fleets of hundreds of boats that bring fish in from the ocean and grind them up in these factories for fertilizer and oil. This particular factory is on an island between here and Atlantic City, opposite Tuckerton, and so hard to get to by car and boat that the president of the company up and said by gum he'd have himself a private landing field on it, and fly up from Delaware in fifteen minutes. So that's where Pop has been since November.

"We have had carpenters here fixing up things about the house, but the money was all used up before they finished so I am still in a mess. I said I would finish plastering up the wallboard seams, etc., myself. It hurt me to see $16 a day going out to a big strong man for plugging up nail holes, which I can do perfectly well, if I had the time. Wages are something awful here. We got the house all covered with white asbestos shingles, the little balcony porch off my bedroom enclosed to make an extra closet and sewing room, shelves and cupboards put in my bedroom and Margaret's, new windows cut in the living room, the bunks torn out, and in the north wing, which wasn't built when you were here, we have an entrance porch and a bedroom for Michael. With love, Josie."

21

My High School Years

A photo I took of my family and our dog with the camera I received for Christmas in 1948.

"I felt sad when I remembered all the dates from that house, and all the necking on that bench at the front door. Life was nothing but dancing and fun then, and a job was merely incidental."

Family finances eased as the post-war economy expanded and summer residents re-turned to the shore. During my high school years, my father was very busy, as his dredging company filled the land for new homeowners and developers who moved onto the island. He was president of the school board, in addition to serving as town commissioner. Mommy wasn't a joiner. She didn't attend the church socials or join the Fire Company's ladies auxiliary, both of which made up a lot of the social activities in the winter. But most women at the time did not have the job of tax collector — increasingly more time consuming — or pound the typewriter.

In 1947, our family joined the Barnegat Light Yacht Club on 76th Street. At the club, I learned to race my sneakbox, and crewed in friends' Comets and Lightnings. Though I grew close to the girls during summer, our friendships were tainted by the impending loss in the fall. This undertow of change — the intense social life alternated with the quiet isolation of the winter, became the rhythm of my life. Not until I was an adult did I become more aware of the subtle variations of summer people, when the difference between a two-week renter, a summer renter and a second-home owner established a pecking order, and people like me were called "natives." From a summer person's point of view, the natives were at the bottom of this order. At the beginning of the season, if one said, "Is anyone down yet?" we knew they didn't mean us. We had been down all year. "Natives" was sometimes said derisively, other times with curiosity, as in, "What do you DO here all winter?" The biggest distinction between the two groups was obvious: the city people were on vacation and the natives, whose families took vacations in the winter, were working.

When I turned thirteen, Mommy and I started the conflicts so common with strong-willed teenage girls and their equally strong-willed mothers. I wanted what the other girls wore, the plaid pleated skirts, cardigan sweaters to button up the back and cotton blouses with Peter Pan collars, not the clothes my mother so lovingly made for me.

My mother's letters registered the drop in the emotional temperature.

"January 14, 1946: Dear Marian: We've had the flux since Christmas, the children and me, but all right now. I was so delighted with that beautiful blouse. It fits me exactly and was one of the things on my list to look for when I got near a city shop. In fact, if I do say so modestly myself, it is very becoming (Tommy agrees). Thank you so much, Marian for such a gorgeous present.

"I am enclosing a letter that Margaret wrote, although I hesitate to do so. I have threatened, punished and explained, but I can't break her of the habit of asking people for things. If she suddenly decides she would like a bright red pocketbook, she will ask family, relatives, friends and even strangers if they have a red pocketbook they want to sell — and the first thing I know is that she comes home with one, or somebody produces one. Well, maybe that is the way to get along in life. So tell Dorothy not to feel that if she has a collarless suit she must hand it over. Margaret complained that 'all' her jackets have collars and wanted me to alter them all, to which I was very unsympathetic. Just one of those daughter and mother situations! My response was to roar, 'If I had as many clothes as you do when I was your age, I would have been in Heaven.' I suppose this disagreement about clothes is an age-old problem. I can remember seething with resentment over what I had to wear, and vowing I would never dictate what <u>my</u> daughter should wear. So here I go, doing it.

"I am making up long lists of what I have to do this winter to have everything spick and span by spring. We got quite a lot of new furniture, I mean new to us, from Reynold's Great-aunt Margaret. Most of it we could not use and sold. Can you imagine me with a six-foot sideboard and two china closets and enormous mahogany dining table? We brought down a lot of maple furniture and for the living room we have an old-fashioned hutch table (it makes a bench), a couple of easy chairs, two wicker armchairs, a chifferobe for linens and a small mahogany chest. We also kept a considerable lot of dishes and silver.

"Oh! I almost forgot to tell you, we got a banquet set no less, of green and gold Limoges china. I used it once. Thanksgiving, and it took me all day to wash the dusty dishes and set the table, and all the next day to wash and put them away, as I didn't dare let the children touch them. You can see how useful they are.

"I have been having an uneventful winter, merely pegging along and trying to get to feel better, which I think I do, although I <u>know</u> another operation is hanging over my head. Bye-bye and write when you can snitch the time from the State of Michigan. I keep hoping I'll get out to Michigan suddenly one day and catch up on all the years. With much love, Josie."

In the fall of 1946, I entered the 10-year-old high school in Barnegat, which was built after the student population outgrew the 19th century building where I attended 6th through 8th grades.

My mother told me, that of course, I must be on the staff of the school newspaper, the *Lighthouse*. I suppose it was natural to want me to follow in her footsteps and I did like words; Mommy had given me that. There was one position available for a freshman and Chloe Oliver, a girl from Beach Haven whose older sister was editor, had her eye on it. To be selected, we had to write an essay about hazing. All I can remember about it was the lipstick the sophomores smeared on my face. I wrote the essay and my mother rewrote my boring lead. Chloe got the reporter's job and they made me a special feature writer. Only one of those mimeographed papers made it into my mother's files. I wrote a short piece about beachcombing, and all the things I dragged home — prescient, as much sooner than I could imagine, I would own a newspaper called the *Beachcomber*.

I had a lackadaisical attitude toward school — a major source of dissent between Mommy and me. I could get by with a minimum of effort and was more interested in having fun than studying, and no teacher challenged me. On an American History test in my junior year, I didn't know some of the answers so made up silly answers to all the questions. The principal wrote my mother — said I should know better, and to do something with me. My mother saved that letter. My parents discussed my education and they decided that I would go to a Quaker boarding school in Pennsylvania as my aunts and grandmother had. Aunt Milly would help foot the bill. I whined and cried and begged not to be sent away. I said I would try harder, and I prevailed.

One Saturday morning in June 1947, when Mommy called me to get out of bed, I couldn't — I tried to sit up but I could not lift my body. The night before, I'd crashed a party in town, although my mother said specifically not to go to Tommy's party, as I was not invited. A friend and I did go, of course my mother found out, so she thought I was playing sick for sympathy, but I literally could not move my upper body. I remember Doctor Dodd coming from Beach Haven, taking both of my hands, and pulling me into a sitting position. I had polio — an irony at the seashore, where prosperous city people brought their children to protect them from the infectious, paralyzing disease. I don't remember being immobile for a long time, but my memory is blocked after the initial doctor's visit.

I found among my mother's papers the prescription written by Doctor Ransohoff in Long Branch, almost two hours north, for an inch and one-quarter lift on my left shoe to counteract the curvature of my spine, which the polio left taut, like a stretched bow. In high school those ugly shoes embarrassed me, but by the time I was in college my spine was straight.[1]

About the time I got polio, Mommy got fulltime music — an FM radio. Daddy hired a man from the phone company to install a telephone pole on the bay side of the house and he screwed an antenna on top so she could listen to WQXR, New York's classical music station. My mother loved music and missed the live music that had been such a large part of her life in Washington and New York. Most Saturday afternoons, she set up the ironing board and turned on the Metropolitan Opera broadcast narrated by the resonant voice of Milton Cross. Next she got a 45-rpm record player and spun Nelson Eddy and Jeannette MacDonald, Mozart and Beethoven symphonies and Enrico Caruso over and over and over. She ironed, darned socks and mended with music playing. As she set the iron on end and twirled around the room to "La Donna e Mobile," she said, "All tasks are easier with music." I feel sad that my mother had to live without it for so many years.

At the end of 1948, Mommy was sick again. In a short letter to Marian she wrote: "Reynold has been very busy, working two shifts and not getting home until eight at night. I have to go have my incision dressed every other day. An infection developed and I've had to take penicillin shots. There should be a federal law against mothers in maidless households getting sick. But the children have been marvelous."

The series of seven shots, including two home visits by Dr. Dodd, cost $28. I don't know if this was the very long incision from the mastectomy six years earlier — but I know of no other. It was just a few months later that a letter from Lowell Thomas[2] perked her up, and she heard from two friends from her Washington years

In June, Mommy took me with her on the bus to New York City to visit Martha Taylor, her buddy from Ionia and Washington, who was moving to California. I remember a sad woman and a small apartment. Mommy told me that Martha had been in love with a married man. She also heard from Grace Leonard, still living and working in Washington, who told her that 1415 Massachusetts Avenue had been demolished. Mommy wrote Marian: "Like Grace, I felt sad when I remembered all the dates from that house, and all the necking on that bench at the front door. Life was nothing but dancing and fun then, and a job was merely incidental."

NOTES

[1] *In 1955, the year my son was born, Jonas Salk released his newly developed polio vaccine to the public and my children were spared the crippling disease. I was lucky that I was left with no aftereffects.*

[2] *In 1949, Lowell Thomas and his son, Lowell Jr., traveled to Lhasa, Tibet, just before the Communist Chinese takeover, where they met the teenaged Dalai Lama; they were the "seventh and eighth" persons from the United States to do so, LT said. He sent Mommy a photograph of the group in front of Potala palace, and also a copy of Lowell Jr.'s book,* Out of This World, *inscribed to my mother "Wish you had been along!" This led to a geography lesson from my mother about Tibet. My mother had an amazing knowledge of culture and geography, including Tibet — even though Frank Carpenter hadn't written about that country.*

22

1950 TO 1951

Letters to and from College

My brother and I pose for photographer Angelo Pinto, summer 1949.

"I suggest that you confine frivolities to the weekends, and spend your evenings in your room — STUDYING. You can never say your homework is all done because you can always put the final exquisite touches to any preparation."

Among the treasures in my bountiful attic — and one that I found years after the original batch of letters in the window seat — was a collapsed carton that originally held a dozen quart cans of prune juice. This final gift from my mother was labeled, in her handwriting, "Letters etc. 1950-1952." After I shook out the tiny black mouse droppings and shards of yellowed paper flakes, I retrieved about 150 letters written to me during that period, from relatives, many girlfriends, a few boyfriends and, most importantly, a precious pack written by my mother during my first two years of college.

On September 26th, 1950, Daddy, Mommy and Michael packed me, my new portable radio, and what I thought was a skimpy amount of clothing — in spite of the half-dozen cashmere sweaters Aunt Milly gave me — into our 1949 Chevrolet and drove me to Keystone Junior College, a coed school near Scranton, Pennsylvania.[1] Again, I hadn't wanted to leave home. I was afraid to leave the security of the island and I didn't want to leave my boyfriend, a year behind me in high school. My parents settled me into my dorm, a rambling, gabled, turreted, multi-roofed 19th century home transformed to house about twenty girls and one housemother.

For a small school, Keystone enrolled a large proportion of foreign students and ex-GIs, which made for a more diverse student body than other small colleges of the era. In addition to my liberal arts courses, my mother insisted I take shorthand, because, she said, I needed it to get any job. I thought that was an old-fashioned concept, but did as I was told. I had learned how to type in high school and — although I didn't know it then — that, plus a business English class and a hands-on journalism course at Keystone would prove invaluable in the future. Our shorthand battle was a continuing theme in letters between my mother and me. The following are excerpts from our letters from the fall of 1950 to the end of the 1951 academic year.

"Dear Mommy: Good news, I'm not homesick at all; in fact, the place is livable. I just registered and bought books and will try to get the rest secondhand. I charged three books at $2.50 each. I have shorthand for two hours at a time, two days a week. I'm going to get on cheerleading, basketball, softball, volleyball, paper staff and Dean's list, if at all possible."

"Dear Poochy: We all miss you terribly, Mike most of all at table-setting time. Today or tonight I'll try to catch up on any memoranda about things you need. ... This is not a real letter, just hello from all your family. Daddy really misses you and I keep waiting for you to come through the door. This may be a financial strain on poor Pop, so I know you will do your best."

"Dear Mommy: Hazing starts Monday. We have to braid our hair in ten pigtails, wear pajamas, boots, robe, carry an umbrella, books in wastebasket, no makeup and a two-square-foot sign around neck with our vital statistics and a rope necklace tied on an onion. ... I'm doing well in all subjects and trying in shorthand, which I despise, detest, deplore, disdain and etc. Don't be dissappointed if I don't get all As and Bs."

"Dear Sweet Pea, I mean Poo-Pee: I am terribly proud you are doing well and I knew you could. Don't let the shorthand get you down. Please stop saying you despise it or you'll begin to believe it. I won't be "dissappointed" if you don't get all As but I will be if you don't learn to spell *disappointed*. Ha! Are you going to drop Commerce because you don't think it will be any help to you or because you don't want to work at it? Oh, Poopy, you could get such good marks if you wanted to. Don't mind my needling you. It's just love and affection. You are on your own now and I'm not there to yak-yak. ... Your tuition and board are paid up to February, and it is up to you now whether you go further than that. It is your own choice. [Keystone accepted me conditionally, and I had to maintain a certain grade average to continue for the second semester.] ... I don't need to remind you that with a roommate, neat and tidy habits are more important. And I repeat, again, my future letters are not going to be full of admonitions. You can just keep this one and read it over every month. Love and a big hug."

"Dear Mommy: The food up here STINKS. I have not bought any cokes and only two ice cream cones since I've been here. In fact, I just this minute finished two bottles of milk at ten cents each, they don't even give you milk with dinner, just tea and coffee, so I spend about 25 cents a day on that. I've been asked to run for secretary of the freshman class. [I must have asked my mother for some campaign slogans when I ran for class secretary. I found a sheet of paper with some suggestions — for example: "For good of the class of fifty-two/Make Tommy Thomas[2] the scribe for you."]

"I have a date for Homecoming Dance, it's a big affair, and alumni from all over come back, could you PLEASE send me $10 to buy a dress. PLEASE. This is a very important dance. I'll skimp on everything else. PLEASE. Did you sign that permission slip? Every other girl in the dorm has unlimited. WRITE!" [Written permission was required to leave campus overnight.]

"Dear Poochy: About the permission, we are sending the blanket permission to the college. Knowing that we are not there to hold a club over your unbowed head, would you please keep in mind these things: with your conditional academic standing, I would like to know that your evenings are spent studying. That you don't go whooshing around in cars on dates. Go in a crowd and keep it impersonal. It is all right for you to go home with a girl for a weekend if you are asked, but we should like to know about any other off campus or weekend plans, and we think they should be kept to a minimum until your nose is academically clean. ...I hope your classmates don't judge the quality of your home environment and culture by the kind of stationery your mother uses. I just pull out whatever is handiest to where I am sitting. That's what a newspaper background does for you; you write on anything.[3]

"You must have thought your poor old mom was not glad to hear your voice over the phone Sunday, she yakked at you so much. But I was flabbergasted when I found you were penniless. I know it is not naturally in the Thomas family make-up to economize, but you will try to realize what is essential and what is not, won't you please?"

My parents had conflicting attitudes toward money. Daddy was used to it being there in the background, somewhere, and if it weren't there right now, well, it would be back, sometime. He had no idea how to budget. Mommy managed the household money and she believed in Saving, with a capital "S".

"Dear Mommy: You ask where the money went — $3 notebook, 50 cents stickers, $1 stationery, 50 cents locker deposit, $1 blotters pencils paper, $1.50 food, 75 cents tennis and ping-pong balls, 75 cents film — total $9.00. ... I can think of no better use for this dictation pad than writing letters, I hate shorthand. I want to drop it next semester but I can't. Got a warning grade, 68. If I flunk out of school, remember, it's you making me take shorthand."

"Dear Poochy: Thank you for sending the shorthand sample; I think your shorthand is all right. I was sure that anybody who could print as artistically as you do could write a nice, flowing shorthand after practice. It will be hard at first, but suddenly it will be fascinating. I'll bet you ... I'm sorry you lost the election, but it will save you an awful lot of time."

"Dear Mommy: Could you and Daddy put me on an allowance? It would be much wiser as I could learn how to handle the money and make it stretch until the next time. Some girls get $20 a month and others $5 or $10 a week. I could do with $3 or $4 a week now that beginning expenses are over. ...Dottie and I are the only ones on the whole campus who don't smoke."

"Dear Pooey: I don't like to pull the stern mother stuff now that you are at college. But I will suggest that you confine frivolities to the weekends, and spend your evenings in your room — STUDYING. I know just how much of a temptation it is to spend lots of time in gay persiflage (I sent you a dictionary) with attractive boys, or draped over the soda fountain, or solving the problems of college, youth, sex in gab parties in some girl's room. All I say is — be moderate. Your studies come first, and there are two rocks in your academic load some other girls may not have — your being there under a condition, and Daddy's darned uncertain business outlook.[4] We all enjoyed your English theme. I thought it was exceptionally good."

"Dear Mommy: I think I could manage on $15 a month, but it would mean less eating than I am used to. I was elected captain of the hockey team after the previous captain left school; she was too homesick. I joined the Glee Club and sing second soprano."

"Dear Poochy: I have been trying desperately to do some writing and have half a story written, and if only I can get it finished, it might be saleable. But just as I think I am going good, Michael comes home with a fever — he never should have gone to school this morning, so I am worrying about him, and then that wretched furnace scared me. It was about eleven at night, with Daddy at a long school board meeting and I in bed, when it starts an awful screeching noise like brakes going on suddenly. By the time I realized what it was, Mike was there ahead of me and flames were shooting out of the switch box. So I turned off everything, actually put my half-finished story near the front door so I could grab it while running out, and quaked and shook until Daddy came home. This morning the repairman came and said it was nothing but a fan belt that needed tightening."

"Dear Mommy: I'm glad to hear that you're writing again. I wasn't so bad that you had to wait until I left for school until you could get anything done. Or was I? ... I'm the only one on the second floor who has any cotton dresses and they travel from girl to girl, and the cashmere sweaters Aunt Milly gave me fly from back to back.

"Dear Poochy: I don't mind if you want to swap clothes, but I do mind too much borrowing. I can't forbid it: I merely ask you not to get in that habit which eventually does not add to your popularity."

This rare letter from Daddy was a scrawl; Mommy typed most of hers.

"Poochy dear: Those marks are not too bad, but I believe you can do better. I want you to get all the fun you can out of being at Keystone, yet don't forget, dear, to grab onto all the knowledge you can — that's the real reason you are there. You're a big girl now and you have to decide when to study and when to play — and I know you can make the right decisions."

"Dear Daddy: Happy to hear from you, didn't know you knew how to write! Don't worry, I can take care of myself. ... I've been studying all day. Honestly, shorthand is HORRIBLE. The teacher dictates at 80 words per minute and I'm always about ten sentences behind, I don't know why Mommy thinks I need this to get a job. Psychology is much more interesting. The gang is going skiing tomorrow but I'm down to 70 cents so I guess I don't go. I was down to 20 cents when I got your dollar. Write again. Thank you for money, much appreciated."

"Dear Poochy: Say this fifty times before you go to sleep — 'Every day, in every way, I love shorthand better.' Thirty years ago this was called Coueism.[5] With your remarkably good vocabulary and reading ability you will find it easy to read once you learn to write it with facility. I don't say for a moment that it is easy to learn — it takes steady drill, drill, drill, but it will give you a good feeling of achievement to have mastered it."

"Poochy dear, Daddy and I love you very much and want you to have as good a time as it is possible, but Daddy can't afford to pay out all that money unless you justify it by hard work. I'm sorry about the skiing, but the exchequer is very low."

"Dear Mommy: Just got back from a girls' basketball game, we lost both games, I couldn't play because of the sprained thumb I got in the last game, which is in a splint. I couldn't take shorthand dictation either so didn't have to go to class. I was heartbroken — Ha! ... Marks came out on Monday. I got a C in Shorthand and Speech, 83 in French, 83 in Sociology and B in Business English. Not too bad, huh? Love to the cats."

"Dear Poo: [a scrawled note on an index card] The ghost walked! Meaning some money came in.[6] Make this last. I'll send more when I can, but please don't spend unless you absolutely need it. Things will be better."

"Dear Poochy: This is the first chance Daddy and I have had to discuss the letter from the Dean, about your staying away all night without permission. You were given unlimited permission to decide for yourself where and when you would go, but we never thought that to mean that you could go anywhere without informing the

<u>college</u> where you were going, and when. ... It is our joint decision, you are now on limited permission and cannot go away for the night or a weekend without advance permission from home."

"Dear Mommy and Daddy: I just received your letter about that staying overnight business. It was very unfair of Dean Mac to write you without saying anything to me. We had a mid-semester vacation two weeks ago from whenever exams ended until Sunday night at 10 and when you go home you don't have to sign out at the Dean's office, just at the dorm, which is what I did when I went to Bobbi's home for Wednesday night."

"Dear Poo: Will you please do this for me? Go to Miss McIntosh, tell her I wrote you about staying out without the proper permission, and tell her you are sorry. That will put you right with her, and it is important to have a good feeling with your Dean. Believe me, a little apology, even when you think you are in the right, can help a lot. Just explain it was a misunderstanding. Now, don't put this off and intend to do it. Do it right away.

"Daddy was very amused by your letter trying to get blood out of a turnip, but can't do much about it right now."

"Dear Mommy: Marks came out Monday: 75 in journalism, that was the highest in the class ... We have quite a time in journalism, six started the class and only three are left. The others couldn't keep up with the work."

"Dear Poochy: Congratulations on the 87 in World Civilization. Now if Stalin and Truman would only try for an 87 in preserving said world civilization, there would be less to worry about."

Having experienced what I thought was real freedom, I didn't want to return for a summer under my parent's roof, so together with friends Judi Breckir and Bobbi Weiss, I applied for a summer job at Grossinger's resort in the Catskills. I wasn't accepted.

"Dear Poo: About the summer job. Did it ever occur to you that a girl with a name like Thomas doesn't stand a chance of getting a job at Grossingers? I think you have to learn about the birds and the bees. You will find there is a great deal of anti-Jewish and anti-Gentile prejudice out in the world. We have a lot of Jewish friends here, as you know, and the question has never come up in our family, as Daddy and I just think people are people; but out in the world that is not the prevalent feeling. You have to recognize that it does exist among many people. You know you have never seen a Jewish girl at the Yacht Club here. Be aware of that and be friends to whom you please. Only you have to be careful not to thoughtlessly hurt the feelings of Jewish friends and not subject them to any anti-Jewish prejudice.[7]

"I want you to get a job this summer, but I would like to have you home, too. Why don't you try the hotels in Beach Haven? Are you interested in the *Beachcomber* job? If so, write to Mr. Craig <u>but not in that scribbly handwriting</u>. Tell him you can type and take shorthand and have a car.

"You say you are glad to hear I am writing again. I was when I wrote you, but haven't had a chance since. Before I can even get the decks cleared, Daddy is in and out of the house, the telephone rings, somebody comes, etc. etc. And of course there has been this school board business and the income tax bookkeeping (what income?). … I have just finished typing something for Mike and now will write a wee sma' note to my absent and much-missed daughter, and then list that laundry all over the bedroom floor, and then, by Allah, I'm going to take an anti-histamine pill and crawl into bed and defy anything short of an atom bomb to get me out."

NOTES

[1] *The following was written for "Life in these United States" at the time I was taken to college:*

"Late one hot, dusty Sunday in September, my husband and son and I were returning from taking out daughter to college. At eight o'clock we drew up at a diner, but thirteen-year-old Mike was sleeping so soundly in the back of the car, we gave up trying to wake him, and ate a big dinner without him.

Two hours later, Mike awoke and demanded food, and we stopped at another diner. By that time we had made over 500 miles through Sunday traffic. My husband was coatless and tieless and grimy, and I was too exhausted even to look for a comb and lipstick.

Mike ordered clam chowder, two hamburgers, French fries, cole slaw, hot rolls, apple pie, and a glass of milk. When the waitress turned to us, my husband said, 'Well, that's going to cost me so much, we'll just have a cup of coffee.' Mike's appetite had been a family joke for months.

When Mike finished, he asked if he could have another glass of milk and some ice cream. Thinking of the miles yet ahead of us, we tried to dissuade him, then tiredly told him to order it.

'Are you sure you two won't have anything to eat?' the waitress asked us for a second time.

We said we weren't hungry, really, and sat watching Mike. Just before he finished, the waitress slid two pieces of pie quietly in front of us.

"'These are on me,' she said. 'Believe me, I know what it's like to go hungry so your kids can eat.'"

[2] *No way was I telling anyone my despised nickname. My roommate dubbed me Tommy; I liked it and it stuck.*

[3] *This letter is typed on the back of a promotional letter from Macmillan Publishing Co.*

[4] *The Korean War caused a construction slump on the island.*

[5] *Emile Coue was a French psychologist who in the 1920s introduced a method of self-improvement based on optimistic autosuggestion.*

[6] *The origin of "The ghost walks," inspired by Shakespeare's* Hamlet, *has a colorful theory. It tells of a 19th-century British theater company that threatened to strike because their salaries had not been paid for several weeks. The leader of the company, a highly acclaimed actor, played the ghost. During a performance, the ghost, in answer to Hamlet's exclamation, "Perchance 'twill walk again," shouted from the wings, "No, I'm damned if the ghost walks any more until our salaries are paid!" Their salaries were paid and the performance continued. From then on, the actors met every payday to determine whether the ghost would walk.*

[7] *It wasn't until years later that I understood why my parents rarely came to a Yacht Club function. Daddy said they joined so Mike and I could sail and race, but they didn't want to be active at a restricted club. It wasn't until the 1970s that the club accepted Jews.*

23
1951 TO 1954
Jo Writes for the Beachcomber

Typing on the Remington upright in the *Beachcomber* office.

"We got those mid-August seashore blues. Last week's wet bathing suits are still wet. Woolens are mildewed. Shoes and belts are moldy. The icebox needs defrosting every day. Cesspools overflow. Zippers jam, lipsticks ooze, girdles stick. In the heavens, flying saucers. Down here below, flies."

In June 1950, a journalist named Donald Craig had started a seasonal, weekly newspaper on Long Beach Island, called the *Beachcomber*. My mother dusted off her typewriter — an even newer one, again compliments of Uncle Bill — and submitted short essays. During the summers of 1951 and 1952, she wrote a garden and cooking column, and also submitted what she called "little bits of this and that." She was so enthusiastic that she gathered her information and started those weekly columns in the dead of winter, while Michael was in high school and I was away at college.

At the end of my freshman year at Keystone, I moved in with friends whose father owned The Baldwin, a rambling, 19th century hotel in Beach Haven. I ran the elevator on the late shift, but in mid-July, I went back home and got a job selling advertising for the *Beachcomber*. I returned each summer through 1954. Mommy, of course, pushed me toward the newspaper job and told me how much salary to ask: "Tell him you want $50 a week," she said. I did, and got it — a good salary for a summer job.

I sold advertising and turned out copy when at the last minute my boss needed "ten more inches." I learned how to re-write news releases, scale photographs, write captions, write a lead, mock up a dummy, lay out a paper and, by the end of two summers, how to put a 36-page tabloid "to bed" each week. My first assignment was to write a history of Barnegat Light, spread it out over eight weeks and sell advertising around it. (My mother checked my copy before I turned it in. Although she made a few suggestions, she approved.) We did all the rough copy in the office and every Thursday drove two hours north, to the printers in Newark, where typesetters used hot lead on now-antique linotype machines. It was a noisy, dirty shop, staffed by rough men with foul mouths. We proofed ads and editorial copy, waited until the papers were off the press, then trailed them back to the island, where newsboys rolled, banded and delivered one to each home on the island. My boss delivered bundles of papers to businesses. Then we did it all over again the next week. Every week was different and I loved it.

After I graduated from Keystone, I transferred as an English major to Cedar Crest College,[1] in Allentown, to be near Aunt Milly. My mother encouraged this, as she knew my aunt would open me up to the world of culture that she experienced in Philadelphia and New York. Aunt Milly introduced me to Bach, T.S. Eliot, Moroccan textiles, George Nakashima, and dancer Martha Graham, with whom she took classes in the late 1930s. She took me to the Barnes Foundation in Philadelphia, to the theater in New York, and for lunch at Princeton's Institute for Advanced Study, where I met Robert Oppenheimer in the cafeteria.[2]

In January 1953, my mother wrote Marian that she "felt wretched." The cancer had metastasized. In February — the same week her mother died — Mommy was back in Paul Kimball Hospital for what is listed on the typewritten bill only as: "Major operation — $35." In April, Daddy met me in Philadelphia to bring me home for Easter vacation. We stopped at a restaurant in Haddonfield — I can picture him sitting across the table fingers wrapped around a cup of coffee as he told me the doctor told him my mother had two years to live. He did not tell my mother. I don't remember crying — it was so unreal. When I got home Mommy seemed fine; it was impossible to imagine her not always in the house with us. She suffered through huge doses of radiation, but struggled to maintain a normal life as long as possible. She wrote her father, now living with his bachelor son Clem, that she didn't feel so well and had to travel back and forth on the long trip to Philadelphia to see the radiologist. My father drove her on the two-lane road through the Pine Barrens to the city, 90 minutes away.

Mommy had more good years than the doctor predicted and continued to write for the *Beachcomber*. The summer of 1953 she wrote "Vacation Cooking" and took over the social "Sand in my Ears" column in which editor Craig called for "names, names, names" of people visiting the island; but my mother wanted to write vignettes similar in style to the *New Yorker's* "Talk of the Town," and substituted her own brand of rambling observation, humor, and editorializing. Her byline was "By Josie."

"In this column the editor expects me to list newcomers to the island, the more the better. So be it. I hereby report that 64,731 people (at least) are summering — spelled with an "i" this week — on the island, each one just as heat bedraggled as I. If any ambitious reader wants the NAMES, just apply to this office." A few weeks later: "In spite of Simon Legree cracking that whip about my shoulders I can't get ALL the names. Here are some"— followed by three long paragraphs of the names of vacationers who arrived on the island that week. Then — "I tried six other real estate offices on the island for more names. At two of them, the line was busy every time I called. Three others answered but were too bushed to give out any news. At the fourth there was merely a loud crash as of a chair falling over. Just one more overworked realtor fainting."

My mother loved creating statistics and was happy when she could refer to a national event — that summer flying saucers made headlines:

"We got those mid-August seashore blues. Last week's wet bathing suits are still wet. Woolens are mildewed. Shoes and belts are moldy. The icebox needs defrosting every day. Cesspools overflow. Zippers jam, lipsticks ooze, girdles stick. The fire at Cedar Run Laundry burned up all our sheets and towels. Lightning struck our hot water heater and our egg man. In the heavens, flying saucers. Down here below, flies. Before there is a loud holler from the Board of Trade, we hurry to say none of these afflictions keep the people away. Our statistical department, using our newest electronic brain, added up over the last Saturday 49,262 rubbers of bridge played, 727 crossword puzzles completed, 5,622 television programs watched, 11,000 martinis consumed — very dry, and the only dry thing on the island. (Typewriter just stalled from heat expansion.) Too hot to sort out the rest of the news this week anyway."

Sometimes she tried to find a local slant for something or someone about whom she wanted to write:

"The Countess of Desmond has absolutely no connection with this island, but I like the story of how she broke her leg falling out of a tree at the age of 91. I dragged in that story when I reported the first Bing cherries at the M&M Market, and the editor left it out. I tied up her great age (she lived to 140) with the old cemetery in Manahawkin but it got the blue pencil. I even tried to slip in a recipe for cherry pie in my cooking column and use her for the introduction. It never worked, and I hereby say farewell to the aged Countess."

Typical of the history my mother like to drop into a column of otherwise local interest is this one:

"Dendrological Note: We have been trying all summer to tell you about that forest of stumps offshore between Harvey Cedars and Surf City. About thirty years ago, during the lowest tide ever reported on this beach, the ocean receded 500 feet farther out than the normal low water mark, and brought to view thousands of cedar stumps. In one of them was found an Indian spearhead. These are no doubt the stumps from the thick forests reported by Henry Hudson when he sailed along this coast three hundred years ago."

She looked back to the beach rambles we took when I was very young:
"Returning to beachcombing, things were different in the good old days when New York City towed its garbage and trash out to sea and dumped it. A northeast wind eventually deposited a large share of it on the beaches of this island. You could find almost anything along the beach then. My three-year-old daughter ignored her Christmas presents and played for months with some faded sand-scraped wooden toys she found one January. On one autumn walk I found eighty-six pencils, one iron bedstead, assorted empty bottles (mostly blue Bromo-Seltzer), a pajama jacket with the label 'George Deman & Co., Ostende, Bruxelles,' a large black suede handbag complete with French label and water soaked illegible address book, and a gold lettered tag from the florist firm of Max Schling at the Savoy-Plaza. The address on it was quite legible: 'Miss Janice Perrine, *S.S. Morro Castle*.' Even as I deciphered it, the *Morro Castle* was lying, a burned derelict, on the beach at Asbury Park.[3]
"The late Louis Wild of Harvey Cedars, who studied art in Paris and then retired to the island to paint and occasionally build a house for somebody, collected a cigar box of old coins during his beachcombings. Some were Elizabethan, some sixteenth-century Dutch and many of them Spanish pieces of eight. He also found a small metal object that exploded when he tried to scrape the sand off it — it cost him the sight of one eye."

My mother segued skillfully from what Craig was looking for to her own style:
" 'We would like information about other beachcombers,' the boss says a couple of issues ago. That made me curious about real beachcombers. The dictionary meaning of the word — those (I quote Webster) 'who hang around the shore looking for wreckage or plunder.' Another phrase I looked up was flotsam and jetsam, words often tossed about casually in nautical circles, referring to anything that drifts up on the beach. According to our 1890 *Britannica,* flotsam and jetsam is, or are, what does not drift up on the beach. In British naval law, flotsam floats on the sea and jetsam sinks to the bottom. If either floats ashore, it ceases to be F and J and becomes, (still speaking legally) wreckage."
My mother's *Britannica* didn't exactly drift up on the beach, but sometime in the 1940s, Daddy did salvage it from a distressed sailboat owned by a couple going south for the winter. The schooner ran aground and tore a hole in its hull in the bay opposite our house. Daddy got his tugboat and went to help. The owners stripped and abandoned the

boat and left the 27-volume set with us; said they would come back and get it next year. Much to my mother's delight, they never did.

NOTES

[1] *While at Cedar Crest, I went to the University of Pennsylvania to research a paper on Henry James and discovered how much I liked poking around in libraries. This made my mother very happy, but I wouldn't utilize the skill until much later in my life. In 2003, at the National Archives in Washington, DC, when I was researching a book about New Jersey shipwrecks and the origins of the United States Coast Guard, I discovered that between 1868 and 1871 my great-grandfather Kinsey had been a Keeper, or Captain, in the Life Saving Service at the Harvey Cedars station. It was a satisfying and exciting discovery.*

[2] *Aunt Milly's influence continued long after I left college. In 1979, on the Dalai Lama's first trip to this country, he visited Aunt Milly in her New York apartment. Two decades after his escape into exile, but before he was as famous as a rock star, I shared tea with him.*

[3] *In September 1934, the* Morro Castle, *an ocean liner on the way back from Cuba, caught fire and burned off Asbury Park. The hulk was close to shore and a tourist attraction until it was towed away a month later.*

24
1954 TO 1957
A Family Tragedy

Mommy and me on my wedding day, Beach Haven, March 11, 1955

"The police found my husband's body on the beach. The same beach where I'd played as a child, where we swam in the summer. He shot himself with the gun he used to shoot the ducks."

I graduated from Cedar Crest and worked another summer at the *Beachcomber*. After Labor Day I kicked around the house, restlessly trying to decide what to do with my life. My mother urged me to "look for a job." I considered teaching, and interviewed with the principal of the new elementary school, who glanced at my English major degree and dismissed me with the scathing remark that I was qualified to be "the wife of a banker or a lawyer." It never crossed my mind to object. Like a well-brought up young woman of the time, I said "Thank You," and walked out of his office — not angry; but I didn't really understand what he meant. I always assumed, prodded by my mother, that I would graduate and get a job. And I hoped it would be off the island. Very few of my graduating class went to work — most got married and started raising a family. I didn't want to be like everyone else; I wanted to follow my mother's path. Travel. Adventure.

That fall Lowell Thomas, whose latest venture was as a producer of the new 3-D movies, sent my mother tickets to the Cinerama Holiday movie, about to open in Philadelphia. In January 1955, she wrote a thank-you note, saying that she had not been able to go:

> "The rest of my family did go to see Cinerama, and were so enthusiastic about it some of them went back the second time with friends. I have had a card from a friend in Washington who has been four times. I see a new edition is coming out, and I am happy that it is doing so marvelously."

Although she never stated it, I must have disappointed my mother when I did not grasp this opportunity with the American Field Service. (Or, perhaps she knew how little time she had left and was happy to have me home.) The plan was to travel to eleven countries throughout Europe and interview AFS exchange students. My cousin George[1] would take the photographs and I would write the news releases to send to their hometown newspapers. Instead, I fell in love with Bill Douglas, the editor of the *Beach Haven Times*. Our paths crossed often that summer as we each covered events or sold ads for our respective newspapers. He was talented, bright, and sometimes a bit crazy in an endearing way.

In March 1955, we married; two weeks later we bought the *Beachcomber*. Craig had built up the weekly he started five years earlier into a viable, popular publication, but his wife wanted to stop the seasonal trek back and forth from their home in North Jersey. We paid $6,000; $1,000 down and $1,000 a year for five years. Bill's parents gave us $1,000 for the down payment. We decided I would manage the *Beachcomber* and Bill would continue with the *Times,* guaranteeing us a winter income. This lasted until early July, when the owner of the *Times* fired Bill because of the growing competition between the two papers. By then it was obvious that I was pregnant.

1955 was a golden year for the Jersey shore; it was a perfect time to buy a business. The Garden State Parkway was completed, connecting New York and North Jersey to Atlantic City, Cape May, and all the small resorts along the coast. A booming economy during President Eisenhower's administration allowed a middle class family to consider not only a summer rental; with a VA loan, they could buy a second home. Families who before the war could not have afforded a car could now own one, and sometimes two.

A ferment of building spread along the coast, and the first lagoon developments were carved out of virgin bay meadows on both the mainland and the island. Creosoted bulkheads evened off the irregular shoreline and dredges buried the bay meadows under an avalanche of sand. Daddy had more work than he could handle and ordered a larger dredge. Depending on location, a waterfront cottage cost between $7,000 and $10,000 with only $500 down. Entrepreneurs bought cheap land and built restaurants and shops.

Developers acquired large expanses of bayside land and plowed under bayberry, cedar and holly trees. (At the drop of every tree and bush, my mother railed in print against the destruction.) Daddy gave Bill and me the choice of two lots on which to build a house, and his parents gave us $1,000 for a down payment. I chose a lot in Barnegat Light because it was lush with growth, but Daddy said, "Oh, they'll knock the trees down to build the house." So we took the lot across the street from my parents, the flat sandlot that had been Michael's and my playground.

In her *Beachcomber* column, my mother chastised the developers who flattened the land, and left standing nothing green:

"I offer the helpful suggestion that this is the place for anyone interested in going into the gnarled root and old stump business. Trees and roots have been bulldozed to make room for new developments — nice flat open places with never a tree or bush left. Why, I ask, why cannot the developers lay out the lots before bulldozing and leave some planting along the boundary lines? It is well known that trees and shrubs are sound deadeners for traffic — and TV."

Mortgage debt made my mother uncomfortable, and she convinced us to build a duplex so we could get income from summer rentals. A builder friend of Daddy's built the three-bedroom house for $11,000 and we watched both it and my belly get bigger during that summer. Mommy pitched in and helped me decide how to finish the inside of the house. She advised, "Don't let those builders put in those tiny triangular corner cupboards. They are out of proportion and impractical. Tell them to..." And she proceeded to tell me what to tell them, although I'm sure that while I was at the office she came across the street and told them herself.

That spring and summer, while our house was being built, Bill and I rented a tiny cottage at the end of the island near Barnegat Lighthouse. The house was built seventy-five years earlier and the ivy that covered the brick chimney on the side had forced its way between the clapboards and twined around the bare studs on the bathroom wall. I thought it was charming until I saw the ants marching in along the vines. We worked hard that summer and were happy.

My mother continued to have radiation as the cancer spread — in 1955, according to the bills, it was to the neck, in 1956 to the chin — $5 for each treatment. I was pregnant for most of the next two years —at the end of November 1955, Billy was born followed by Elizabeth in December 1956. I drove my mother to Philadelphia as often as possible and she tolerated the weekly treatments well enough to take an interest in shopping. On one trip, after the treatment, she spotted a black wool coat in a shop window and bought it. It was very expensive but she said she didn't care. I kept it for years after my mother died, finally giving it to a friend whom it fit. I became closer to my mother. Now that I had my own home, my own children, and was beginning to realize how difficult and complicated motherhood was, the mother-daughter conflict of my teenage years diminished. I was eager to take her advice, and she helped out with the children.

In March 1957, Mommy wrote to her sister:

"Dear Marian: Congratulations on another grandson. Little boys are nice. Pooch's little Billy is the sweetest, most companionable little child one could ask for. He has mouse colored hair and a wistful little face and beautiful hazel eyes and a real sense of humor. He just loves to play tricks and giggle. The little girl (we call her Lizzie-potts) is turning into a charmer. So just listen to Grandma boast. I simply can't resist the two of them and they keep me worn out all the time. It seems there is always one or the other being deposited upon me when I am busiest. I have yelled NO into the telephone four times today, being determined to clean up this desk.

"Reynold takes Billy with him a lot on his rounds in the car, and they jabber at each other like two monkeys. Pooch is terribly busy, although a new washer-dryer helps some. I don't know how she is going to manage this summer with two children and a job, as she had enough trouble to get one taken care of last year. I am looking forward to spring and some sunshine. Josie"

There was not much sunshine that spring. On April 26th my husband shot himself. Just writing it down brings it back again — the fear, the astonishment, the disbelief. He came home the night before, drunk and in a rage. He knocked me across the room, screamed, "You aren't fit to live." I couldn't calm him. He pushed me out the door and I fell down three brick steps onto the gravel — sobbing, bleeding, shocked, and frightened. He jumped into his red Mercury convertible and sped down the street. I went back into the house and grabbed a child under each arm and ran across the street to my parents. My father called the police. I was afraid he'd gone to our friend John's house, where, at John's suggestion, their shotguns were stowed with the duck-hunting gear. I nursed Lizzie while Mommy held Billy. We put the children in bed. We waited. He didn't come back. My parents went to their room and I dozed on the couch, dreaming, tossing — waking fully as the sun rose over the ocean, streaming through the window. With daylight came security. I lived in a small town. I felt safe. The police would keep him away from the house. Mommy and I took the children home, fed them, changed their diapers. And waited some more.

That morning, I remember for some reason that I had on a pair of khaki shorts and a striped sleeveless blouse. As I looked out the living room window, I saw my father and brother as they walked in harmony across the street and into my yard. Their heads were bent; their bodies drooped. I called out the open door. They looked up. Their faces were set, grim. My father had been crying. My father never cried. I knew they were going to tell me something terrible. That picture is clear in my mind, even now, although what followed is lost. I don't remember who spoke or what they said, only my response, "Oh, my God. My poor children." The police found Bill's body on the beach. The same beach where I'd played as a child, where we swam in the summer. He shot himself with the gun he used to shoot the ducks.

It wasn't until after Bill died that I realized he was an alcoholic — I didn't even know what that meant until I was told. It also came out that, before he came to the island, he'd been fired from his public relations job at Publicker Industries, a distillery in Philadelphia. We all drank a lot then, but I didn't know he had a bottle of scotch hidden in the garage. It was almost a relief to learn that mental illness was in Bill's family; it took some of the burden of guilt from my shoulders. I never told my children their father had killed himself, I said it was an accident, but, of course — and foolish me — in a small town, by the time they were teenagers, they learned the truth. In the 1950s shame attached itself to suicide. I asked myself what I did wrong? What could I have done differently?

That cruelest April of 1957, I had no choice but to pull myself together. I had two babies and a business to run. I just got on with it. In 1957, there was no time to mourn, to weep and wail, to try to understand, to dwell on what had happened. My newspaper, my children, my friends, and my parents pulled me through. It wasn't until September, after the last issue was on the stands, that I collapsed and had hysterics. I sobbed for 45 minutes in a friend's house. I also suffered from a recurring nightmare — Bill would come back and surprise me, telling me it was all a joke.

The first issue of the *Beachcomber* was Memorial Day, just a month after the funeral. Our good friend John, who had been selling real estate with Bill during the winter, took over as ad manager; my college roommate quit her job in New York, moved in with me, and took care of my children; another college friend quit her job, moved in, and sold advertising. All our writers were freelance. I became editor, publisher, distribution manager, and whatever else I had to do. That whole summer is a blur but the paper came out each week. Mommy turned in as much copy as I could use, and sometimes more. I paid her usual rate that summer, but she never cashed the checks until she was sure I had enough money to make it through the winter — she also taught me how to balance a checkbook and manage the business end of the paper; she set up alphabetical files and showed me how to use them. In August she wrote her sister:

"I have been helping with the *Beachcomber* all summer, having no regular column but just giving a hand where needed, but Margaret has been running it alone, managing it, I mean. She has a fulltime staff of four and a girl who lives with her and keeps house and takes care of the two babies and everything has worked out all right except for me being so tired all the time.

"The last issue of the paper is Labor Day and I don't know how Poochy will do this winter. She can live on her social security payments, but the house mortgage and car payments are another thing. I simply am not up to taking care of both children, and it is almost impossible to get a good person for what she can afford. The babies are terribly cute. Little Lizzie looks like that baby picture of me — in fatness I mean — but has blue eyes and dark hair.

"Reynold is all tied up in his school board business. He is now president of the board of a new high school on the mainland and they hope to open this September, so they have meetings almost every day and he spends more time on it than on the dredging, which Mike is looking after. I tell him he needs to take a couple of weeks off, but can't make much impression on him. I'd like to drive out to Michigan but don't know if we can manage it. And I am so tired I just take each day as it comes. I really went through a bad time with the shock of all this trouble of Pooch's, but everything is working out and she is doing fine and proving very capable. Love to all. Josie."

NOTE

[1] *For the rest of his life, George traveled to almost every country in the world, more than 130, he said. When China opened its doors to outsiders, off George went, a front-runner. Magazines vied for his pictures. By the fall of 1979 he had been three times. I was in Paris that fall, when Daddy called. George had died of a heart attack in the middle of the night in the village of Lushan, Yangtze Province, in western China. Despondent, desolate, I flew home, much saddened by the loss of my prickly, perfectionist cousin. Aunt Milly and Uncle Bill, George's wife and my daughter and I buried his ashes on a hill in Pennsylvania, releasing his spirit very close to the land on which I had first felt it*

25
1958 TO 1959
Jo's Cancer Returns

My mother next to our Bay Terrace house, 1958

*"Even when I'm dying no one will believe me;
I always look so damn healthy."*

Whether or not I was capable enough to manage the paper was a concern of some business owners — one realtor asked my father who would run the paper. Daddy told him, "Poochy will." His response: "But she's just a girl."

I got through the winter without any financial worries, published special issues of the *Beachcomber* for Thanksgiving and Christmas, became active in a new community theater group, played poker and bridge with friends, read lots of books, and took care of my children. I was not introspective. I think I was numb, and just going through the motions of living.

My parents took some road trips, the getaways that my mother had craved for years — to Virginia and Western Pennsylvania, but not Michigan. My mother took day trips with Mary Hartman. They explored historic sites and visited second-hand bookstores on the mainland in south and central New Jersey. She and Daddy would sometimes do something special when he drove her to Atlantic City to see one of her doctors — dinner at a favorite restaurant, or a visit to friends off the island.

I found this scribbled note Daddy wrote about their twenty-eighth wedding anniversary in February 1959:

"I had forgotten our wedding anniversary the year before. This year I took Jo to Ventnor Clinic; she thought I'd forgotten again. On our way back we stopped for lunch at Smithville Inn. I'd made reservations for our favorite table. The waitress brought cocktails as soon as we sat down, then Mrs. Noyes brought out a white orchid I'd ordered for Josie's blue dress. She got over being mad and was happy. That was our last celebration."

Mommy remained strong enough that she could write during the summer of 1958. She liked to drive slowly in the car, looking for story ideas. In one column she acknowledged frustrated drivers trying to pass her as she meandered along the road:

"I am probably the recipient of more black looks from other motorists than any other legal driver in Ocean County. This is because I still cling to the shreds of the antiquated idea that it is possible to drive a car and at the same time take in the sights. A newspaper writer picks up lots of news that way. Or did once. So if you are driving along and see a lady of uncertain age veering back and forth over the white line, with a pencil in one hand, a notebook in the other, and Heaven help the steering wheel — it's probably me. If you want to get by, honk, and if I'm not too absorbed composing that deathless prose you find only in the *Beachcomber*, I'll get out of your way. Maybe."

My brother Michael had followed me to Keystone, graduated, and in 1957 lived at home and worked with my father in the dredging business. Mike's first love was boats, and he focused that passion on racing a hydroplane: a light, fast craft designed to skim over the water at high speed. He built his first hydroplane in high school; it had a very loud outboard motor and when it whizzed by the house, Mommy turned up the music on the radio to drown out the raucous whine and retreated to the room furthest from the bay. She was so afraid he would flip the boat.[1]

On Memorial Day 1959, the new Manahawkin Causeway was dedicated and my mother wrote the lead to one of the stories: "We don't know how the Indians got from the mainland to the island, but we'll bet that if they didn't swim, they used a canoe, or hollowed out log, or whatever it was that Indians used. But we do know what they did not use — a two-mile long, four-bridge, two-lane dual roadway, eight and a half million dollar causeway. Way back in the pre-resort era, cattlemen brought their herds across the bay in scows to graze on the island. In 1816 a stagecoach line was built from Camden to Tuckerton, an active Revolutionary War trading port. In 1822 the first resort hotel, a rough lodge catering to duck hunters, was built and they came across in sailboats. In 1872 the railway brought vacationers to the mainland side of the bay and visitors took a steamboat to the island…."

A week later, she wrote about children:

"Many people have children but only a few of them come into the office and tell us what funny things they do. Two prizes this week: Mom was being annoyed by little Becky and told her to go out and water the tomato plants — a few minutes later Mom heard strange noises in the kitchen. Becky had very carefully pulled up the plants and brought them to the sink — to water them. What else? … Ego-Boosting Department: Overheard while pounding our typewriter late one night — very small girl to mother, gazing up at sign, "What's the *Beachcomber*, Mommy?" "That's a newspaper dear, like the *New York Times*." Thank you, mother, whoever you are. … A little boy in Harvey Cedars who shall remain nameless[2] was advised that it was time to come to dinner; he demurred, telling us that he was busy pulling the skin off his peeling arms and chest because he wanted to feed it to his turtles for their dinner."

Two months before my mother died, she wrote this short essay, again mining the rescued *Encyclopedia Britannica*. That spring was the last time she was able to go to the beach:

"The beach at sundown, particularly in May, has a magical open quality that disappears as the days get hotter. We took one of our rare walks on the beach after the heavy northwest winds this week. Hundreds of thousands of infinitesimally tiny clams washed up along the high water mark — none measured more than half an inch long, and if you bent down and watched closely for a moment, which we did, you could see tiny tongues of living clams reaching out and wiggling, searching for water or wet sand, as their shells slowly opened. Our *pelecypoda* department, *mollusca* division, informs us that they are baby turkey clams — surf clams stirred up by the heavy winds and turbulent seas.

"Another discovery was a small starfish rolled up into a tight little ball. In the Caribbean we saw very large ones that cling to the deck of a boat and won't let go; but we had never met up with one of these obstinate little creatures that won't open up and look like a star no matter how much we tickle it."

At the beginning of that summer, I met Gunter Buchholz, a German architect who, together with a friend, had rented a houseboat pulled up on shore. We eyed each other on the street and met at the same Scandinavian Bar where, in the 1930s, my parents and

Aunt Dot went folk dancing. In four weeks I was hooked. I walked into my mother's bedroom, all excited because I thought she would approve of a German man. When I told her I was in love and wanted to marry him she must have metaphorically rolled her eyes, as she had heard this before. She did not approve. I said, "But you said that German men were the most charming men in the world." She answered, "Yes, but not to <u>marry</u>." I wanted to introduce him, but she said she was too sick. She was right — again.

At the end of July, Mommy was in Philadelphia's Albert Einstein Hospital. Hospice care did not yet exist, and no one suggested or encouraged a person to spend their last days at home. Shortly before she died, while Daddy and Michael stood at the foot of the bed, I held my mother's hand and studied the strength, determination and intelligence in her face. I remembered she had once told me, "Even when I'm dying no one will believe me; I always look so damn healthy."

In the July 30, 1959 *Beachcomber*, I wrote an obituary. After a concise survey of my mother's life and work I concluded:

"Josephine Thomas has been largely responsible for the sparkle and subtle humor in the *Beachcomber* since its inception in 1950. Although we had to tiptoe and remain in absolute silence while she typed, the reams of copy from her Underwood were always more than worth the wait. It was her acute eye for the heart of a story, her power of observing the infinite details that make up the personality of a story, and her quick wit, which assured her success in journalism, and endeared her to co-workers, friends and family. We deeply mourn the passing of a talented writer and a loving mother."

It never occurred to my father or me to write of my mother's death to Lowell Thomas, such an iconic figure in my childhood — but in March 1960 I received a letter from him. While playing golf, he met a man from Harvey Cedars who told him my mother had died the previous year. "I want to tell you how distressed we are to hear about this," he wrote. "Josephine was like a member of our family. We all admired her greatly and had much affection for her. She was an exceptional woman, and it left a large void both in our household and in our office when she departed those many, many years ago."

Beachcomber founder Donald Craig wrote to tell me how much he liked and respected her: "She meant a lot to me as a friend and as your ma, which is an unusual combination. And she often and oftener made me proud to be running the *Beachcomber* because of her wonderful copy. It seemed to me that her heart was always in writing, that she resented all the pulls on her, including the *Beachcomber*, which kept her from what she considered serious writing. It's tragic in a way that she never had the chance to get back to it. But on the other hand, she might never have got to what she really wanted to say, even if she had lived to be old. The fact that you were able to bully or cajole her into writing for you for the past years was a great thing, because it made her produce, and she couldn't help but do that distinctively. Your write-up was sensitive and touching."

After the funeral, Aunt Dot wrote to Aunt Milly:[3]

"I'm so glad you could be with Reynold and his family during this terrible time. My heart winced to see him so suddenly a broken old man. Perhaps with rest and an upturn in his business he will look more like his old, debonair self. I understand that his business is very bad — those months of Jo in and out of the hospital took their toll of him emotionally and physically. The only bright spot was when I saw him drive off, sitting between Margaret and Michael, both so handsome and strong. Brother has always been so right in all his relationships. He was a kind, considerate husband. I am sure his children will both do everything they possibly can to ease things for him here on out. Margaret seemed more outgoing, not so cold, and she said several things since Jo's death that made me think she might begin to think of someone other than herself. I never saw one human being worship another as Jo did Margaret. She was the vulnerable spot in Jo's armor. I doubt if she could have sustained Margaret's death if it had been the other way around."

I am not a violent person. Very few times have I acted or reacted violently. In the middle of the winter after Mommy died the children were visiting their Douglas grandparents and I was sitting alone in the living room, calmly, I thought, cutting my fingernails, when grief erupted from within me. Deep, wrenching sobs bent me double and I heaved the scissors across the room, then picked up the teacup from the coffee table and pitched that against the fieldstone fireplace. Then I overturned the coffee table, covered with books. Still sobbing, I collapsed on my bed. Later I realized I was lamenting both my husband and my mother's death. I had suppressed the grief when Bill died and now another loss overlapped the first one. I didn't cry over my mother again until 1972, when, in a women's studies course, our assignment was to write about our mothers. Asked to read it aloud, many in the class, including me, were sobbing. As I am now.

NOTES

[1] *By the 1960s, Michael raced bigger and faster boats, as far distant as Tampa Bay and Puget Sound. In October 1963, he set a world record at the President's Cup race on the Potomac and received a congratulatory letter from President Kennedy; in 1966, he won a gold medal in Venice, Italy. In 1967, Michael made his Unlimited class debut driving* Miss Budweiser *in the British Columbia Cup race, where his top speed was 105 miles per hour. He was acclaimed Rookie of the Year. In October that year, my brother flipped not a hydroplane — a fear in the back of all our minds — but a bulldozer, as he loaded it onto a flatbed trailer while on a dredging job on the mainland. He was crushed and died instantly. On the phone, we told my father, on vacation in Florida, only that he had been in a serious accident. Aunt Milly, Daddy's doctor and I met him at 30th Street Station in Philadelphia. As he walked down the platform and saw the three of us standing there he guessed what had happened. He said later, "Thank God your mother wasn't alive to see this."*

[2] *"Remain nameless" means it was her grandson, Billy. Both children made it into the paper over the years, anonymously, and otherwise.*

[3] *Uncle Bill retired from Bethlehem Steel in 1960 and he and my aunt moved to Manhattan. Aunt Milly divided her energies between Zen Buddhism and the Japanese Tea Ceremony. Uncle Bill died in 1983, just a few months after my father. I thought that, with her active life, Aunt Milly would be fine, but without her husband, son and brother, she was a lost soul and, in her last months, didn't recognize me. She died in 1988. Their ashes were divided between Dai Bosatsu Zendo in the Catskills and the First Presbyterian Church in Bethlehem.*

Epilogue

Elizabeth and Billy, the Christmas after their father died, 1957

We never live in just one era — the layers of history are within us and string out behind us. In this house the history is beneath me, around me, surrounds me. Through my mother's letters and diaries, and all the family letters, I bring the past alive and, as I approach the end of my life, I hold dear to me all those who have died before me — some in the normal course of life, but too often not. If life had progressed smoothly for my family and me, my brother Michael, who died in 1967, and my daughter Elizabeth, who died in 1989, would be here to share memories of our parents.

The window seat that overlooks the bay is empty of family files now — Aunt Maggie's Limoges china is stored there. My mother's letters, diaries and other papers — the raw material for a book she hoped to write when my brother and I were grown, and that I have used for this book — fill a three-foot wide drawer in a steel filing cabinet. Four years after my father died in 1983, my former husband and I remodeled this 1934 cottage in which I spent my childhood. We expanded it slightly, but kept the same cottage feeling and the same New Jersey cedar cupboards and bookshelves where my parents' books stand in line with mine.

Now, I sit at the computer where my mother sat at her sewing machine. From her sewing room window she saw the dunes protecting the ocean, three blocks to the east across Kinsey Cove; today houses and tall Japanese pines block the distant view. I look out the window and see my garden, which was Mommy's garden, and look across the street to the cove where she watched Daddy crawling through the rushing water to rescue a birdbath during the 1938 hurricane. I played with my grandchildren in the sandy yard where she played, for too short a time, with hers. I cook in her kitchen, now just a little larger, with recipes she saved; stir with her wooden spoons; and use the salad bowl she salvaged from a destroyed house after the 1944 hurricane. I followed my mother's path of words, but, even though I have her sewing cabinet, with drawers full of buttons and spools of thread marked "nineteen cents," I was never interested in sewing; but when forced to sew a hem, I do thread a needle the way she showed me: cut a piece of thread, spit on it, twist and insert in eye of needle.

Today, if my mother returned to sit with me on the window seat, she would see only a few changes. Way off across the bay to the northwest, the tower of Oyster Creek Nuclear generating station rises on the horizon. In the middle distance, the shack on Sandy Island was rebuilt after fire destroyed the old one. The new structure stands slightly higher, and gives some dimension to the island, which has eroded on the narrow northern tip that used to be directly opposite the house.

Mommy would see the same watery vista, the land, the seascape of her life here. Nervous as she felt around water, she would be happy to see a newer, higher bulkhead that protects the house from the rising water level.

Our house is now better shielded against winter; there are pine trees on two sides, tall fences, insulation in the walls, and double windows. The land between the house and the bay has been raised, and beach grass grows between the deck and bulkhead. When the spray freezes on each spike of grass, the yard becomes a field of gracefully arched icicles, which reflect the low, glimmering winter sun. In winter, the obstreperous northwest wind whips waves topped with white horses across the bay; they splash over the bulkhead and coat the windows with speckled salt spray.

Now, in the winter of my life, days of freezing weather have transformed the bay into a solid mass of buckled plates of ice. Under a sunny sky, the ice reflects shades of blue and silver. Repeating cycles of freeze and thaw jam buckled plates of ice against the bulkhead. Moving ice pushes channel markers askew, if it doesn't lift them out altogether.

Bundled in a down coat, I walk, bent against the wind, along 80th Street to the beach. I pass unoccupied houses, where once the empty lots of my childhood offered a variety of sand, grass, marsh and bayberry bushes as playgrounds.

The walk on the winter beach is invigorating, visceral. Where the winter-hardened sand freezes it crunches as I step. The strong northeast wind pushes the churning surf almost to the foot of the dunes. I stand bent against the gritty wind and watch the turbulent breakers, white as far as the horizon. Ice frosts the jetties; sea smoke hovers over the water. An incoming wave sweeps the beach clean, reshapes a patch of shells with a rattling, clacking sound then leaves a new wrack line of sea-borne detritus. I step over a sturdy waterlogged timber with rusty iron spikes, a remnant of a shipwreck or a storm-dismembered seawall.

I walk alone, but am escorted by phantoms of my past. Family and friends walk the beach with me. I am a receptacle for the ghosts I carry within me. I am happy to live in this expansive space, to be on the edge of the land. It's good for my soul to have all that water before me.

I remember something Rachel Carson wrote:

"Perhaps something of the strength and serenity and endurance of the sea, of this spirit beyond time and place, transfers itself to us, to us of the land world as we confront its vast and lonely expanse from the shore — our last outpost."

AUTHOR'S NOTE

Editing my mother's diary of the Washington years was a job mainly of cutting and judicious pruning. Innumerable references to dances with handsome shavetails (all carefully chaperoned), movies and plays (she and her girl friends must have seen every one), and eating (she adored Chinese food) had to go. Many acquaintances, both male and female, were left behind in order to emphasize relationships that lasted over a period of several years. I corrected obvious typographical errors but allowed her the spelling she had learned. Stylistically, Jo was a natural writer and eminently readable; so aside from inserting some commas, the writing is hers.

Endnotes clarify both my mother's and my references — the everyday things that defined her world and the greater world around her — with which today's readers might not be familiar. (Even though the World War I Armistice was signed in November 1918, a great many soldiers did not return until September 1919, and stayed in the camps surrounding Washington until they were mustered out.) To immerse myself in the Washington years I read periodicals at the New York Public Library and all books at the Washingtonia Division of the D.C. Public Library relating to the District during the war, and scanned four years of the *Washington Evening Star* and *The Washington Post* on microfilm. I read oral histories and unpublished manuscripts at the Gelman Library of George Washington University and The Historical Society of Washington, D.C. I found Frank Carpenter's papers and books at the Library of Congress. I gained additional information about the Carpenters from Amy Hague, Curator of Manuscripts at the Sophia Smith Collection at Smith College, where Frances Carpenter deposited some of her papers. After much patience and perseverance, I uncovered pages of my mother's War Department work at the National Archives. (I recognized her handwriting and initials on letters.)

To get a sense of the city's scale before the beltway, I walked through the neighborhoods where she lived and worked, searching for buildings from my mother's time, and looked at every 1917 to 1921 photograph that I could get my hands on. Some searches were in vain: I thumbed the files of Barney Neighborhood House hoping to find photographs or references to its wartime activities — nothing. But imagine the thrill when I discovered a photo of my mother's smiling face sitting under the statue of Columbus on the Capitol steps in the 1923 National Geographic book *The Capital of Our Country*.

During the months I was in Washington, I drove to Bluemont, Virginia. Using my mother's diary as a guide, I found the road out of town to the Carpenters' property — it was a real rush to see the stone gateposts inscribed "Joannasberg, 1896." I drove halfway up the driveway, saw farmers working and dogs running around, but felt timorous so turned around and went back to Washington. It wasn't until recently, through the Internet and Susan Freis Falknor at the Friends of Bluemont, that I met Lester Querry, who researches historic homes in the area, and he invited me to visit. Les put me in touch with Margo Foster, who in 1967, with her husband, Rockwood Hoar Foster, bought the Carpenters' 414-acre estate. She lives there now with her son Adam. This time I drove along the winding driveway, up the hill and to the house, and was welcomed by the Fosters. Except for an enclosed porch, it was unchanged since my mother's time. Diary in hand, the Fosters showed me the house, the grounds, and the library, and I found my mother's basement office and her upstairs bedroom. The white bathroom, with the large deep bathtub that overflowed, has not been modernized, and I burst into tears when I realized I was standing by the tub where my mother took her cold baths.

I traveled to Ionia, Michigan, and was guided by Marie and Michael Hurd, cousins I had never met. Susan Brooks at the Hall-Fowler Library shared their photos with me and LaVonne Bennett searched the Ionia Community Library's microfilm. Editor Emeritus Russell C. Gregory at the *Ionia Sentinel* made several suggestions, adding, "Your mother would not get lost were she to return here, although, God help her if she tried the same inside or outside the Beltway in Washington."

To expand my knowledge of my mother's work for Lowell Thomas, I visited the Marist College Archives and Special Collections in Poughkeepsie, New York, which houses the Lowell Thomas archive. I went before LT's papers and photographs had been digitized, and the late Dr. Fred D. Crawford, Associate Professor, Central Michigan University, who was researching a biography of Thomas, supported me from the beginning. Whenever he found a tidbit about my mother, he sent it to me. Now the archives can be searched at: http://library.marist.edu/archives/LTP/LTP. I met LT only once, in 1974, for lunch in Manhattan, and we corresponded for several years. By the time I was interested in my mother's life before I was born — which, when I was young, seemed like ancient history — he had died.

A Google search led me to a number of websites about the men my mother interviewed for Thomas' books. The most useful was http://luckner-society.com. I received help from Mackenzie Gregory in Australia and Michael Buschow in Germany. Paul Crespel in London related some details about Admiral Max Horton. Wendy Sprague in Colorado saw my query on the Luckner site and told her aunt, Janis Jack, whose husband's father and uncle were the medical officers on the *Mopelia* in 1929. They have a 16-mm film of the cruise and put it on a DVD for me. A clip can be found at http://www.down-the-shore.com/josephine.html

Aside from my own memory, family letters and diaries were the primary source for Part 2, in addition to stories in the *Beach Haven Times*, and my mother's published writing in the *Beachcomber* between 1950 and 1959. I received photographs and information about Ridgewood from Peggy Norris at the Ridgewood Public Library.

I am greatly indebted to friends and colleagues who assisted me as I tackled my mother's story. Early on, my friend Fiona Foster said, "This could be a book." David Foster led me to "Washington History," the magazine of the Historical Society of Washington, D.C., which published a segment of my mother's diary, "The Washington Diary of a War Worker, 1918-1919," in its Fall/Winter 1998-99 issue. Colleen McKnight, Krysta Harden, and editors Lynn Cothern and Jane Freundel Levey offered many helpful suggestions. I thank Anita Josephson, Madeleine Blais, Victoria Lassonde, Whitney Ransome, Leslee Ganss, Ashley Roberts, Perdita Buchan, Jim De Francesco and Steve Seplow for insightful feedback after reading various iterations of the completed manuscript.

I am most indebted, of course, to my dear mother, who hated to throw anything away.

MARGARET THOMAS BUCHHOLZ is co-author of *Great Storms of the Jersey Shore,* author of *New Jersey Shipwrecks: 350 Years in the Graveyard of the Atlantic,* and editor of *Shore Chronicles: Diaries and Travelers Tales from the Jersey Shore 1764-1955.* Her essays about the shore have also been included in anthologies and collections. Buchholz was publisher of the Long Beach Island newspaper the *Beachcomber* from 1955 to 1987 and is still an editor. She currently lives year-round in her childhood home (described in this book) in Harvey Cedars, New Jersey, on Barnegat Bay, where her family has been coming since 1833.

DOWN THE SHORE PUBLISHING specializes in books, calendars, videos and cards about New Jersey and the Shore. For a free catalog of all our titles or to be included on our mailing list, just send us a request:

email: info@down-the-shore.com

Down The Shore Publishing
P.O. Box 100 • West Creek, NJ 08092

www.down-the-shore.com